English Romantic Poets : Critical Assessment

English Romantic Poets : Critical Assessment

M.P. Kotter

CYBER TECH PUBLICATIONS
4264/3, Ansari Road, Daryaganj, New Delhi-110002 (India)
Ph.: 011-23244078. Fax: 011-23280028
E-Mail: cyberpublicationsdelhi@yahoo.com

English Romantic Poets : Critical Assessment
M.P. Kotter

First Edition 2009

Published by :

G.S. Rawat for **Cyber Tech Publications**
4264/3, Ansari Road, Daryaganj, New Delhi-110002 (India)
Ph.: 011-23244078. Fax: 011-23280028
E-Mail: cyberpublicationsdelhi@yahoo.com

Printed at : **Amit Enterprises**, Maujpur, Delhi, (9810878184)

Preface

The British Romantic writers lived through a period of rapid social change and the violent political upheavals of the French Revolution and its aftermath, and responded fully to these changes in their writing. We will focus on a selection of the poetry and prose written during this period, from the Fall of the Bastille (1789) to the Reform Act (1832). The writers to be studied will include poets such as Blake, Robinson, Wordsworth, Coleridge, Shelley, Byron, Hemans, Tighe, and Keats, the political writings of Burke, Williams, Wollstonecraft and Godwin, selections from the work of the main essayists, such as Hazlitt and De Quincey; and several novels that represent the Gothic tradition or the reaction against it. In addition to considering the literary texts, we will also look at some of the theoretical writings of the period, such as Wordsworth's Preface to Lyrical Ballads and Shelley's Defence of Poetry.

There will be a limited number of lectures during the course. Much of the important work will take place in discussion sessions and in small groups who will report on the poems or other writings they have chosen to study.

Undersigned is confident enough that this work of him would be informative to the students and readers alike.

—***Author***

Contents

1

The Age of Romanticism (1800-1850)

THE SECOND CREATIVE PERIOD OF ENGLISH LITERATURE

The first half of the nineteenth century records the triumph of Romanticism in literature and of democracy in government; and the two movements are so closely associated, in so many nations and in so many periods of history, that one must wonder if there be not some relation of cause and effect between them. Just as we understand the tremendous energizing influence of Puritanism in the matter of English liberty by remembering that the common people had begun to read, and that their book was the Bible, so we may understand this age of popular government by remembering that the chief subject of romantic literature was the essential nobleness of common men and the value of the individual.

As we read now that brief portion of history which lies between the Declaration of Independence (1776) and the English Reform Bill of 1832, we are in the presence of such mighty political upheavals that "the age of revolution" is the only name by which we can adequately characterize it. Its great historic movements become intelligible only when we read what was written in this period; for the French Revolution and the American commonwealth, as well as the establishment of a true democracy in England by the Reform

Bill, were the inevitable results of ideas which literature had spread rapidly through the civilized world. Liberty is fundamentally an ideal; and that ideal--beautiful, inspiring, compelling, as a loved banner in the wind--was kept steadily before men's minds by a multitude of books and pamphlets as far apart as Burns's Poems and Thomas Paine's Rights of Man,--all read eagerly by the common people, all proclaiming the dignity of common life, and all uttering the same passionate cry against every form of class or caste oppression.

First the dream, the ideal in some human soul; then the written word which proclaims it, and impresses other minds with its truth and beauty; then the united and determined effort of men to make the dream a reality,--that seems to be a fair estimate of the part that literature plays, even in our political progress.

HISTORICAL SUMMARY

The period we are considering begins in the latter half of the reign of George III and ends with the accession of Victoria in 1837. When on a foggy morning in November, 1783, King George entered the House of Lords and in a trembling voice recognized the independence of the United States of America, he unconsciously proclaimed the triumph of that free government by free men which had been the ideal of English literature for more than a thousand years; though it was not till 1832, when the Reform Bill became the law of the land, that England herself learned the lesson taught her by America, and became the democracy of which her writers had always dreamed.

The half century between these two events is one of great turmoil, yet of steady advance in every department of English life. The storm center of the political unrest was the French Revolution, that frightful uprising which proclaimed the natural rights of man and the abolition of class distinctions. Its effect on the whole civilized world is beyond computation.

Patriotic clubs and societies multiplied in England, all asserting the doctrine of Liberty, Equality, Fraternity, the watchwords of the Revolution. Young England, led by Pitt the younger, hailed the new French republic and offered it friendship; old England, which pardons no revolutions but her own, looked with horror on the turmoil in France and, misled by Burke and the nobles of the realm, forced the two nations into war. Even Pitt saw a blessing in this at first; because the sudden zeal for fighting a foreign nation--which by some horrible perversion is generally called patriotism--might turn men's thoughts from their own to their neighbors' affairs, and so prevent a threatened revolution at home.

The causes of this threatened revolution were not political but economic. By her invention in steel and machinery, and by her monopoly of the carrying trade, England had become the workshop of the world. Her wealth had increased beyond her wildest dreams; but the unequal distribution of that wealth was a spectacle to make angels weep. The invention of machinery at first threw thousands of skilled hand workers out of employment; in order to protect a few agriculturists, heavy duties were imposed on corn and wheat, and bread rose to famine prices just when laboring men had the least money to pay for it. There followed a curious spectacle. While England increased in wealth, and spent vast sums to support her army and subsidize her allies in Europe, and while nobles, landowners, manufacturers, and merchants lived in increasing luxury, a multitude of skilled laborers were clamoring for work. Fathers sent their wives and little children into the mines and factories, where sixteen hours' labor would hardly pay for the daily bread; and in every large city were riotous mobs made up chiefly of hungry men and women. It was this unbearable economic condition, and not any political theory, as Burke supposed, which occasioned the danger of another English revolution.

It is only when we remember these conditions that we can understand two books, Adam Smith's Wealth of Nations and Thomas Paine's Rights of Man, which can hardly be considered as literature, but which exercised an enormous influence in England. Smith was a Scottish thinker, who wrote to uphold the doctrine that labor is the only source of a nation's wealth, and that any attempt to force labor into unnatural channels, or to prevent it by protective duties from freely obtaining the raw materials for its industry, is unjust and destructive. Paine was a curious combination of Jekyll and Hyde, shallow and untrustworthy personally, but with a passionate devotion to popular liberty.

His Rights of Man published in London in 1791, was like one of Burns's lyric outcries against institutions which oppressed humanity. Coming so soon after the destruction of the Bastille, it added fuel to the flames kindled in England by the French Revolution. The author was driven out of the country, on the curious ground that he endangered the English constitution, but not until his book had gained a wide sale and influence.

All these dangers, real and imaginary, passed away when England turned from the affairs of France to remedy her own economic conditions. The long Continental war came to an end with Napoleon's overthrow at Waterloo, in 1815; and England, having gained enormously in prestige abroad, now turned to the work of reform at home.

The destruction of the African slave trade; the mitigation of horribly unjust laws, which included poor debtors and petty criminals in the same class; the prevention of child labor; the freedom of the press; the extension of manhood suffrage; the abolition of restrictions against Catholics in Parliament; the establishment of hundreds of popular schools, under the leadership of Andrew Bell and Joseph Lancaster,--these are but a few of the reforms which mark the progress of civilization in a single half century. When England, in 1833, proclaimed the emancipation of all slaves in all her colonies, she unconsciously proclaimed her final emancipation from barbarism.

LITERARY CHARACTERISTICS OF THE AGE

It is intensely interesting to note how literature at first reflected the political turmoil of the age; and then, when the turmoil was over and England began her mighty work of reform, how literature suddenly developed a new creative spirit, which shows itself in the poetry of Wordsworth, Coleridge, Byron, Shelley, Keats, and in the prose of Scott, Jane Austen, Lamb, and De Quincey,--a wonderful group of writers, whose patriotic enthusiasm suggests the Elizabethan days, and whose genius has caused their age to be known as the second creative period of our literature. Thus in the early days, when old institutions seemed crumbling with the Bastille, Coleridge and Southey formed their youthful scheme of a "Pantisocracy on the banks of the Susquehanna,"--an ideal commonwealth, in which the principles of More's Utopia should be put in practice. Even Wordsworth, fired with political enthusiasm, could write,

Bliss was it in that dawn to be alive,

But to be young was very heaven.

The essence of Romanticism was, it must be remembered, that literature must reflect all that is spontaneous and unaffected in nature and in man, and be free to follow its own fancy in its own way. We have already noted this characteristic in the work of the Elizabethan dramatists, who followed their own genius in opposition to all the laws of the critics. In Coleridge we see this independence expressed in "Kubla Khan" and "The Ancient Mariner," two dream pictures, one of the populous Orient, the other of the lonely sea. In Wordsworth this literary independence led him inward to the heart of common things. Following his own instinct, as Shakespeare does, he too

Finds tongues in trees, books in the running brooks,

Sermons in stones, and good in everything.

And so, more than any other writer of the age, he invests the common life of nature, and the souls of common men and women, with glorious significance. These two poets, Coleridge and Wordsworth, best represent the romantic genius of the age in which they lived, though Scott had a greater literary reputation, and Byron and Shelley had larger audiences.

The second characteristic of this age is that it is emphatically an age of poetry. The previous century, with its practical outlook on life, was largely one of prose; but now, as in the Elizabethan Age, the young enthusiasts turned as naturally to poetry as a happy man to singing. The glory of the age is in the poetry of Scott, Wordsworth, Coleridge, Byron, Shelley, Keats, Moore, and Southey. Of its prose works, those of Scott alone have attained a very wide reading, though the essays of Charles Lamb and the novels of Jane Austen have slowly won for their authors a secure place in the history of our literature. Coleridge and Southey (who with Wordsworth form the trio of so-called Lake Poets) wrote far more prose than poetry; and Southey's prose is much better than his verse. It was characteristic of the spirit of this age, so different from our own, that Southey could say that, in order to earn money, he wrote in verse "what would otherwise have been better written in prose."

It was during this period that woman assumed, for the first time, an important place in our literature. Probably the chief reason for this interesting phenomenon lies in the fact that woman was for the first time given some slight chance of education, of entering into the intellectual life of the race; and as is always the case when woman is given anything like a fair opportunity she responded magnificently. A secondary reason may be found in the nature of the age itself, which was intensely emotional. The French Revolution stirred all Europe to its depths, and during the following half century every great movement in literature, as in politics and religion, was characterized by strong emotion; which is all the more noticeable by contrast with the cold, formal, satiric spirit of the early eighteenth century. As woman is naturally more emotional than man, it may well be that the spirit of this emotional age attracted her, and gave her the opportunity to express herself in literature.

As all strong emotions tend to extremes, the age produced a new type of novel which seems rather hysterical now, but which in its own day delighted multitudes of readers whose nerves were somewhat excited, and who reveled in "bogey" stories of supernatural terror. Mrs. Anne Radcliffe (1764-1823) was one of the most successful writers of this school of exaggerated romance. Her novels, with their azure-eyed heroines, haunted castles, trapdoors, bandits, abductions, rescues in the nick of time, and a general medley of overwrought joys and horrors, were immensely popular, not only with the crowd of novel readers, but also with men of unquestioned literary genius, like Scott and Byron.

In marked contrast to these extravagant stories is the enduring work of Jane Austen, with her charming descriptions of everyday life, and of Maria Edgeworth, whose wonderful pictures of Irish life suggested to Walter Scott the idea of writing his Scottish romances. Two other women who attained a more or less lasting fame were Hannah More, poet, dramatist, and novelist, and Jane Porter, whose Scottish Chiefs and Thaddeus of Warsaw are still in demand in our libraries. Beside these were Fanny Burney (Madame D'Arblay) and several other writers whose works, in the early part of the nineteenth century, raised woman to the high place in literature which she has ever since maintained.

In this age literary criticism became firmly established by the appearance of such magazines as the Edinburgh Review (1802), The Quarterly Review (1808), Blackwood's Magazine (1817), the Westminster Review (1824), The Spectator (1828), The Athenaeum (1828), and Fraser's Magazine (1830). These magazines, edited by such men as Francis Jeffrey, John Wilson (who is known to us as Christopher North), and John Gibson Lockhart, who gave us the Life of Scott, exercised an immense influence on all subsequent literature. At first their criticisms were largely destructive, as when Jeffrey hammered Scott, Wordsworth, and Byron most unmercifully; and Lockhart could find no good in either Keats or Tennyson; but with added wisdom, criticism assumed its true function of construction. And when these magazines began to seek and to publish the works of unknown writers, like Hazlitt, Lamb, and Leigh Hunt, they discovered the chief mission of the modern magazine, which is to give every writer of ability the opportunity to make his work known to the world.

THE POETS OF ROMANTICISM

William Wordsworth (1770-1850)

It was in 1797 that the new romantic movement in our literature assumed definite form. Wordsworth and Coleridge retired to the Quantock Hills, Somerset, and there formed the deliberate purpose to make literature "adapted to interest mankind permanently," which, they declared, classic poetry could never do. Helping the two poets was Wordsworth's sister Dorothy, with a woman's love for flowers and all beautiful things; and a woman's divine sympathy for human life even in its lowliest forms. Though a silent partner, she furnished perhaps the largest share of the inspiration which resulted in the famous Lyrical Ballads of 1798.

In their partnership Coleridge was to take up the "supernatural, or at least romantic"; while Wordsworth was "to give the charm of novelty to things of everyday... by awakening the mind's attention from the lethargy of custom and directing it to the loveliness and the wonders of the world before us."

The whole spirit of their work is reflected in two poems of this remarkable little volume, "The Rime of the Ancient Mariner," which is Coleridge's masterpiece, and "Lines Written a Few Miles above Tintern Abbey," which expresses Wordsworth's poetical creed, and which is one of the noblest and most significant of our poems. That the Lyrical Ballads attracted no attention, and was practically ignored by a public that would soon go into raptures over Byron's Childe Harold and Don Juan, is of small consequence. Many men will hurry a mile to see skyrockets, who never notice Orion and the Pleiades from their own doorstep. Had Wordsworth and Coleridge written only this one little book, they would still be among the representative writers of an age that proclaimed the final triumph of Romanticism.

LIFE OF WORDSWORTH

To understand the life of him who, in Tennyson's words, "uttered nothing base," it is well to read first The Prelude, which records the impressions made upon Wordsworth's mind from his earliest recollection until his full manhood, in 1805, when the poem was completed. Outwardly his long and uneventful life divides itself naturally into four periods: (1) his childhood and youth, in the Cumberland Hills, from 1770 to 1787; (2) a period of uncertainty, of storm and stress, including his university life at Cambridge, his travels abroad, and his revolutionary experience, from 1787 to 1797; (3) a short but significant period of finding himself and his work, from 1797 to 1799; (4) a long period of retirement in the northern lake region, where he was born, and where for a full half century he lived so close to nature that her influence is reflected in all his poetry. When one has outlined these four periods he has told almost all that can be told of a life which is marked, not by events, but largely by spiritual experiences.

Wordsworth was born in 1770 at Cockermouth, Cumberland, where the Derwent,

Fairest of all rivers, loved

To blend his murmurs with my nurse's song,

And from his alder shades and rocky falls,

And from his fords and shallows, sent a voice

That flowed along my dreams.

It is almost a shock to one who knows Wordsworth only by his calm and noble poetry to read that he was of a moody and violent temper, and that his mother despaired of him alone among her five children. She died when he was but eight years old, but not till she had exerted an influence which lasted all his life, so that he could remember her as "the heart of all our learnings and our loves."

The father died some six years later, and the orphan was taken in charge by relatives, who sent him to school at Hawkshead, in the beautiful lake region. Here, apparently, the unroofed school of nature attracted him more than the discipline of the classics, and he learned more eagerly from the flowers and hills and stars than from his books; but one must read Wordsworth's own record, in The Prelude, to appreciate this.

Three things in this poem must impress even the casual reader: first, Wordsworth loves to be alone, and is never lonely, with nature; second, like every other child who spends much time alone in the woods and fields, he feels the presence of some living spirit, real though unseen, and companionable though silent; third, his impressions are exactly like our own, and delightfully familiar.

When he tells of the long summer day spent in swimming, basking in the sun, and questing over the hills; or of the winter night when, on his skates, he chased the reflection of a star in the black ice; or of his exploring the lake in a boat, and getting suddenly frightened when the world grew big and strange,--in all this he is simply recalling a multitude of our own vague, happy memories of childhood. He goes out into the woods at night to tend his woodcock snares; he runs across another boy's snares, follows them, finds a woodcock caught, takes it, hurries away through the night. And then,

I heard among the solitary hills

Low breathings coming after me, and sounds

Of undistinguishable motion.

That is like a mental photograph. Any boy who has come home through the woods at night will recognize it instantly. Again he tells as of going bird's-nesting on the cliffs:

Oh, when I have hung
Above the raven's nest, by knots of grass
And half-inch fissures in the slippery rock
But ill-sustained, and almost (so it seemed)
Suspended by the blast that blew amain,
Shouldering the naked crag,--oh, at that time,
While on the perilous ridge I hung alone,
With what strange utterance did the loud dry wind
Blow through my ear! The sky seemed not a sky
Of earth,--and with what motion moved the clouds!

No man can read such records without finding his own boyhood again, and his own abounding joy of life, in the poet's early impressions.

The second period of Wordsworth's life begins with his university course at Cambridge, in 1787. In the third book of The Prelude we find a dispassionate account of student life, with its trivial occupations, its pleasures and general aimlessness. Wordsworth proved to be a very ordinary scholar, following his own genius rather than the curriculum, and looking forward more eagerly to his vacation among the hills than to his examinations. Perhaps the most interesting thing in his life at Cambridge was his fellowship with the young political enthusiasts, whose spirit is expressed in his remarkable poem on the French Revolution,--a poem which is better than a volume of history to show the hopes and ambitions that stirred all Europe in the first days of that mighty upheaval. Wordsworth made two trips to France, in 1790 and 1791, seeing things chiefly through the rosy spectacles of the young Oxford Republicans. On his second visit he joined the Girondists, or the moderate Republicans, and only the decision of his relatives, who cut off his allowance and hurried him back to England, prevented his going headlong to the guillotine with the leaders of his party. Two things rapidly cooled Wordsworth's revolutionary enthusiasm, and ended the only dramatic interest of his placid life. One was the excesses of the Revolution itself, and especially the execution of Louis XVI; the other was the rise of Napoleon, and the slavish adulation accorded by France to this most vulgar and dangerous of tyrants. His coolness soon grew to disgust and opposition, as shown by his subsequent poems; and this brought upon him the censure of Shelley, Byron, and other extremists, though it gained the friendship of Scott, who from the first had no sympathy with the Revolution or with the young English enthusiasts.

Of the decisive period of Wordsworth's life, when he was living with his sister Dorothy and with Coleridge at Alfoxden, we have already spoken. The importance of this decision to give himself to poetry is evident when we remember that, at thirty years of age, he was without money or any definite aim or occupation in life. He considered the law, but confessed he had no sympathy for its contradictory precepts and practices; he considered the ministry, but though strongly inclined to the Church, he felt himself not good enough for the sacred office; once he had wanted to be a soldier and serve his country, but had wavered at the prospect of dying of disease in a foreign land and throwing away his life without glory or profit to anybody. An apparent accident, which looks more to us like a special Providence, determined his course. He had taken care of a young friend, Raisley Calvert, who died of consumption and left Wordsworth heir to a few hundred pounds, and to the request that he should give his life to poetry. It was this unexpected gift which enabled Wordsworth to retire from the world and follow his genius. All his life he was poor, and lived in an atmosphere of plain living and high thinking. His poetry brought him almost nothing in the way of money rewards, and it was only by a series of happy accidents that he was enabled to continue his work. One of these accidents was that he became a Tory, and soon accepted the office of a distributor of stamps, and was later appointed poet laureate by the government,--which occasioned Browning's famous but ill-considered poem of "The Lost Leader":

Just for a handful of silver he left us,

Just for a riband to stick in his coat.

The last half century of Wordsworth's life, in which he retired to his beloved lake district and lived successively at Grasmere and Rydal Mount, remind one strongly of Browning's long struggle for literary recognition. It was marked by the same steadfast purpose, the same trusted ideal, the same continuous work, and the same tardy recognition by the public. His poetry was mercilessly ridiculed by nearly all the magazine critics, who seized upon the worst of his work as a standard of judgment; and book after book of poems appeared without meeting any success save the approval of a few loyal friends. Without doubt or impatience he continued his work, trusting to the future to recognize and approve it. His attitude here reminds one strongly of the poor old soldier whom he met in the hills, who refused to beg or to mention his long service or the neglect of his country, saying with noble simplicity,

My trust is in the God of Heaven

And in the eye of him who passes me.

Such work and patience are certain of their reward, and long before Wordsworth's death he felt the warm sunshine of general approval. The wave of popular enthusiasm for Scott and Byron passed by, as their limitations were recognized; and Wordsworth was hailed by critics as the first living poet, and one of the greatest that England had ever produced. On the death of Southey (1843) he was made poet laureate, against his own inclination. The late excessive praise left him quite as unmoved as the first excessive neglect. The steady decline in the quality of his work is due not, as might be expected, to self-satisfaction at success, but rather to his intense conservatism, to his living too much alone and failing to test his work-by the standards and judgment of other literary men. He died tranquilly in 1850, at the age of eighty years, and was buried in the churchyard at Grasmere. Such is the brief outward record of the world's greatest interpreter of nature's message; and only one who is acquainted with both nature and the poet can realize how inadequate is any biography; for the best thing about Wordsworth must always remain unsaid. It is a comfort to know that his life, noble, sincere, "heroically happy," never contradicted his message. Poetry was his life; his soul was in all his work; and only by reading what he has written can we understand the man.

THE POETRY OF WORDSWORTH

There is often a sense of disappointment when one reads Wordsworth for the first time; and this leads us to speak first of two difficulties which may easily prevent a just appreciation of the poet's worth. The first difficulty is in the reader, who is often puzzled by Wordsworth's absolute simplicity. We are so used to stage effects in poetry, that beauty unadorned is apt to escape our notice,--like Wordsworth's "Lucy":

A violet by a mossy stone,

Half hidden from the eye;

Fair as a star, when only one

Is shining in the sky.

Wordsworth set himself to the task of freeing poetry from all its "conceits," of speaking the language of simple truth, and of portraying man and nature as they are; and in this good work we are apt to miss the beauty, the passion, the intensity, that hide themselves under his simplest lines. The second difficulty is in the poet, not in the reader. It must be confessed that Wordsworth is not always melodious; that he is seldom graceful, and only occasionally inspired. When he is inspired, few poets can be compared with him; at other times the bulk of his verse is so wooden and prosy that we wonder how a poet could have written it. Moreover he is absolutely without humor, and so he often fails to see the small step that separates the sublime from the ridiculous. In no other way can we explain "The Idiot Boy," or pardon the serious absurdity of "Peter Bell" and his grieving jackass.

On account of these difficulties it is well to avoid at first the longer works and begin with a good book of selections. When we read these exquisite shorter poems, with their noble lines that live forever in our memory, we realize that Wordsworth is the greatest poet of nature that our literature has produced. If we go further, and study the poems that impress us, we shall find four remarkable characteristics:

(1) Wordsworth is sensitive as a barometer to every subtle change in the world about him. In The Prelude he compares himself to an aeolian harp, which answers with harmony to every touch of the wind; and the figure is strikingly accurate, as well as interesting, for there is hardly a sight or a sound, from a violet to a mountain and from a bird note to the thunder of the cataract, that is not reflected in some beautiful way in Wordsworth's poetry.

(2) Of all the poets who have written of nature there is none that compares with him in the truthfulness of his representation. Burns, like Gray, is apt to read his own emotions into natural objects, so that there is more of the poet than of nature even in his mouse and mountain daisy; but Wordsworth gives you the bird and the flower, the wind and the tree and the river, just as they are, and is content to let them speak their own message.

(3) No other poet ever found such abundant beauty in the common world. He had not only sight, but insight, that is, he not only sees clearly and describes accurately, but penetrates to the heart of things and

always finds some exquisite meaning that is not written on the surface. It is idle to specify or to quote lines on flowers or stars, on snow or vapor. Nothing is ugly or commonplace in his world; on the contrary, there is hardly one natural phenomenon which he has not glorified by pointing out some beauty that was hidden from our eyes.

(4) It is the life of nature which is everywhere recognized; not mere growth and cell changes, but sentient, personal life; and the recognition of this personality in nature characterizes all the world's great poetry. In his childhood Wordsworth regarded natural objects, the streams, the hills, the flowers, even the winds, as his companions; and with his mature belief that all nature is the reflection of the living God, it was inevitable that his poetry should thrill with the sense of a Spirit that "rolls through all things." Cowper, Burns, Keats, Tennyson,--all these poets give you the outward aspects of nature in varying degrees; but Wordsworth gives you her very life, and the impression of some personal living spirit that meets and accompanies the man who goes alone through the woods and fields. We shall hardly find, even in the philosophy of Leibnitz, or in the nature myths of our Indians, any such impression of living nature as this poet awakens in us. And that suggests another delightful characteristic of Wordsworth's poetry, namely, that he seems to awaken rather than create an impression; he stirs our memory deeply, so that in reading him we live once more in the vague, beautiful wonderland of our own childhood.

Such is the philosophy of Wordsworth's nature poetry. If we search now for his philosophy of human life, we shall find four more doctrines, which rest upon his basal conception that man is not apart from nature, but is the very "life of her life."

(1) In childhood man is sensitive as a wind harp to all natural influences; he is an epitome of the gladness and beauty of the world. Wordsworth explains this gladness and this sensitiveness to nature by the doctrine that the child comes straight from the Creator of nature:

Our birth is but a sleep and a forgetting:

The Soul that rises with us, our life's Star,

Hath had elsewhere its setting,

And cometh from afar:

Not in entire forgetfulness

And not in utter nakedness,

But trailing clouds of glory do we come

From God, who is our home.

In this exquisite ode, which he calls "Intimations of Immortality from Recollections of Early Childhood (1807), Wordsworth sums up his philosophy of childhood; and he may possibly be indebted here to the poet Vaughan, who, more than a century before had proclaimed in "The Retreat" the same doctrine. This kinship with nature and with God, which glorifies childhood, ought to extend through a man's whole life and ennoble it. This is the teaching of "Tintern Abbey," in which the best part of our life is shown to be the result of natural influences. According to Wordsworth, society and the crowded unnatural life of cities tend to weaken and pervert humanity; and a return to natural and simple living is the only remedy for human wretchedness.

(2) The natural instincts and pleasures of childhood are the true standards of a man's happiness in this life. All artificial pleasures soon grow tiresome. The natural pleasures, which a man so easily neglects in his work, are the chief means by which we may expect

permanent and increasing joy. In "Tintern Abbey," "The Rainbow," "Ode to Duty," and "Intimations of Immortality" we see this plain teaching; but we can hardly read one of Wordsworth's pages without finding it slipped in unobtrusively, like the fragrance of a wild flower.

(3) The truth of humanity, that is, the common life which labors and loves and shares the general heritage of smiles and tears, is the only subject of permanent literary interest. Burns and the early poets of the Revival began the good work of showing the romantic interest of common life; and Wordsworth continued it in "Michael," "The Solitary Reaper," "To a Highland Girl," "Stepping Westward," The Excursion, and a score of lesser poems. Joy and sorrow, not of princes or heroes, but "in widest commonalty spread," are his themes; and the hidden purpose of many of his poems is to show that the keynote of all life is happiness,--not an occasional thing, the result of chance or circumstance, but a heroic thing, to be won, as one would win any other success, by work and patience.

(4) To this natural philosophy of man Wordsworth adds a mystic element, the result of his own belief that in every natural object there is a reflection of the living God. Nature is everywhere transfused and illumined by Spirit; man also is a reflection of the divine Spirit; and we shall never understand the emotions roused by a flower or a sunset until we learn that nature appeals through the eye of man to his inner spirit. In a word, nature must be "spiritually discerned." In "Tintern Abbey" the spiritual appeal of nature is expressed in almost every line; but the mystic conception of man is seen more clearly in "Intimations of Immortality," which Emerson calls "the high-water mark of poetry in the nineteenth century." In this last splendid ode Wordsworth adds to his spiritual

interpretation of nature and man the alluring doctrine of preexistence, which has appealed so powerfully to Hindoo and Greek in turn, and which makes of human life a continuous, immortal thing, without end or beginning.

Wordsworth's longer poems, since they contain much that is prosy and uninteresting, may well be left till after we have read the odes, sonnets, and short descriptive poems that have made him famous. As showing a certain heroic cast of Wordsworth's mind, it is interesting to learn that the greater part of his work, including The Prelude and The Excursion, was intended for a place in a single great poem, to be called The Recluse, which should treat of nature, man, and society. The Prelude, treating of the growth of a poet's mind, was to introduce the work. The Home at Grasmere, which is the first book of The Recluse, was not published till 1888, long after the poet's death. The Excursion (1814) is the second book of The Recluse; and the third was never completed, though Wordsworth intended to include most of his shorter poems in this third part, and so make an immense personal epic of a poet's life and work. It is perhaps just as well that the work remained unfinished. The best of his work appeared in the Lyrical Ballads (1798) and in the sonnets, odes, and lyrics of the next ten years; though "The Duddon Sonnets" (1820), "To a Skylark" (1825), and "Yarrow Revisited" (1831) show that he retained till past sixty much of his youthful enthusiasm. In his later years, however, he perhaps wrote too much; his poetry, like his prose, becomes dull and unimaginative; and we miss the flashes of insight, the tender memories of childhood, and the recurrence of noble lines--each one a poem--that constitutes the surprise and the delight of reading Wordsworth.

The outward shows of sky and earth,
Of hill and valley, he has viewed;
And impulses of deeper birth
Have come to him in solitude.

In common things that round us lie
Some random truths he can impart--
The harvest of a quiet eye
That broods and sleeps on his own heart.

SAMUEL TAYLOR COLERIDGE (1772-1834)

A grief without a pang, void, dark and drear,
A stifled, drowsy, unimpassioned grief,
Which finds no natural outlet, no relief,
In word, or sigh, or tear.

In the wonderful "Ode to Dejection," from which the above fragment is taken, we have a single strong impression of Coleridge's whole life,--a sad, broken, tragic life, in marked contrast with the peaceful existence of his friend Wordsworth. For himself, during the greater part of his life, the poet had only grief and remorse as his portion; but for everybody else, for the audiences that were charmed by the brilliancy of his literary lectures, for the friends who gathered about him to be inspired by his ideals and conversation, and for all his readers who found unending delight in the little volume which holds his poetry, he had and still has a cheering message, full of beauty and hope and inspiration. Such is Coleridge, a man of grief who makes the world glad.

LIFE. In 1772 there lived in Ottery St. Mary, Devonshire, a queer little man, the Rev. John Coleridge, vicar of the parish church and master of the local grammar school. In the former capacity he preached profound sermons, quoting to open-mouthed rustics long passages from the Hebrew, which he told them was the very tongue of the Holy Ghost. In the latter capacity he wrote for his boys a new Latin grammar, to mitigate some of the difficulties of traversing that terrible jungle by means of ingenious bypaths and short cuts. For instance, when his boys found the ablative a somewhat difficult case to understand, he told them to think of it as the quale-quare-quidditive case, which of course makes its meaning perfectly clear. In both these capacities the elder Coleridge was a sincere man, gentle and kindly, whose memory was "like a religion" to his sons and daughters. In that same year was born Samuel Taylor Coleridge, the youngest of thirteen children.

He was an extraordinarily precocious child, who could read at three years of age, and who, before he was five, had read the Bible and the Arabian Nights, and could remember an astonishing amount from both books. From three to six he attended a "dame" school; and from six till nine (when his father died and left the family destitute) he was in his father's school, learning the classics, reading an enormous quantity of English books, avoiding novels, and delighting in cumbrous theological and metaphysical treatises. At ten he was sent to the Charity School of Christ's Hospital, London, where he met Charles Lamb, who records his impression of the place and of Coleridge in one of his famous essays. Coleridge seems to have remained in this school for seven or eight years without visiting his home,--a poor, neglected boy, whose comforts and entertainments were all within himself. Just as, when a little child, he used to wander over the fields with a stick in his hand, slashing the tops from weeds and thistles, and thinking himself to be the mighty champion of Christendom against the infidels, so now he would lie on the roof of the school, forgetting the play of his fellows and the roar of the London streets, watching the white clouds drifting over and following them in spirit into all sorts of romantic adventures.

At nineteen this hopeless dreamer, who had read more books than an old professor, entered Cambridge as a charity student. He remained for nearly three years, then ran away because of a trifling debt and enlisted in the Dragoons, where he served several months before he was discovered and brought back to the university. He left in 1794 without taking his degree; and presently we find him with the youthful

Southey,--a kindred spirit, who had been fired to wild enthusiasm by the French Revolution,--founding his famous Pantisocracy for the regeneration of human society. "The Fall of Robespierre," a poem composed by the two enthusiasts, is full of the new revolutionary spirit. The Pantisocracy, on the banks of the Susquehanna, was to be an ideal community, in which the citizens combined farming and literature; and work was to be limited to two hours each day. Moreover, each member of the community was to marry a good woman, and take her with him. The two poets obeyed the latter injunction first, marrying two sisters, and then found that they had no money to pay even their traveling expenses to the new Utopia.

During all the rest of his career a tragic weakness of will takes possession of Coleridge, making it impossible for him, with all his genius and learning, to hold himself steadily to any one work or purpose. He studied in Germany; worked as a private secretary, till the drudgery wore upon his free spirit; then he went to Rome and remained for two years, lost in study. Later he started The Friend, a paper devoted to truth and liberty; lectured on poetry and the fine arts to enraptured audiences in London, until his frequent failures to meet his engagements scattered his hearers; was offered an excellent position and a half interest (amounting to some L2000) in the Morning Post and The Courier, but declined it, saying "that I would not give up the country and the lazy reading of old folios for two thousand times two thousand pounds,--in short, that beyond L350 a year I considered money a real evil." His family, meanwhile, was almost entirely neglected; he lived apart, following his own way, and the wife and children were left in charge of his friend Southey. Needing money, he was on the point of becoming a Unitarian minister, when a small pension from two friends enabled him to live for a few years without regular employment.

A terrible shadow in Coleridge's life was the apparent cause of most of his dejection. In early life he suffered from neuralgia, and to ease the pain began to use opiates. The result on such a temperament was almost inevitable. He became a slave to the drug habit; his naturally weak will lost all its directing and sustaining force, until, after fifteen years of pain and struggle and despair, he gave up and put himself in charge of a physician, one Mr. Gillman, of Highgate. Carlyle, who visited him at this time, calls him "a king of men," but records that "he gave you the idea of a life that had been full of sufferings, a life heavy-laden, half-vanquished, still swimming painfully in seas of manifold physical and other bewilderment."

The shadow is dark indeed; but there are gleams of sunshine that occasionally break through the clouds. One of these is his association with Wordsworth and his sister Dorothy, in the Quantock hills, out of which came the famous Lyrical Ballads of 1798. Another was his loyal devotion to poetry for its own sake. With the exception of his tragedy Remorse, which through Byron's influence was accepted at Drury Lane Theater, and for which he was paid L400, he received almost nothing for his poetry. Indeed, he seems not to have desired it; for he says: "Poetry has been to me its own exceeding great reward; it has soothed my afflictions; it has multiplied and refined my enjoyments; it has endeared solitude, and it has given me the habit of wishing to discover the good and the beautiful in all that meets and surrounds me." One can better understand his exquisite verse after such a declaration. A third ray of sunlight came from the admiration of his contemporaries; for though he wrote comparatively little, he was by his talents and learning a leader among literary men, and his conversations were as eagerly listened to as were those of Dr. Johnson. Wordsworth says of him that, though other men of the age had done some wonderful things, Coleridge was the only wonderful man he had ever known. Of his lectures on literature a contemporary says: "His words seem to flow as from a person repeating with grace and energy some delightful poem." And of his conversation it is recorded: "Throughout a long-drawn summer's day would this man talk to you in low, equable but clear and musical tones, concerning things human and divine; marshalling all history, harmonizing all experiment, probing the depths of your consciousness, and revealing visions of glory and terror to the imagination."

The last bright ray of sunlight comes from Coleridge's own soul, from the gentle, kindly nature which made men love and respect him in spite of his weaknesses, and which caused Lamb to speak of him humorously as "an archangel a little damaged." The universal law of suffering seems to be that it refines and softens humanity; and Coleridge was no exception to the law. In his poetry we find a note of human sympathy, more tender and profound than can be found in Wordsworth or, indeed, in any other of the great English poets. Even in his later poems, when he has lost his first inspiration and something of the splendid imaginative power that makes his work equal to the best of Blake's, we find a soul tender, triumphant, quiet, "in the stillness of a great peace." He died in 1834, and was buried in Highgate Church. The last stanza of the boatman's song, in Remorse, serves better to express the world's judgment than any epitaph:

Hark! the cadence dies away

On the quiet moon-lit sea;

The boatmen rest their oars and say,

Miserere Domini!

Works of Coleridge

The works of Coleridge naturally divide themselves into three classes,--the poetic, the critical, and the philosophical, corresponding to the early, the middle, and the later periods of his career. Of his poetry Stopford Brooke well says: "All that he did excellently might be bound up in twenty pages, but it should be bound in pure gold." His early poems show the influence of Gray and Blake, especially of the latter. When Coleridge begins his "Day Dream" with the line, "My eyes make pictures when they're shut," we recall instantly

Blake's haunting Songs of Innocence. But there is this difference between the two poets,--in Blake we have only a dreamer; in Coleridge we have the rare combination of the dreamer and the profound scholar. The quality of this early poetry, with its strong suggestion of Blake, may be seen in such poems as "A Day Dream," "The Devil's Thoughts," "The Suicide's Argument," and "The Wanderings of Cain." His later poems, wherein we see his imagination bridled by thought and study, but still running very freely, may best be appreciated in "Kubla Khan," "Christabel," and "The Rime of the Ancient Mariner." It is difficult to criticise such poems; one can only read them and wonder at their melody, and at the vague suggestions which they conjure up in the mind. "Kubla Khan" is a fragment, painting a gorgeous Oriental dream picture, such as one might see in an October sunset. The whole poem came to Coleridge one morning when he had fallen asleep over Purchas, and upon awakening he began to write hastily,

In Xanadu did Kubla Khan

A stately pleasure-dome decree:

Where Alph, the sacred river, ran

Through caverns measureless to man

Down to a sunless sea.

He was interrupted after fifty-four lines were written, and he never finished the poem.

"Christabel" is also a fragment, which seems to have been planned as the story of a pure young girl who fell under the spell of a sorcerer, in the shape of the woman Geraldine. It is full of a strange melody, and contains many passages of exquisite poetry; but it trembles with a strange, unknown horror, and so suggests the supernatural terrors of the popular hysterical novels, to which we have referred. On this account it is not wholesome reading; though one flies in the face of Swinburne and of other critics by venturing to suggest such a thing.

"The Rime of the Ancient Mariner" is Coleridge's chief contribution to the Lyrical Ballads of 1798, and is one of the world's masterpieces. Though it introduces the reader to a supernatural realm, with a phantom ship, a crew of dead men, the overhanging curse of the albatross, the polar spirit, and the magic breeze, it nevertheless manages to create a sense of absolute reality concerning these manifest absurdities. All the mechanisms of the poem, its meter, rime, and melody are perfect; and some of its descriptions of the lonely sea have never been equaled. Perhaps we should say suggestions, rather than descriptions; for Coleridge never describes things, but makes a suggestion, always brief and always exactly right, and our own imagination instantly supplies the details. It is useless to quote fragments; one must read the entire poem, if he reads nothing else of the romantic school of poetry.

Among Coleridge's shorter poems there is a wide variety, and each reader must be left largely to follow his own taste. The beginner will do well to read a few of the early poems, to which we have referred, and then try the "Ode to France," "Youth and Age," "Dejection," "Love Poems," "Fears in Solitude," "Religious Musings," "Work Without Hope," and the glorious "Hymn Before Sunrise in the Vale of Chamouni." One exquisite little poem from the Latin, "The Virgin's Cradle Hymn," and his version of Schiller's Wallenstein, show Coleridge's remarkable power as a translator. The latter is one of the best poetical translations in our literature.

Of Coleridge's prose works, the Biographia, Literaria, or Sketches of My Literary Life and Opinions (1817), his collected Lectures on Shakespeare (1849), and Aids to Reflection (1825) are the most interesting from a literary view point. The first is an explanation and criticism of Wordsworth's theory of poetry, and contains more sound sense and illuminating ideas on the general subject of poetry than any other book in our language. The Lectures, as refreshing as a west wind in midsummer, are remarkable for their attempt to sweep away the arbitrary rules which for two centuries had stood in the way of literary criticism of Shakespeare, in order to study the works themselves. No finer analysis and appreciation of the master's genius has ever been written. In his philosophical work Coleridge introduced the idealistic philosophy of Germany into England. He set himself in line with Berkeley, and squarely against Bentham, Malthus, Mill, and all the materialistic tendencies which were and still are the bane of English philosophy. The Aids to Reflection is Coleridge's most profound work, but is more interesting to the student of religion and philosophy than to the readers of literature.

ROBERT SOUTHEY (1774-1843)

Closely associated with Wordsworth and Coleridge is Robert Southey; and the three, on account of their residence in the northern lake district, were referred to contemptuously as the "Lakers" by the Scottish magazine reviewers. Southey holds his place in this group more by personal association than by his literary gifts. He was born at Bristol, in 1774; studied at Westminster School, and at Oxford, where he found himself in perpetual conflict with the authorities on account of his independent views. He finally left the university and joined Coleridge in his scheme of a Pantisocracy. For more than fifty years he labored steadily at literature, refusing to consider any other occupation. He considered himself seriously as one of the greatest writers of the day, and a reading of his ballads--which connected him at once with the romantic school--leads us to think that, had he written less, he might possibly have justified his own opinion of himself. Unfortunately he could not wait for inspiration, being obliged to support not only his own family but also, in large measure, that of his friend Coleridge.

Southey gradually surrounded himself with one of the most extensive libraries in England, and set himself to the task of of writing something every working day. The results of his industry were one hundred and nine volumes, besides some hundred and fifty articles for the magazines, most of which are now utterly forgotten. His most ambitious poems are Thalaba, a tale of Arabian enchantment; The Curse of Kehama, a medley of Hindoo mythology; Madoc, a legend of a Welsh prince who discovered the western world; and Roderick, a tale of the last of the Goths. All these, and many more, although containing some excellent passages, are on the whole exaggerated and unreal, both in manner and in matter. Southey wrote far better prose than poetry, and his admirable Life of Nelson is still often read. Besides these are his Lives of British Admirals, his lives of Cowper and Wesley, and his histories of Brazil and of the Peninsular War.

Southey was made Poet Laureate in 1813, and was the first to raise that office from the low estate into which it had fallen since the death of Dryden. The opening lines of Thalaba, beginning,

How beautiful is night!

A dewy freshness fills the silent air,

are still sometimes quoted; and a few of his best known short poems, like "The Scholar," "Auld Cloots," "The Well of St. Keyne," "The Inchcape Rock," and "Lodore," will repay the curious reader. The beauty of Southey's character, his patience and helpfulness, make him a worthy associate of the two greater poets with whom he is generally named.

WALTER SCOTT (1771-1832)

We have already called attention to two significant movements of the eighteenth century, which we must for a moment recall if we are to appreciate Scott, not simply as a delightful teller of tales, but as a tremendous force in modern literature. The first is the triumph of romantic poetry in Wordsworth and Coleridge; the second is the success of our first English novelists, and the popularization of literature by taking it from the control of a few patrons and critics and putting it into the hands of the people as one of the forces which mold our modern life. Scott is an epitome of both these movements. The poetry of Wordsworth and Coleridge was read by a select few, but Scott's Marmion and Lady of the Lake aroused a whole nation to enthusiasm, and for the first time romantic poetry became really popular. So also the novel had been content to paint men and women of the present, until the wonderful series of Waverley novels appeared, when suddenly, by the magic of this "Wizard of the North," all history seemed changed.

The past, which had hitherto appeared as a dreary region of dead heroes, became alive again, and filled with a multitude of men and women who had the surprising charm of reality. It is of small consequence that Scott's poetry and prose are both faulty; that his poems are read chiefly for the story, rather than for their poetic excellence; and that much of the evident crudity and barbarism of the Middle Ages is ignored or forgotten in Scott's writings. By their vigor, their freshness, their rapid action, and their breezy, out-of-door atmosphere, Scott's novels attracted thousands of readers who else had known nothing of the delights of literature. He is, therefore, the greatest known factor in establishing and in popularizing that romantic element in prose and poetry which has been for a hundred years the chief characteristic of our literature.

Life

Scott was born in Edinburgh, on August 15, 1771. On both his mother's and father's side he was descended from old Border families, distinguished more for their feuds and fighting than for their intellectual attainments. His father was a barrister, a just man, who often lost clients by advising them to be, first of all, honest in their lawsuits. His mother was a woman of character and education, strongly imaginative, a teller of tales which stirred young Walter's enthusiasm by revealing the past as a world of living heroes.

As a child, Scott was lame and delicate, and was therefore sent away from the city to be with his grandmother in the open country at Sandy Knowe, in Roxburghshire, near the Tweed. This grandmother was a perfect treasure-house of legends concerning the old Border feuds. From her wonderful tales Scott developed that intense love of Scottish history and tradition which characterizes all his work.

By the time he was eight years old, when he returned to Edinburgh, Scott's tastes were fixed for life. At the high school he was a fair scholar, but without enthusiasm, being more interested in Border stories than in the text-books. He remained at school only six or seven years, and then entered his father's office to study law, at the same time attending lectures at the university. He kept this up for some six years without developing any interest in his profession, not even when he passed his examinations and was admitted to the Bar, in 1792. After nineteen years of desultory work, in which he showed far more zeal in gathering Highland legends than in gaining clients, he had won two small legal offices which gave him enough income to support him comfortably. His home, meanwhile, was at Ashestiel on the Tweed, where all his best poetry was written.

Scott's literary work began with the translation from the German of Buerger's romantic ballad of Lenore (1796) and of Goethe's Goetz von Berlichingen (1799); but there was romance enough in his own loved Highlands, and in 1802-1803 appeared three volumes of his Minstrelsy of the Scottish Border, which he had been collecting for many years. In 1805, when Scott was 34 years old, appeared his first original work, The Lay of the Last Minstrel. Its success was immediate, and when Marmion (1808) and The Lady of the Lake (1810) aroused Scotland and England to intense enthusiasm, and brought unexpected fame to the author,--without in the least spoiling his honest and lovable nature,--Scott gladly resolved to abandon the law, in which he had won scant success, and give himself wholly to literature.

Unfortunately, however, in order to increase his earnings, he entered secretly into partnership with the firms of Constable and the brothers Ballantyne, as printer-publishers,--a sad mistake, indeed, and the cause of that tragedy which closed the life of Scotland's greatest writer.

The year 1811 is remarkable for two things in Scott's life. In this year he seems to have realized that, notwithstanding the success of his poems, he had not yet "found himself"; that he was not a poetic genius, like Burns; that in his first three poems he had practically exhausted his material, though he still continued to write verse; and that, if he was to keep his popularity, he must find some other work. The fact that, only a year later, Byron suddenly became the popular favorite, shows how correctly Scott had judged himself and the reading public, which was even more fickle than usual in this emotional age. In that same year, 1811, Scott bought the estate of Abbotsford, on the Tweed, with which place his name is forever associated. Here he began to spend large sums, and to dispense the generous hospitality of a Scotch laird, of which he had been dreaming for years. In 1820 he was made a baronet; and his new title of Sir Walter came nearer to turning his honest head than had all his literary success. His business partnership was kept secret, and during all the years when the Waverley novels were the most popular books in the world, their authorship remained unknown; for Scott deemed it beneath the dignity of his title to earn money by business or literature, and sought to give the impression that the enormous sums spent at Abbotsford in improving the estate and in entertaining lavishly were part of the dignity of the position and came from ancestral sources.

It was the success of Byron's Childe Harold, and the comparative failure of Scott's later poems, Rokeby, The Bridal of Triermain, and The Lord of the Isles, which led our author into the new field, where he was to be without a rival. Rummaging through a cabinet one day in search of some fishing tackle, Scott found the manuscript of a story which he had begun and laid aside nine years before. He read this old story eagerly, as if it had been another's work; finished it within three weeks, and published it without signing his name. The success of this first novel, Waverley (1814), was immediate and unexpected. Its great sales and the general chorus of praise for its unknown author were without precedent; and when Guy Mannering, The Antiquary, Black Dwarf, Old Mortality, Rob Roy, and The Heart of Midlothian appeared within the next four years, England's delight and wonder knew no bounds. Not only at home, but also on the Continent, large numbers of these fresh and fascinating stories were sold as fast as they could be printed.

During the seventeen years which followed the appearance of Waverley, Scott wrote on an average nearly two novels per year, creating an unusual number of characters and illustrating many periods of Scotch, English, and French history, from the time of the Crusades to the fall of the Stuarts. In addition to these historical novels, he wrote Tales of a Grandfather, Demonology and Witchcraft, biographies of Dryden and of Swift, the Life of Napoleon, in nine volumes, and a large number of articles for the reviews and magazines. It was an extraordinary amount of literary work, but it was not quite so rapid and spontaneous as it seemed. He had been very diligent in looking up old records, and we must remember that, in nearly all his poems and novels, Scott was drawing upon a fund of legend, tradition, history, and poetry, which he had been gathering for forty years, and which his memory enabled him to produce at will with almost the accuracy of an encyclopedia.

For the first six years Scott held himself to Scottish history, giving us in nine remarkable novels the whole of Scotland, its heroism, its superb faith and enthusiasm, and especially its clannish loyalty to its hereditary chiefs; giving us also all parties and characters, from Covenanters to Royalists, and from kings to beggars. After reading these nine volumes we know Scotland and Scotchmen as we can know them in no other way. In 1819 he turned abruptly from Scotland, and in Ivanhoe, the most popular of his works, showed what a mine of neglected wealth lay just beneath the surface of English history. It is hard to realize now, as we read its rapid, melodramatic action, its vivid portrayal of Saxon and Norman character, and all its picturesque details, that it was written rapidly, at a time when the author was suffering from disease and could hardly repress an occasional groan from finding its way into the rapid dictation.

It stands to-day as the best example of the author's own theory that the will of a man is enough to hold him steadily, against all obstacles, to the task of "doing what he has a mind to do." Kenilworth, Nigel, Peveril, and Woodstock, all written in the next few years, show his grasp of the romantic side of English annals; Count Robert and The Talisman show his enthusiasm for the heroic side of the Crusaders' nature; and Quentin Durward and Anne of Geierstein suggest another mine of romance which he discovered in French history.

For twenty years Scott labored steadily at literature, with the double object of giving what was in him, and of earning large sums to support the lavish display which he deemed essential to a laird of Scotland. In 1826, while he was blithely at work on Woodstock, the crash came. Not even the vast earnings of all these popular novels could longer keep the wretched business of Ballantyne on its feet, and the firm failed, after years of mismanagement. Though a silent partner, Scott assumed full responsibility, and at fifty-five years of age, sick, suffering, and with all his best work behind him, he found himself facing a debt of over half a million dollars. The firm could easily have compromised with its creditors; but Scott refused to hear of bankruptcy laws under which he could have taken refuge. He assumed the entire debt as a personal one, and set resolutely to work to pay every penny. Times were indeed changed in England when, instead of a literary genius starving until some wealthy patron gave him a pension, this man, aided by his pen alone, could confidently begin to earn that enormous amount of money. And this is one of the unnoticed results of the popularization of literature. Without a doubt Scott would have accomplished the task, had he been granted only a few years of health. He still lived at Abbotsford, which he had offered to his creditors, but which they generously refused to accept; and in two years, by miscellaneous work, had paid some two hundred thousand dollars of his debt, nearly half of this sum coming from his Life of Napoleon.

A new edition of the Waverley novels appeared, which was very successful financially, and Scott had every reason to hope that he would soon face the world owing no man a penny, when he suddenly broke under the strain. In 1830 occurred a stroke of paralysis from which he never fully recovered; though after a little time he was again at work, dictating with splendid patience and resolution. He writes in his diary at this time: "The blow is a stunning one, I suppose, for I scarcely feel it. It is singular, but it comes with as little surprise as if I had a remedy ready, yet God knows I am at sea in the dark, and the vessel leaky."

It is good to remember that governments are not always ungrateful, and to record that, when it became known that a voyage to Italy might improve Scott's health, the British government promptly placed a naval vessel at the disposal of a man who had led no armies to the slaughter, but had only given pleasure to multitudes of peaceable men and women by his stories. He visited Malta, Naples, and Rome; but in his heart he longed for Scotland, and turned homeward after a few months of exile. The river Tweed, the Scotch hills, the trees of Abbotsford, the joyous clamor of his dogs, brought forth the first exclamation of delight which had passed Scott's lips since he sailed away. He died in September of the same year, 1832, and was buried with his ancestors in the old Dryburgh Abbey.

Works of Scott

Scott's work is of a kind which the critic gladly passes over, leaving each reader to his own joyous and uninstructed opinion. From a literary view point the works are faulty enough, if one is looking for faults; but it is well to remember that they were intended to give delight, and that they rarely fail of their object. When one has read the stirring Marmion or the more enduring Lady of the Lake, felt the heroism of the Crusaders in The Talisman, the picturesqueness of chivalry in Ivanhoe, the nobleness of soul of a Scotch peasant girl in The Heart of Midlothian, and the quality of Scotch faith in Old Mortality, then his own opinion of Scott's genius will be of more value than all the criticisms that have ever been written.

At the outset we must confess frankly that Scott's poetry is not artistic, in the highest sense, and that it lacks the deeply imaginative and suggestive qualities which make a poem the noblest and most enduring work of humanity. We read it now, not for its poetic excellence, but for its absorbing story interest. Even so, it serves an admirable purpose. Marmion and The Lady of the Lake, which are often the first long poems read by the beginner in literature, almost invariably lead to a deeper interest in the subject; and many readers owe to these poems an introduction to the delights of poetry.

They are an excellent beginning, therefore, for young readers, since they are almost certain to hold the attention, and to lead indirectly to an interest in other and better poems. Aside from this, Scott's poetry is marked by vigor and youthful abandon; its interest lies in its vivid pictures, its heroic characters, and especially in its rapid action and succession of adventures, which hold and delight us still, as they held and delighted the first wondering readers. And one finds here and there terse descriptions, or snatches of song and ballad, like the "Boat Song" and "Lochinvar," which are among the best known in our literature.

In his novels Scott plainly wrote too rapidly and too much. While a genius of the first magnitude, the definition of genius as "the infinite capacity for taking pains" hardly belongs to him. For details of life and history, for finely drawn characters, and for tracing the logical consequences of human action, he has usually no inclination. He sketches a character roughly, plunges him into the midst of stirring incidents, and the action of the story carries us on breathlessly to the end.

So his stories are largely adventure stories, at the best; and it is this element of adventure and glorious action, rather than the study of character, which makes Scott a perennial favorite of the young. The same element of excitement is what causes mature readers to turn from Scott to better novelists, who have more power to delineate human character, and to create, or discover, a romantic interest in the incidents of everyday life rather than in stirring adventure.

Notwithstanding these limitations, it is well--especially in these days, when we hear that Scott is outgrown--to emphasize four noteworthy things that he accomplished.

(1) He created the historical novel; and all novelists of the last century who draw upon history for their characters and events are followers of Scott and acknowledge his mastery.

(2) His novels are on a vast scale, covering a very wide range of action, and are concerned with public rather than with private interests. So, with the exception of The Bride of Lammermoor, the love story in his novels is generally pale and feeble; but the strife and passions of big parties are magnificently portrayed. A glance over even the titles of his novels shows how the heroic side of history for over six hundred years finds expression in his pages; and all the parties of these six centuries--Crusaders, Covenanters, Cavaliers,

Roundheads, Papists, Jews, Gypsies, Rebels--start into life again, and fight or give a reason for the faith that is in them. No other novelist in England, and only Balzac in France, approaches Scott in the scope of his narratives.

(3) Scott was the first novelist in any language to make the scene an essential element in the action. He knew Scotland, and loved it; and there is hardly an event in any of his Scottish novels in which we do not breathe the very atmosphere of the place, and feel the presence of its moors and mountains. The place, morever, is usually so well chosen and described that the action seems almost to be the result of natural environment. Perhaps the most striking illustration of this harmony between scene and incident is found in Old Mortality, where Morton approaches the cave of the old Covenanter, and where the spiritual terror inspired by the fanatic's struggle with imaginary fiends is paralleled by the physical terror of a gulf and a roaring flood spanned by a slippery tree trunk. A second illustration of the same harmony of scene and incident is found in the meeting of the arms and ideals of the East and West, when the two champions fight in the burning desert, and then eat bread together in the cool shade of the oasis, as described in the opening chapter of The Talisman. A third illustration is found in that fascinating love scene, where Ivanhoe lies wounded, raging at his helplessness, while the gentle Rebecca alternately hides and reveals her love as she describes the terrific assault on the castle, which goes on beneath her window. His thoughts are all on the fight; hers on the man she loves; and both are natural, and both are exactly what we expect under the circumstances. These are but striking examples of the fact that, in all his work, Scott tries to preserve perfect harmony between the scene and the action.

(4) Scott's chief claim to greatness lies in the fact that he was the first novelist to recreate the past; that he changed our whole conception of history by making it to be, not a record of dry facts, but a stage on which living men and women played their parts. Carlyle's criticism is here most pertinent: "These historical novels have taught this truth... unknown to writers of history: that the bygone ages of the world were actually filled by living men, not by protocols, state papers, controversies, and abstractions of men." Not only the pages of history, but all the hills and vales of his beloved Scotland are filled with living characters,--lords and ladies, soldiers, pirates, gypsies, preachers, schoolmasters, clansmen, bailiffs, dependents,--all Scotland is here before our eyes, in the reality of life itself. It is astonishing, with his large numbers of characters, that Scott never repeats himself. Naturally he is most at home in Scotland, and with humble people. Scott's own romantic interest in feudalism caused him to make his lords altogether too lordly; his aristocratic maidens are usually bloodless, conventional, exasperating creatures, who talk like books and pose like figures in an old tapestry. But when he describes characters like Jeanie Deans, in The Heart of Midlothian, and the old clansman, Evan Dhu, in Waverley, we know the very soul of Scotch womanhood and manhood.

Perhaps one thing more should be said, or rather repeated, of Scott's enduring work. He is always sane, wholesome, manly, inspiring. We know the essential nobility of human life better, and we are better men and women ourselves, because of what he has written.

GEORGE GORDON, LORD BYRON (1788-1824)

There are two distinct sides to Byron and his poetry, one good, the other bad; and those who write about him generally describe one side or the other in superlatives. Thus one critic speaks of his "splendid and imperishable excellence of sincerity and strength"; another of his "gaudy charlatanry, blare of brass, and big bow-wowishness." As both critics are fundamentally right, we shall not here attempt to reconcile their differences, which arise from viewing one side of the man's nature and poetry to the exclusion of the other. Before his exile from England, in 1816, the general impression made by Byron is that of a man who leads an irregular life, poses as a romantic hero, makes himself out much worse than he really is, and takes delight in shocking not only the conventions but the ideals of English society.

His poetry of this first period is generally, though not always, shallow and insincere in thought, and declamatory or bombastic in expression. After his exile, and his meeting with Shelley in Italy, we note a gradual improvement, due partly to Shelley's influence and partly to his own mature thought and experience. We have the impression now of a disillusioned man who recognizes his true character, and who, though cynical and pessimistic, is at least honest in his unhappy outlook on society. His poetry of this period is generally less shallow and rhetorical, and though he still parades his feelings in public, he often surprises us by being manly and sincere. Thus in the third canto of Childe Harold, written just after his exile, he says:

In my youth's summer I did sing of one,

The wandering outlaw of his own dark mind;

and as we read on to the end of the splendid fourth canto--with its poetic feeling for nature, and its stirring rhythm that grips and holds the reader like martial music--we lay down the book with profound regret that this gifted man should have devoted so much of his talent to describing trivial or unwholesome intrigues and posing as the hero of his own verses. The real tragedy of Byron's life is that he died just as he was beginning to find himself.

Life

Byron was born in London in 1788, the year preceding the French Revolution. We shall understand him better, and judge him more charitably, if we remember the tainted stock from which he sprang. His father was a dissipated spendthrift of unspeakable morals; his mother was a Scotch heiress, passionate and unbalanced.

The father deserted his wife after squandering her fortune; and the boy was brought up by the mother who "alternately petted and abused" him. In his eleventh year the death of a granduncle left him heir to Newstead Abbey and to the baronial title of one of the oldest houses in England. He was singularly handsome; and a lameness resulting from a deformed foot lent a suggestion of pathos to his make-up. All this, with his social position, his pseudo-heroic poetry, and his dissipated life,--over which he contrived to throw a veil of romantic secrecy,--made him a magnet of attraction to many thoughtless young men and foolish women, who made the downhill path both easy and rapid to one whose inclinations led him in that direction. Naturally he was generous, and easily led by affection. He is, therefore, largely a victim of his own weakness and of unfortunate surroundings.

At school at Harrow, and in the university at Cambridge, Byron led an unbalanced life, and was more given to certain sports from which he was not debarred by lameness, than to books and study. His school life, like his infancy, is sadly marked by vanity, violence, and rebellion against every form of authority; yet it was not without its hours of nobility and generosity. Scott describes him as "a man of real goodness of heart, and the kindest and best feelings, miserably thrown away by his foolish contempt of public opinion."

While at Cambridge, Byron published his first volume of poems, Hours of Idleness, in 1807. A severe criticism of the volume in the Edinburgh Review wounded Byron's vanity, and threw him into a violent passion, the result of which was the now famous satire called English Bards and Scotch Reviewers, in which not only his enemies, but also Scott, Wordsworth, and nearly all the literary men of his day, were satirized in heroic couplets after the manner of Pope's Dunciad. It is only just to say that he afterwards made friends with Scott and with others whom he had abused without provocation; and it is interesting to note, in view of his own romantic poetry, that he denounced all masters of romance and accepted the artificial standards of Pope and Dryden. His two favorite books were the Old Testament and a volume of Pope's poetry. Of the latter he says, "His is the greatest name in poetry... all the rest are barbarians."

In 1809 Byron, when only twenty-one years of age, started on a tour of Europe and the Orient. The poetic results of this trip were the first two cantos of Childe Harold's Pilgrimage, with their famous descriptions of romantic scenery. The work made him instantly popular, and his fame overshadowed Scott's completely. As he says himself, "I awoke one morning to find myself famous," and presently he styles himself "the grand Napoleon of the realms of rhyme." The worst element in Byron at this time was his insincerity, his continual posing as the hero of his poetry. His best works were translated, and his fame spread almost as rapidly on the Continent as in England. Even Goethe was deceived, and declared that a man so wonderful in character had never before appeared in literature, and would never appear again. Now that the tinsel has worn off, and we can judge the man and his work dispassionately, we see how easily even the critics of the age were governed by romantic impulses.

The adulation of Byron lasted only a few years in England. In 1815 he married Miss Milbanke, an English heiress, who abruptly left him a year later. With womanly reserve she kept silence; but the public was not slow to imagine plenty of reasons for the separation. This, together with the fact that men had begun to penetrate the veil of romantic secrecy with which Byron surrounded himself and found a rather brassy idol beneath, turned the tide of public opinion against him. He left England under a cloud of distrust and disappointment, in 1816, and never returned. Eight years were spent abroad, largely in Italy, where he was associated with Shelley until the latter's tragic death in 1822.

His house was ever the meeting place for Revolutionists and malcontents calling themselves patriots, whom he trusted too greatly, and with whom he shared his money most generously. Curiously enough, while he trusted men too easily, he had no faith in human society or government, and wrote in 1817: "I have simplified my politics to an utter detestation of all existing governments." During his exile he finished Childe Harold, The Prisoner of Chillon, his dramas Cain and Manfred, and numerous other works, in some of which, as in Don Juan, he delighted in revenging himself upon his countrymen by holding up to ridicule all that they held most sacred.

In 1824 Byron went to Greece to give himself and a large part of his fortune to help that country in its struggle for liberty against the Turks. How far he was led by his desire for posing as a hero, and how far by a certain vigorous Viking spirit that was certainly in him, will never be known.

The Greeks welcomed him and made him a leader, and for a few months he found himself in the midst of a wretched squabble of lies, selfishness, insincerity, cowardice, and intrigue, instead of the heroic struggle for liberty which he had anticipated. He died of fever, in Missolonghi, in 1824. One of his last poems, written there on his thirty-sixth birthday, a few months before he died, expresses his own view of his disappointing life:

My days are in the yellow leaf,

The flowers and fruits of love are gone:

The worm, the canker, and the grief

Are mine alone.

Works of Byron

In reading Byron it is well to remember that he was a disappointed and embittēred man, not only in his personal life, but also in his expectation of a general transformation of human society. As he pours out his own feelings, chiefly, in his poetry, he is the most expressive writer of his age in voicing the discontent of a multitude of Europeans who were disappointed at the failure of the French Revolution to produce an entirely new form of government and society.

One who wishes to understand the whole scope of Byron's genius and poetry will do well to begin with his first work, Hours of Idleness, written when he was a young man at the university. There is very little poetry in the volume, only a striking facility in rime, brightened by the devil-may-care spirit of the Cavalier poets; but as a revelation of the man himself it is remarkable. In a vain and sophomoric preface he declares that poetry is to him an idle experiment, and that this is his first and last attempt to amuse himself in that line. Curiously enough, as he starts for Greece on his last, fatal journey, he again ridicules literature, and says that the poet is a "mere babbler." It is this despising of the art which alone makes him famous that occasions our deepest disappointment. Even in his magnificent passages, in a glowing description of nature or of a Hindoo woman's exquisite love, his work is frequently marred by a wretched pun, or by some cheap buffoonery, which ruins our first splendid impression of his poetry.

Byron's later volumes, Manfred and Cain, the one a curious, and perhaps unconscious, parody of Faust, the other of Paradise Lost, are his two best known dramatic works. Aside from the question of their poetic value, they are interesting as voicing Byron's excessive individualism and his rebellion against society. The best known and the most readable of Byron's works Mazeppa, The Prisoner of Chillon, and Childe Harold's Pilgrimage. The first two cantos of Childe Harold (1812) are perhaps more frequently read than any other work of the same author, partly because of their melodious verse, partly because of their descriptions of places along the lines of European travel; but the last two cantos (1816-1818) written after his exile from England, have more sincerity, and are in every way better expressions of Byron's mature genius. Scattered through all his works one finds magnificent descriptions of natural scenery, and exquisite lyrics of love and despair; but they are mixed with such a deal of bombast and rhetoric, together with much that is unwholesome, that the beginner will do well to confine himself to a small volume of well-chosen selections.

Byron is often compared with Scott, as having given to us Europe and the Orient, just as Scott gave us Scotland and its people; but while there is a certain resemblance in the swing and dash of the verses, the resemblance is all on the surface, and the underlying difference between the two poets is as great as that between Thackeray and Bulwer-Lytton. Scott knew his country well,--its hills and valleys which are interesting as the abode of living and lovable men and women. Byron pretended to know the secret, unwholesome side of Europe, which generally hides itself in the dark; but instead of giving us a variety of living men, he never gets away from his own unbalanced and egotistical self. All his characters, in Cain, Manfred, The Corsair, The Giaour, Childe Harold, Don Juan, are tiresome repetitions of himself,--a vain, disappointed, cynical man, who finds no good in life or love or anything. Naturally, with such a disposition, he is entirely incapable of portraying a true woman. To nature alone, especially in her magnificent moods, Byron remains faithful; and his portrayal of the night and the storm and the ocean in Childe Harold are unsurpassed in our language.

PERCY BYSSHE SHELLEY (1792-1822)

Make me thy lyre, even as the forest is:
What if my leaves are falling like its own!
The tumult of thy mighty harmonies

Will take from both a deep, autumnal tone,
Sweet though in sadness. Be thou, spirit fierce,
My spirit! Be thou me, impetuous one!

In this fragment, from the "Ode to the West Wind," we have a suggestion of Shelley's own spirit, as reflected in all his poetry. The very spirit of nature, which appeals to us in the wind and the cloud, the sunset and the moonrise, seems to have possessed him, at times, and made him a chosen instrument of melody. At such times he is a true poet, and his work is unrivaled. At other times, unfortunately, Shelley joins with Byron in voicing a vain rebellion against society. His poetry, like his life, divides itself into two distinct moods. In one he is the violent reformer, seeking to overthrow our present institutions and to hurry the millennium out of its slow walk into a gallop. Out of this mood come most of his longer poems, like Queen Mab, Revolt of Islam, Hellas, and The Witch of Atlas, which are somewhat violent diatribes against government, priests, marriage, religion, even God as men supposed him to be. In a different mood, which finds expression Alastor, Adonais, and his wonderful lyrics, Shelley is like a wanderer following a vague, beautiful vision, forever sad and forever unsatisfied. In the latter mood he appeals profoundly to all men who have known what it is to follow after an unattainable ideal.

Shelley's Life

There are three classes of men who see visions, and all three are represented in our literature. The first is the mere dreamer, like Blake, who stumbles through a world of reality without noticing it, and is happy in his visions. The second is the seer, the prophet, like Langland, or Wyclif, who sees a vision and quietly goes to work, in ways that men understand, to make the present world a little more like the ideal one which he sees in his vision. The third, who appears in many forms,--as visionary, enthusiast, radical, anarchist, revolutionary, call him what you will,--sees a vision and straightway begins to tear down all human institutions, which have been built up by the slow toil of centuries, simply because they seem to stand in the way of his dream. To the latter class belongs Shelley, a man perpetually at war with the present world, a martyr and exile, simply because of his inability to sympathize with men and society as they are, and because of his own mistaken judgment as to the value and purpose of a vision.

Shelley was born in Field Place, near Horsham, Sussex, in 1792. On both his father's and his mother's side he was descended from noble old families, famous in the political and literary history of England. From childhood he lived, like Blake, in a world of fancy, so real that certain imaginary dragons and headless creatures of the neighboring wood kept him and his sisters in a state of fearful expectancy. He learned rapidly, absorbed the classics as if by intuition, and, dissatisfied with ordinary processes of learning, seems to have sought, like Faustus, the acquaintance of spirits, as shown in his "Hymn to Intellectual Beauty":

While yet a boy, I sought for ghosts, and sped
Through many a listening chamber, cave and ruin,
And starlight wood, with fearful steps pursuing
Hopes of high talk with the departed dead.

Shelley's first public school, kept by a hard-headed Scotch master, with its floggings and its general brutality, seemed to him like a combination of hell and prison; and his active rebellion against existing institutions was well under way when, at twelve years of age, he entered the famous preparatory school at Eton. He was a delicate, nervous, marvelously sensitive boy, of great physical beauty; and, like Cowper, he suffered torments at the hands of his rough schoolfellows. Unlike Cowper, he was positive, resentful, and brave to the point of rashness; soul and body rose up against tyranny; and he promptly organized a rebellion against the brutal fagging system. "Mad Shelley" the boys called him, and they chivied him like dogs around a little coon that fights and cries defiance to the end. One finds what he seeks in this world, and it is not strange that Shelley, after his Eton experiences, found causes for rebellion in all existing forms of human society, and that he left school "to war among mankind," as he says of himself in the Revolt of Islam. His university days are but a repetition of his earlier experiences. While a student at Oxford he read some scraps of Hume's philosophy, and immediately published a pamphlet called "The Necessity of Atheism." It was a crude, foolish piece of work, and Shelley distributed it by post to every one to whom it might give offense. Naturally this brought on a conflict with the authorities, but Shelley would not listen to reason or make any explanation, and was expelled from the university in 1811.

Shelley's marriage was even more unfortunate. While living in London, on a generous sister's pocket money, a certain young schoolgirl, Harriet Westbrook, was attracted by Shelley's crude revolutionary doctrines. She promptly left school, as her own personal part in the general rebellion, and refused to return or even to listen to her parents upon the subject. Having been taught by Shelley, she threw herself upon his protection; and this unbalanced couple were presently married, as they said, "in deference to anarch custom." The two infants had already proclaimed a rebellion against the institution of marriage, for which they proposed to substitute the doctrine of elective affinity. For two years they wandered about England, Ireland, and Wales, living on a small allowance from Shelley's father, who had disinherited his son because of his ill-considered marriage. The pair soon separated, and two years later Shelley, having formed a strong friendship with one Godwin,--a leader of young enthusiasts and a preacher of anarchy,--presently showed his belief in Godwin's theories by eloping with his daughter Mary. It is a sad story, and the details were perhaps better forgotten. We should remember that in Shelley we are dealing with a tragic blend of high-mindedness and light-headedness.

Byron wrote of him, "The most gentle, the most amiable, and the least worldly-minded person I ever met!"

Led partly by the general hostility against him, and partly by his own delicate health, Shelley went to Italy in 1818, and never returned to England. After wandering over Italy he finally settled in Pisa, beloved of so many English poets,--beautiful, sleepy Pisa, where one looks out of his window on the main street at the busiest hour of the day, and the only living thing in sight is a donkey, dozing lazily, with his head in the shade and his body in the sunshine. Here his best poetry was written, and here he found comfort in the friendship of Byron, Hunt, and Trelawney, who are forever associated with Shelley's Italian life. He still remained hostile to English social institutions; but life is a good teacher, and that Shelley dimly recognized the error of his rebellion is shown in the increasing sadness of his later poems:

O world, O life, O time!
On whose last steps I climb,
Trembling at that where I had stood before;
When will return the glory of your prime?
No more--oh, never more!
Out of the day and night
A joy has taken flight;
Fresh spring, and summer, and winter hoar,
Move my faint heart with grief, but with delight
No more--oh, never more!

In 1822, when only thirty years of age, Shelley was drowned while sailing in a small boat off the Italian coast. His body was washed ashore several days later, and was cremated, near Viareggio, by his friends, Byron, Hunt, and Trelawney. His ashes might, with all reverence, have been given to the winds that he loved and that were a symbol of his restless spirit; instead, they found a resting place near the grave of Keats, in the English cemetery at Rome. One rarely visits the spot now without finding English and American visitors standing in silence before the significant inscription, Cor Cordium.

Works of Shelley

As a lyric poet, Shelley is one of the supreme geniuses of our literature; and the reader will do well to begin with the poems which show him at his very best. "The Cloud," "To a Skylark," "Ode to the West Wind," "To Night,"--poems like these must surely set the reader to searching among Shelley's miscellaneous works, to find for himself the things "worthy to be remembered."

In reading Shelley's longer poems one must remember that there are in this poet two distinct men: one, the wanderer, seeking ideal beauty and forever unsatisfied; the other, the unbalanced reformer, seeking the overthrow of present institutions and the establishment of universal happiness. Alastor, or the Spirit of Solitude (1816) is by far the best expression of Shelley's greater mood. Here we see him wandering restlessly through the vast silences of nature, in search of a loved dream-maiden who shall satisfy his love of beauty. Here Shelley is the poet of the moonrise, and of the tender exquisite fancies that can never be expressed. The charm of the poem lies in its succession of dreamlike pictures; but it gives absolutely no impressions of reality. It was written when Shelley, after his long struggle, had begun to realize that the world was too strong for him. Alastor is therefore the poet's confession, not simply of failure, but of undying hope in some better thing that is to come.

Prometheus Unbound (1818-1820), a lyrical drama, is the best work of Shelley's revolutionary enthusiasm, and the most characteristic of all his poems. Shelley's philosophy (if one may dignify a hopeless dream by such a name) was a curious aftergrowth of the French Revolution, namely, that it is only the existing tyranny of State, Church, and society which keeps man from growth into perfect happiness. Naturally Shelley forgot, like many other enthusiasts, that Church and State and social laws were not imposed upon man from without, but were created by himself to minister to his necessities. In Shelley's poem the hero, Prometheus, represents mankind itself,--a just and noble humanity, chained and tortured by Jove, who is here the personification of human institutions. In due time Demogorgon (which is Shelley's name for Necessity) overthrows the tyrant Jove and releases Prometheus (Mankind), who is presently united to Asia, the spirit of love and goodness in nature, while the earth and the moon join in a wedding song, and everything gives promise that they shall live together happy ever afterwards.

Shelley here looks forward, not back, to the Golden Age, and is the prophet of science and evolution. If we compare his Titan with similar characters in Faust and Cain, we shall find this interesting difference,--that while Goethe's Titan is cultured and self-reliant, and Byron's stoic and hopeless, Shelley's hero is patient under torture, seeing help and hope beyond his suffering. And he marries Love that the earth may be peopled with superior beings who shall substitute brotherly love for the present laws and conventions of society. Such is his philosophy; but the beginner will read this poem, not chiefly for its thought, but for its youthful enthusiasm, for its marvelous imagery, and especially for its ethereal music. Perhaps we should add here that Prometheus is, and probably always will be, a poem for the chosen few who can appreciate its peculiar spiritlike beauty. In its purely pagan conception of the world, it suggests, by contrast, Milton's Christian philosophy in Paradise Regained.

Shelley's revolutionary works, Queen Mab (1813), The Revolt of Islam (1818), Hellas (1821), and The Witch of Atlas (1820), are to be judged in much the same way as is Prometheus Unbound. They are largely invectives against religion, marriage, kingcraft, and priestcraft, most impractical when considered as schemes for reform, but abounding in passages of exquisite beauty, for which alone they are worth reading. In the drama called The Cenci (1819), which is founded upon a morbid Italian story, Shelley for the first and only time descends to reality. The heroine, Beatrice, driven to desperation by the monstrous wickedness of her father, kills him and suffers the death penalty in consequence. She is the only one of Shelley's characters who seems to us entirely human.

Far different in character is Epipsychidion (1821), a rhapsody celebrating Platonic love, the most impalpable, and so one of the most characteristic, of all Shelley's works. It was inspired by a beautiful Italian girl, Emilia Viviani, who was put into a cloister against her will, and in whom Shelley imagined he found his long-sought ideal of womanhood. With this should be read Adonais (1821), the best known of all Shelley's longer poems. Adonais is a wonderful threnody, or a song of grief, over the death of the poet Keats. Even in his grief Shelley still preserves a sense of unreality, and calls in many shadowy allegorical figures,--Sad Spring, Weeping Hours, Glooms, Splendors, Destinies,--all uniting in bewailing the loss of a loved one. The whole poem is a succession of dream pictures, exquisitely beautiful, such as only Shelley could imagine; and it holds its place with Milton's Lycidas and Tennyson's In Memoriam as one of the three greatest elegies in our language.

In his interpretation of nature Shelley suggests Wordsworth, both by resemblance and by contrast. To both poets all natural objects are symbols of truth; both regard nature as permeated by the great spiritual life which animates all things; but while Wordsworth finds a spirit of thought, and so of communion between nature and the soul of man, Shelley finds a spirit of love, which exists chiefly for its own delight; and so "The Cloud," "The Skylark," and "The West Wind," three of the most beautiful poems in our language, have no definite message for humanity. In his "Hymn to

Intellectual Beauty" Shelley is most like Wordsworth; but in his "Sensitive Plant," with its fine symbolism and imagery, he is like nobody in the world but himself.

Comparison is sometimes an excellent thing; and if we compare Shelley's exquisite "Lament," beginning "O world, O life, O time," with Wordsworth's "Intimations of Immortality," we shall perhaps understand both poets better. Both poems recall many happy memories of youth; both express a very real mood of a moment; but while the beauty of one merely saddens and disheartens us, the beauty of the other inspires us with something of the poet's own faith and hopefulness. In a word, Wordsworth found and Shelley lost himself in nature.

JOHN KEATS (1795-1821)

Keats was not only the last but also the most perfect of the Romanticists. While Scott was merely telling stories, and Wordsworth reforming poetry or upholding the moral law, and Shelley advocating impossible reforms, and Byron voicing his own egoism and the political discontent of the times, Keats lived apart from men and from all political measures, worshiping beauty like a devotee, perfectly content to write what was in his own heart, or to reflect some splendor of the natural world as he saw or dreamed it to be.

He had, moreover, the novel idea that poetry exists for its own sake, and suffers loss by being devoted to philosophy or politics or, indeed, to any cause, however great or small. As he says in "Lamia":

... Do not all charms fly
At the mere touch of cold philosophy?
There was an awful rainbow once in heaven:
We know her woof, her texture; she is given
In the dull catalogue of common things.
Philosophy will clip an Angel's wings,

Conquer all mysteries by rule and line,
Empty the haunted air, and gnomed mine--
Unweave a rainbow, as it erewhile made
The tender-person'd Lamia melt into a shade.

Partly because of this high ideal of poetry, partly because he studied and unconsciously imitated the Greek classics and the best works of the Elizabethans, Keats's last little volume of poetry is unequaled by the work of any of his contemporaries. When we remember that all his work was published in three short years, from 1817 to 1820, and that he died when only twenty-five years old, we must judge him to be the most promising figure of the early nineteenth century, and one of the most remarkable in the history of literature.

Life

Keats's life of devotion to beauty and to poetry is all the more remarkable in view of his lowly origin. He was the son of a hostler and stable keeper, and was born in the stable of the Swan and Hoop Inn, London, in 1795. One has only to read the rough stable scenes from our first novelists, or even from Dickens, to understand how little there was in such an atmosphere to develop poetic gifts. Before Keats was fifteen years old both parents died, and he was placed with his brothers and sisters in charge of guardians.

Their first act seems to have been to take Keats from school at Enfield, and to bind him as an apprentice to a surgeon at Edmonton. For five years he served his apprenticeship, and for two years more he was surgeon's helper in the hospitals; but though skillful enough to win approval, he disliked his work, and his thoughts were on other things. "The other day, during a lecture," he said to a friend, "there came a sunbeam into the room, and with it a whole troop of creatures floating in the ray; and I was off with them to Oberon and fairyland." A copy of Spenser's

Faery Queen, which had been given him by Charles Cowden Clark, was the prime cause of his abstraction. He abandoned his profession in 1817, and early in the same year published his first volume of Poems. It was modest enough in spirit, as was also his second volume, Endymion (1818); but that did not prevent brutal attacks upon the author and his work by the self-constituted critics of Blackwood's Magazine and the Quarterly. It is often alleged that the poet's spirit and ambition were broken by these attacks; but Keats was a man of strong character, and instead of quarreling with his reviewers, or being crushed by their criticism, he went quietly to work with the idea of producing poetry that should live forever. As Matthew Arnold says, Keats "had flint and iron in him"; and in his next volume he accomplished his own purpose and silenced unfriendly criticism.

For the three years during which Keats wrote his poetry he lived chiefly in London and in Hampstead, but wandered at times over England and Scotland, living for brief spaces in the Isle of Wight, in Devonshire, and in the Lake district, seeking to recover his own health, and especially to restore that of his brother. His illness began with a severe cold, but soon developed into consumption; and added to this sorrow was another,--his love for Fannie Brawne, to whom he was engaged, but whom he could not marry on account of his poverty and growing illness. When we remember all this personal grief and the harsh criticism of literary men, the last small volume, Lamia, Isabella, The Eve of St. Agnes, and Other Poems (1820), is most significant, as showing not only Keats's wonderful poetic gifts, but also his beautiful and indomitable spirit. Shelley, struck by the beauty and promise of "Hyperion," sent a generous invitation to the author to come to Pisa and live with him; but Keats refused, having little sympathy with Shelley's revolt against society.

The invitation had this effect, however, that it turned Keats's thoughts to Italy, whither he soon went in the effort to save his life. He settled in Rome with his friend Severn, the artist, but died soon after his arrival, in February, 1821. His grave, in the Protestant cemetery at Rome, is still an object of pilgrimage to thousands of tourists; for among all our poets there is hardly another whose heroic life and tragic death have so appealed to the hearts of poets and young enthusiasts.

The Work of Keats

"None but the master shall praise us; and none but the master shall blame" might well be written on the fly leaf of every volume of Keats's poetry; for never was there a poet more devoted to his ideal, entirely independent of success or failure. In strong contrast with his contemporary, Byron, who professed to despise the art that made him famous, Keats lived for poetry alone, and, as Lowell pointed out, a virtue went out of him into everything he wrote. In all his work we have the impression of this intense loyalty to his art; we have the impression also of a profound dissatisfaction that the deed falls so far short of the splendid dream. Thus after reading Chapman's translation of Homer he writes:

Much have I travelled in the realms of gold,
And many goodly states and kingdoms seen;
Round many western islands have I been
Which bards in fealty to Apollo hold.
Oft of one wide expanse had I been told
That deep-browed Homer ruled as his demesne;
Yet did I never breathe its pure serene
Till I heard Chapman speak out loud and bold:
Then felt I like some watcher of the skies
When a new planet swims into his ken;
Or like stout Cortez when with eagle eyes
He stared at the Pacific--and all his men
Looked at each other with a wild surmise--
Silent, upon a peak in Darien.

In this striking sonnet we have a suggestion of Keats's high ideal, and of his sadness because of his own ignorance, when he published his first little volume of poems in 1817. He knew no Greek; yet Greek literature absorbed and fascinated him, as he saw its broken and imperfect reflection in an English translation. Like Shakespeare, who also was but poorly educated in the schools, he had a marvelous faculty of discerning the real spirit of the classics,--a faculty denied to many great scholars, and to most of the "classic" writers of the preceding century,--and so he set himself to the task of reflecting in modern English the spirit of the old Greeks.

The imperfect results of this attempt are seen in his next volume, Endymion, which is the story of a young shepherd beloved by a moon goddess. The poem begins with the striking lines:

A thing of beauty is a joy forever;

Its loveliness increases; it will never

Pass into nothingness; but still will keep

A bower quiet for us; and a sleep

Full of sweet dreams, and health, and quiet breathing,

which well illustrate the spirit of Keats's later work, with its perfect finish and melody.

It has many quotable lines and passages, and its "Hymn to Pan" should be read in connection with Wordsworth's famous sonnet beginning, "The world is too much with us." The poem gives splendid promise, but as a whole it is rather chaotic, with too much ornament and too little design, like a modern house. That Keats felt this defect strongly is evident from his modest preface, wherein he speaks of Endymion, not as a deed accomplished, but only as an unsuccessful attempt to suggest the underlying beauty of Greek mythology.

Keats's third and last volume, Lamia, Isabella, The Eve of St. Agnes, and Other Poems (1820), is the one with which the reader should begin his acquaintance with this master of English verse. It has only two subjects, Greek mythology and mediaeval romance. "Hyperion" is a magnificent fragment, suggesting the first arch of a cathedral that was never finished. Its theme is the overthrow of the Titans by the young sun-god Apollo. Realizing his own immaturity and lack of knowledge, Keats laid aside this work, and only the pleadings of his publisher induced him to print the fragment with his completed poems.

Throughout this last volume, and especially in "Hyperion," the influence of Milton is apparent, while Spenser is more frequently suggested in reading Endymion.

Of the longer poems in the volume, "Lamia" is the most suggestive. It is the story of a beautiful enchantress, who turns from a serpent into a glorious woman and fills every human sense with delight, until, as a result of the foolish philosophy of old Apollonius, she vanishes forever from her lover's sight. "The Eve of St. Agnes," the most perfect of Keats's mediaeval poems, is not a story after the manner of the metrical romances, but rather a vivid painting of a romantic mood, such as comes to all men, at times, to glorify a workaday world. Like all the work of Keats and Shelley, it has an element of unreality; and when we read at the end,

And they are gone; aye, ages long ago
These lovers fled away into the storm,

it is as if we were waking from a dream,--which is the only possible ending to all of Keats's Greek and mediaeval fancies. We are to remember, however, that no beautiful thing, though it be intangible as a dream, can enter a man's life and leave him quite the same afterwards. Keats's own word is here suggestive. "The imagination," he said, "may be likened to Adam's dream; he awoke and found it true."

It is by his short poems that Keats is known to the majority of present-day readers. Among these exquisite shorter poems we mention only the four odes, "On a Grecian

Urn," "To a Nightingale," "To Autumn," and "To Psyche." These are like an invitation to a feast; one who reads them will hardly be satisfied until he knows more of such delightful poetry. Those who study only the "Ode to a Nightingale" may find four things,--a love of sensuous beauty, a touch of pessimism, a purely pagan conception of nature, and a strong individualism,--which are characteristic of this last of the romantic poets.

As Wordsworth's work is too often marred by the moralizer, and Byron's by the demagogue, and Shelley's by the reformer, so Keats's work suffers by the opposite extreme of aloofness from every human interest; so much so, that he is often accused of being indifferent to humanity. His work is also criticised as being too effeminate for ordinary readers. Three things should be remembered in this connection.

First, that Keats sought to express beauty for its own sake; that beauty is as essential to normal humanity as is government or law; and that the higher man climbs in civilization the more imperative becomes his need of beauty as a reward for his labors.

Second, that Keats's letters are as much an indication of the man as is his poetry; and in his letters, with their human sympathy, their eager interest in social problems, their humor, and their keen insight into life, there is no trace of effeminacy, but rather every indication of a strong and noble manhood.

The third thing to remember is that all Keats's work was done in three or four years, with small preparation, and that, dying at twenty-five, he left us a body of poetry which will always be one of our most cherished possessions. He is often compared with "the marvelous boy" Chatterton, whom he greatly admired, and to whose memory he dedicated his Endymion; but though both died young, Chatterton was but a child, while Keats was in all respects a man. It is idle to prophesy what he might have done, had he been granted a

Tennyson's long life and scholarly training. At twenty five his work was as mature as was Tennyson's at fifty, though the maturity suggests the too rapid growth of a tropical plant which under the warm rains and the flood of sunlight leaps into life, grows, blooms in a day, and dies.

As we have stated, Keats's work was bitterly and unjustly condemned by the critics of his day. He belonged to what was derisively called the cockney school of poetry, of which Leigh Hunt was chief, and Proctor and Beddoes were fellow-workmen. Not even from Wordsworth and Byron, who were ready enough to recommend far less gifted writers, did Keats receive the slightest encouragement.

Like young Lochinvar, "he rode all unarmed and he rode all alone." Shelley, with his sincerity and generosity, was the first to recognize the young genius, and in his noble Adonais--written, alas, like most of our tributes, when the subject of our praise is dead--he spoke the first true word of appreciation, and placed Keats, where he unquestionably belongs, among our greatest poets.

The fame denied him in his sad life was granted freely after his death. Most fitly does he close the list of poets of the romantic revival, because in many respects he was the best workman of them all. He seems to have studied words more carefully than did his contemporaries, and so his poetic expression, or the harmony of word and thought, is generally more perfect than theirs.

More than any other he lived for poetry, as the noblest of the arts. More than any other he emphasized beauty, because to him, as shown by his "Grecian Urn," beauty and truth were one and inseparable. And he enriched the whole romantic movement by adding to its interest in common life the spirit, rather than the letter, of the classics and of Elizabethan poetry. For these reasons Keats is, like Spenser, a poet's poet; his work profoundly influenced Tennyson and, indeed, most of the poets of the present era.

PROSE WRITERS OF THE ROMANTIC PERIOD

Aside from the splendid work of the novel writers--Walter Scott, whom we have considered, and Jane Austen, to whom we shall presently return--the early nineteenth century is remarkable for the development of a new and valuable type of critical prose writing. If we except the isolated work of Dryden and of Addison, it is safe to say that literary criticism, in its modern sense, was hardly known in England until about the year 1825. Such criticism as existed seems to us now to have been largely the result of personal opinion or prejudice. Indeed we could hardly expect anything else before some systematic study of our literature as a whole had been attempted.

In one age a poem was called good or bad according as it followed or ran counter to so-called classic rules; in another we have the dogmatism of Dr. Johnson; in a third the personal judgment of Lockhart and the editors of the Edinburgh Review and the Quarterly, who so violently abused Keats and the Lake poets in the name of criticism. Early in the nineteenth century there arose a new school of criticism which was guided by knowledge of literature, on the one hand, and by what one might call the fear of God on the other. The latter element showed itself in a profound human sympathy,--the essence of the romantic movement,--and its importance was summed up by De Quincey when he said, "Not to sympathize is not to understand." These new critics, with abundant reverence for past masters, could still lay aside the dogmatism and prejudice which marked Johnson and the magazine editors, and read sympathetically the work of a new author, with the sole idea of finding what he had contributed, or tried to contribute, to the magnificent total of our literature. Coleridge, Hunt, Hazlitt, Lamb, and De Quincey were the leaders in this new and immensely important development; and we must not forget the importance of the new periodicals, like the Londen Magazine, founded in 1820, in which Lamb, De Quincey, and Carlyle found their first real encouragement.

Of Coleridge's Biographica Literaria and his Lectures on Shakespeare we have already spoken. Leigh Hunt (1784-1859) wrote continuously for more than thirty years, as editor and essayist; and his chief object seems to have been to make good literature known and appreciated. William Hazlitt (1778-1830), in a long series of lectures and essays, treated all reading as a kind of romantic journey into new and pleasant countries. To his work largely, with that of Lamb, was due the new interest in Elizabethan literature, which so strongly influenced Keats's last and best volume of poetry. For those interested in the art of criticism, and in the appreciation of literature, both Hunt and Hazlitt will well repay study; but we must pass over their work to consider the larger literary interest of Lamb and De Quincey, who were not simply critics of other men's labor, but who also produced some delightful work of their own, which the world has carefully put away among the "things worthy to be remembered."

CHARLES LAMB (1775-1834)

In Lamb and Wordsworth we have two widely different views of the romantic movement; one shows the influence of nature and solitude, the other of society. Lamb was a lifelong friend of Coleridge, and an admirer and defender of the poetic creed of Wordsworth; but while the latter lived apart from men, content with nature and with reading an occasional moral lesson to society, Lamb was born and lived in the midst of the London streets. The city crowd, with its pleasures and occupations, its endless little comedies and tragedies, alone interested him. According to his own account, when he paused in the crowded street tears would spring to his eyes,--tears of pure pleasure at the abundance of so much good life; and when he wrote, he simply interpreted that crowded human life of joy and sorrow, as Wordsworth interpreted the woods and waters, without any desire to change or to reform them. He has given us the best pictures we possess of Coleridge, Hazlitt, Landor, Hood, Cowden

Clarke, and many more of the interesting men and women of his age; and it is due to his insight and sympathy that the life of those far-off days seems almost as real to us as if we ourselves remembered it. Of all our English essayists he is the most lovable; partly because of his delicate, old-fashioned style and humor, but more because of that cheery and heroic struggle against misfortune which shines like a subdued light in all his writings.

Life

In the very heart of London there is a curious, old-fashioned place known as the Temple,--an enormous, rambling, apparently forgotten structure, dusty and still, in the midst of the endless roar of the city streets. Originally it was a chapter house of the Knights Templars, and so suggests to us the spirit of the Crusades and of the Middle Ages; but now the building is given over almost entirely to the offices and lodgings of London lawyers. It is this queer old place which, more than all others, is associated with the name of Charles Lamb. "I was born," he says, "and passed the first seven years of my life in the Temple. Its gardens, its halls, its fountain, its river... these are my oldest recollections." He was the son of a poor clerk, or rather servant, of one of the barristers, and was the youngest of seven children, only three of whom survived infancy. Of these three, John, the elder, was apparently a selfish creature, who took no part in the heroic struggle of his brother and sister. At seven years, Charles was sent to the famous "Bluecoat" charity school of Christ's Hospital. Here he remained seven years; and here he formed his lifelong friendship for another poor, neglected boy, whom the world remembers as Coleridge.

When only fourteen years old, Lamb left the charity school and was soon at work as a clerk in the South Sea House. Two years later he became a clerk in the famous India House, where he worked steadily for thirty-three years, with the exception of six weeks, in the winter of 1795-1796, spent within the walls of an asylum. In 1796 Lamb's sister Mary, who was as talented and remarkable as Lamb himself, went violently insane and killed her own mother.

For a long time after this appalling tragedy she was in an asylum at Hoxton; then Lamb, in 1797, brought her to his own little house, and for the remainder of his life cared for her with a tenderness and devotion which furnishes one of the most beautiful pages in our literary history. At times the malady would return to Mary, giving sure warning of its terrible approach; and then brother and sister might be seen walking silently, hand in hand, to the gates of the asylum, their cheeks wet with tears. One must remember this, as well as Lamb's humble lodgings and the drudgery of his daily work in the-big commercial house, if he would appreciate the pathos of "The Old Familiar Faces," or the heroism which shines through the most human and the most delightful essays in our language.

When Lamb was fifty years of age the East India Company, led partly by his literary fame following his first Essays of Elia, and partly by his thirty-three years of faithful service, granted him a comfortable pension; and happy as a boy turned loose from school he left India House forever to give himself up to literary work.

He wrote to Wordsworth, in April, 1825, "I came home forever on Tuesday of last week--it was like passing from life into eternity." Curiously enough Lamb seems to lose power after his release from drudgery, and his last essays, published in 1833, lack something of the grace and charm of his earlier work. He died at Edmonton in 1834; and his gifted sister Mary sank rapidly into the gulf from which his strength and gentleness had so long held her back. No literary man was ever more loved and honored by a rare circle of friends; and all who knew him bear witness to the simplicity and goodness which any reader may find for himself between the lines of his essays.

Works

The works of Lamb divide themselves naturally into three periods. First, there are his early literary efforts, including the poems signed "C. L." in Coleridge's Poems on Various Subjects (1796); his romance Rosamund Gray (1798); his poetical drama John Woodvil (1802); and various other immature works in prose and poetry. This period comes to an end in 1803, when he gave up his newspaper work, especially the contribution of six jokes, puns, and squibs daily to the Morning Post at sixpence apiece. The second period was given largely to literary criticism; and the Tales from Shakespeare (1807)--written by Charles and Mary Lamb, the former reproducing the tragedies, and the latter the comedies--may be regarded as his first successful literary venture. The book was written primarily for children; but so thoroughly had brother and sister steeped themselves in the literature of the Elizabethan period that young and old alike were delighted with this new version of Shakespeare's stories, and the Tales are still regarded as the best of their kind in our literature. In 1808 appeared his Specimens of English Dramatic Po..us Contemporary with Shakespeare. This carried out the splendid critical work of Coleridge, and was the most noticeable influence in developing the poetic qualities of Keats, as shown in his last volume.

The third period includes Lamb's criticisms of life, which are gathered together in his Essays of Elia (1823), and his Last Essays of Elia, which were published ten years later. These famous essays beg.n in 1820 with the appearance of the new London Magazine and were continued for many years, such subjects as the "Dissertation on Roast Pig," "Old China," "Praise of Chimney Sweepers," "Imperfect Sympathies," "A Chapter on Ears," "Mrs. Battle's Opinions on Whist," "Mackery End," "Grace Before Meat," "Dream Children," and many others being chosen apparently at random, but all leading to a delightful interpretation of the life of London, as it appeared to a quiet little man who walked unnoticed through its crowded streets. In the first and last essays which we have mentioned, "Dissertation on Roast Pig" and "Dream Children," we have the extremes of Lamb's humor and pathos.

The style of all these essays is gentle, old-fashioned, irresistibly attractive. Lamb was especially fond of old writers and borrowed unconsciously from the style of Burton's Anatomy of Melancholy and from Browne's Religio Medici and from the early English dramatists. But this style had become a part of Lamb by long reading, and he was apparently unable to express his new thought without using their old quaint expressions. Though these essays are all criticisms or appreciations of the life of his age, they are all intensely personal. In other words, they are an excellent picture of Lamb and of humanity. Without a trace of vanity or self-assertion, Lamb begins with himself, with some purely personal mood or experience, and from this he leads the reader to see life and literature as he saw it. It is this wonderful combination of personal and universal interests, together with Lamb's rare old style and quaint humor, which make the essays remarkable. They continue the best tradition of Addison and Steele, our first great essayists; but their sympathies are broader and deeper, and their humor more delicious than any which preceded them.

THOMAS DE QUINCY (1785-1859)

In De Quincey the romantic element is even more strongly developed than in Lamb, not only in his critical work, but also in his erratic and imaginative life. He was profoundly educated, even more so than Coleridge, and was one of the keenest intellects of the age; yet his wonderful intellect seems always subordinate to his passion for dreaming. Like Lamb, he was a friend and associate of the Lake poets, making his headquarters in Wordsworth's old cottage at Grasmere for nearly twenty years. Here the resemblance ceases, and a marked contrast begins. As a man, Lamb is the most human and lovable of all our essayists; while De Quincey is the most uncanny and incomprehensible. Lamb's modest works breathe the two essential qualities of sympathy and humor; the greater number of De Quincey's essays, while possessing more or less of both these qualities, are characterized chiefly by their brilliant style. Life, as seen through De Quincey's eyes, is nebulous and chaotic, and there is a suspicion of the fabulous in all that he wrote. Even in The Revolt of the Tartars the romantic element is uppermost, and in much of De Quincey's prose the element of unreality is more noticeable than in Shelley's poetry. Of his subject-matter, his facts, ideas, and criticisms, we are generally suspicious; but of his style, sometimes stately and sometimes headlong, now gorgeous as an Oriental dream, now musical as Keats's Endymion, and always, even in the most violent contrasts, showing a harmony between the idea and the expression such as no other English writer, with the possible exception of Newman, has ever rivaled,--say what you will of the marvelous brilliancy of De Quincey's style, you have still only half expressed the truth. It is the style alone which makes these essays immortal.

Life

De Quincey was born in Manchester in 1785. In neither his father, who was a prosperous merchant, nor his mother, who was a quiet, unsympathetic woman, do we see any suggestion of the son's almost uncanny genius. As a child he was given to dreams, more vivid and intense but less beautiful than those of the young Blake to whom he bears a strong resemblance. In the grammar school at Bath he displayed astonishing ability, and acquired Greek and Latin with a rapidity that frightened his slow tutors. At fifteen he not only read Greek, but spoke it fluently; and one of his astounded teachers remarked, "That boy could harangue an Athenian mob better than you or I could address an English one." From the grammar school at Manchester, whither he was sent in 1800, he soon ran away, finding the instruction far below his abilities, and the rough life absolutely intolerable to his sensitive nature. An uncle, just home from India, interceded for the boy lest he be sent back to the school, which he hated; and with an allowance of a guinea a week he started a career of vagrancy, much like that of Goldsmith, living on the open hills, in the huts of shepherds and charcoal burners, in the tents of gypsies, wherever fancy led him. His fear of the Manchester school finally led him to run away to London, where, without money or friends, his life was even more extraordinary than his gypsy wanderings. The details of this vagrancy are best learned in his Confessions of an English Opium-Eater, where we meet not simply the facts of his life, but also the confusion of dreams and fancies in the midst of which he wandered like a man lost on the mountains, with storm clouds under his feet hiding the familiar earth. After a year of vagrancy and starvation he was found by his family and allowed to go to Oxford, where his career was marked by the most brilliant and erratic scholarship. When ready for a degree, in 1807, he passed his written tests successfully, but felt a sudden terror at the thought of the oral examination and disappeared from the university, never to return.

It was in Oxford that De Quincey began the use of opium; to relieve the pains of neuralgia, and the habit increased until he was an almost hopeless slave to the drug. Only his extraordinary will power enabled him to break away from the habit, after some thirty years of misery. Some peculiarity of his delicate constitution enabled De Quincey to take enormous quantities of opium, enough to kill several ordinary men; and it was largely opium, working upon a sensitive imagination, which produced his gorgeous dreams, broken by intervals of weakness and profound depression. For twenty years he resided at Grasmere in the companionship of the Lake poets; and here, led by the loss of his small fortune, he began to write, with the idea of supporting his family. In 1821 he published his first famous work, the Confessions of an English Opium-Eater, and for nearly forty years afterwards he wrote industriously, contributing to various magazines an astonishing number of essays on a great variety of subjects. Without thought of literary fame, he contributed these articles anonymously; but fortunately, in 1853, he began to collect his own works, and the last of fourteen volumes was published just after his death.

In 1830, led by his connection with Blackwood's Magazine, to which he was the chief contributor, De Quincey removed with his family to Edinburgh, where his erratic genius and his singularly childlike ways produced enough amusing anecdotes to fill a volume. He would take a room in some place unknown to his friends and family; would live in it for a few years, until he had filled it, even to the bath tub, with books and with his own chaotic manuscripts, allowing no one to enter or disturb his den; and then, when the place became too crowded, he would lock the door and go away and take another lodging, where he repeated the same extraordinary performance. He died in Edinburgh in 1859. Like Lamb, he was a small, boyish figure, gentle, and elaborately courteous. Though excessively shy, and escaping as often as possible to solitude, he was nevertheless fond of society, and his wide knowledge and vivid imagination made his conversations almost as prized as those of his friend Coleridge.

Works

De Quincey's works may be divided into two general classes. The first includes his numerous critical articles, and the second his autobiographical sketches. All his works, it must be remembered, were contributed to various magazines, and were hastily collected just before his death. Hence the general impression of chaos which we get from reading them.

From a literary view point the most illuminating of De Quincey's critical works is his. Literary Reminiscences. This contains brilliant appreciations of Wordsworth, Coleridge, Lamb, Shelley, Keats, Hazlitt, and Landor, as well as some interesting studies of the literary figures of the age preceding.

Among the best of his brilliant critical essays are On the Knocking at the Gate in Macbeth (1823), which is admirably suited to show the man's critical genius, and Murder Considered as One of the Fine Arts (1827), which reveals his grotesque humor Other suggestive critical works, if one must choose among such a multitude, are his Letters to a Young Man (1823), Joan of Arc (1847), The Revolt of the Tartars (1840), and The English Mail-Coach (1849). In the last-named essay the "Dream Fugue" is one of the most imaginative of all his curious works.

Of De Quincey's autobiographical sketches the best known is his Confessions of an English Opium-Eater (1821). This is only partly a record of opium dreams, and its chief interest lies in glimpses it gives us of De Quincey's own life and wanderings. This should be followed by Suspiria de Profundis (1845), which is chiefly a record of gloomy and terrible dreams produced by opiates. The most interesting parts of his Suspiria, showing De Quincey's marvelous insight into dreams, are those in which we are brought face to face with the strange feminine creations "Levana," "Madonna," "Our Lady of Sighs," and "Our Lady of Darkness." A series of nearly thirty articles which he collected in 1853, called Autobiographic Sketches, completes the revelation of the author's own life. Among his miscellaneous works may be mentioned, in order to show his wide range of subjects, Klosterheim, a novel, Logic of Political Economy, the Essays on Style and Rhetoric, Philosophy of Herodotus, and his articles on Goethe, Pope, Schiller, and Shakespeare which he contributed to the Encyclopedia Britannica.

De Quincey's style is a revelation of the beauty of the English language, and it profoundly influenced Ruskin and other prose writers of the Victorian Age. It has two chief faults,--diffuseness, which continually leads De Quincey away from his object, and triviality, which often makes him halt in the midst of a marvelous paragraph to make some light jest or witticism that has some humor but no mirth in it.

Notwithstanding these faults, De Quincey's prose is still among the few supreme examples of style in our language. Though he was profoundly influenced by the seventeenth-century writers, he attempted definitely to create a new style which should combine the best elements of prose and poetry. In consequence, his prose works are often, like those of Milton, more imaginative and melodious than much of our poetry. He has been well called "the psychologist of style," and as such his works will never be popular; but to the few who can appreciate him he will always be an inspiration to better writing. One has a deeper respect for our English language and literature after reading him.

SECONDARY WRITERS OF ROMANTICISM

One has only to glance back over the authors we have been studying--Wordsworth, Coleridge, Southey, Byron, Shelley, Keats, Scott, Lamb, De Quincey--to realize the great change which swept over the life and literature of England in a single half century, under two influences which we now know as the French Revolution in history and the Romantic Movement in literature. In life men had rebelled against the too strict authority of state and society; in literature they rebelled even more vigorously against the bonds of classicism, which had sternly repressed a writer's ambition to follow his own ideals and to express them in his own way. Naturally such an age of revolution was essentially poetic,--only the Elizabethan Age surpasses it in this respect,--and it produced a large number of minor writers, who followed more or less closely the example of its great leaders.

Among novelists we have Jane Austen, Frances Burney, Maria Edgeworth, Jane Porter, and Susan Ferrier,--all women, be it noted; among the poets, Campbell, Moore, Hogg ("the Ettrick Shepherd"), Mrs. Hemans, Heber, Keble, Hood, and "Ingoldsby" (Richard Barham); and among miscellaneous writers, Sidney Smith, "Christopher North" (John Wilson), Chalmers, Lockhart, Leigh Hunt, Hazlitt,

Hallam, and Landor. Here is an astonishing variety of writers, and to consider all their claims to remembrance would of itself require a volume. Though these are generally classed as secondary writers, much of their work has claims to popularity, and some of it to permanence. Moore's Irish Melodies, Campbell's lyrics, Keble's Christian Year, and Jane Porter's Thaddeus of Warsaw and Scottish Chiefs have still a multitude of readers, where Keats, Lamb, and De Quincey are prized only by the cultured few; and Hallam's historical and critical works are perhaps better known than those of Gibbon, who nevertheless occupies a larger place in our literature. Among all these writers we choose only two, Jane Austen and Walter Savage Landor, whose works indicate a period of transition from the Romantic to the Victorian Age.

JANE AUSTEN (1775-1817)

We have so lately rediscovered the charm and genius of this gifted young woman that she seems to be a novelist of yesterday, rather than the contemporary of Wordsworth and Coleridge; and few even of her readers realize that she did for the English novel precisely what the Lake poets did for English poetry,--she refined and simplified it, making it a true reflection of English life. Like the Lake poets, she met with scanty encouragement in her own generation. Her greatest novel, Pride and Prejudice, was finished in 1797, a year before the appearance of the famous Lyrical Ballads of Wordsworth and Coleridge; but while the latter book was published and found a few appreciative readers, the manuscript of this wonderful novel went begging for sixteen years before it found a publisher.

As Wordsworth began with the deliberate purpose of making poetry natural and truthful, so Miss Austen appears to have begun writing with the idea of presenting the life of English country society exactly as it was, in opposition to the romantic extravagance of Mrs. Radcliffe and her school. But there was this difference,--that Miss Austen had in large measure the saving gift of humor, which Wordsworth sadly lacked. Maria Edgeworth, at the same time, set a sane and excellent example in her tales of Irish life, The Absentee and Castle Rackrent; and Miss Austen followed up the advantage with at least six works, which have grown steadily in value until we place them gladly in the first rank of our novels of common life. It is not simply for her exquisite charm, therefore, that we admire her, but also for her influence in bringing our novels back to their true place as an expression of human life. It is due partly, at least, to her influence that a multitude of readers were ready to appreciate Mrs. Gaskell's Cranford, and the powerful and enduring work of George Eliot.

Life

Jane Austen's life gives little opportunity for the biographer, unless, perchance, he has something of her own power to show the beauty and charm of commonplace things. She was the seventh child of Rev. George Austen, rector of Steventon, and was born in the parsonage of the village in 1775. With her sisters she was educated at home, and passed her life very quietly, cheerfully, in the doing of small domestic duties, to which love lent the magic lamp that makes all things beautiful. She began to write at an early age, and seems to have done her work on a little table in the family sitting room, in the midst of the family life. When a visitor entered, she would throw a paper or a piece of sewing over her work, and she modestly refused to be known as the author of novels which we now count among our treasured possessions. With the publishers she had little success. Pride and Prejudice went begging, as we have said, for sixteen years; and Northanger Abbey (1798) was sold for a trivial sum to a publisher, who laid it aside and forgot it, until the appearance and moderate success of Sense and Sensibility in 1811. Then, after keeping the manuscript some fifteen years, he sold it back to the family, who found another publisher.

An anonymous article in the Quarterly Review, following the appearance of Emma in 1815, full of generous appreciation of the charm of the new-writer, was the beginning of Jane Austen's fame; and it is only within a few years that we have learned that the friendly and discerning critic was Walter Scott. He continued to be her admirer until her early death; but these two, the greatest writers of fiction in their age, were never brought together. Both were home-loving people, and Miss Austen especially was averse to publicity and popularity. She died, quietly as she had lived, at Winchester, in 1817, and was buried in the cathedral. She was a bright, attractive, little woman, whose sunny qualities are unconsciously reflected in all her books.

Works

Very few English writers ever had so narrow a field of work as Jane Austen. Like the French novelists, whose success seems to lie in choosing the tiny field that they know best, her works have an exquisite perfection that is lacking in most of our writers of fiction. With the exception of an occasional visit to the watering place of Bath, her whole life was spent in small country parishes, whose simple country people became the characters of her novels.

Her brothers were in the navy, and so naval officers furnish the only exciting elements in her stories; but even these alleged heroes lay aside their imposing martial ways and act like themselves and other people. Such was her literary field, in which the chief duties were of the household, the chief pleasures in country gatherings, and the chief interests in matrimony.

Life, with its mighty interests, its passions, ambitions, and tragic struggles, swept by like a great river; while the secluded interests of a country parish went round and round quietly, like an eddy behind a sheltering rock. We can easily understand, therefore, the limitations of Jane Austen; but within her own field she is unequaled. Her characters are absolutely true to life, and all her work has the perfection of a delicate miniature painting. The most widely read of her novels is Pride and Prejudice; but three others, Sense and Sensibility, Emma, and Mansfield Park, have slowly won their way to the front rank of fiction.

From a literary view point Northanger Abbey is perhaps the best; for in it we find that touch of humor and delicate satire with which this gentle little woman combated the grotesque popular novels of the Udolpho type. Reading any of these works, one is inclined to accept the hearty indorsement of Sir Walter Scott: "That young lady has a talent for describing the involvements and feelings and characters of ordinary life which is to me the most wonderful I ever met with.

The big bowwow strain I can do myself, like any now going; but the exquisite touch which renders ordinary commonplace things and characters interesting from the truth of the description and the sentiment, is denied to me. What a pity such a gifted creature died so early!"

WALTER SAVAGE LANDOR (1775-1864)

While Hazlitt, Lamb, De Quincey, and other romantic critics went back to early English literature for their inspiration, Landor shows a reaction from the prevailing Romanticism by his imitation of the ancient classic writers. His life was an extraordinary one and, like his work, abounded in sharp contrasts. On the one hand, there are his egoism, his unncontrollable anger, his perpetual lawsuits, and the last sad tragedy with his children, which suggests King Lear and his daughters; on the other hand there is his steady devotion to the classics and to the cultivation of the deep wisdom of the ancients, which suggests Pindar and Cicero. In his works we find the wild extravagance of Gebir, followed by the superb classic style and charm of Pericles and Aspasia. Such was Landor, a man of high ideals, perpetually at war with himself and the world.

Life

Lander's stormy life covers the whole period from Wordsworth's childhood to the middle of the Victorian Era. He was the son of a physician, and was born at Warwick, in 1775.

From his mother he inherited a fortune; but it was soon scattered by large expenditures and law quarrels; and in his old age, refused help by his own children, only Browning's generosity kept Landor from actual want.

At Rugby, and at Oxford, his extreme Republicanism brought him into constant trouble; and his fitting out a band of volunteers to assist the Spaniards against Napoleon, in 1808, allies him with Byron and his Quixotic followers.

The resemblance to Byron is even more strikingly shown in the poem Gebir, published in 1798, a year made famous by the Lyrical Ballads of Wordsworth and Coleridge.

A remarkable change in Lander's life is noticeable in 1821, when, at forty-six years of age, after having lost his magnificent estate of Llanthony Abbey, in Glamorganshire, and after a stormy experience in Como, he settled down for a time at Fiesole near Florence. To this period of calm after storm we owe the classical prose works for which he is famous.

The calm, like that at the center of a whirlwind, lasted but a short time, and Landor, leaving his family in great anger, returned to Bath, where he lived alone for more than twenty years. Then, in order to escape a libel suit, the choleric old man fled back to Italy. He died at Florence, in 1864. The spirit of his whole life may be inferred from the defiant farewell which he flung to it:

I strove with none, for none was worth my strife;
Nature I loved, and next to Nature Art;
I warmed both hands before the fire of life;
It sinks, and I am ready to depart.

Works

Landor's reaction from Romanticism is all the more remarkable in view of his early efforts, such as Gebir, a wildly romantic poem, which rivals any work of Byron or Shelley in its extravagance. Notwithstanding its occasional beautiful and suggestive lines, the work was not and never has been successful; and the same may be said of all his poetical works.

His first collection of poems was published in 1795, his last a full half century later, in 1846. In the latter volume, The Hellenics,--which included some translations of his earlier Latin poems, called Idyllia Heroica,--one has only to read "The Hamadryad," and compare it with the lyrics of the first volume, in order to realize the astonishing literary vigor of a man who published two volumes, a half century apart, without any appreciable diminution of poetical feeling. In all these poems one is impressed by the striking and original figures of speech which Landor uses to emphasize his meaning.

It is by his prose works, largely, that Landor has won a place in our literature; partly because of their intrinsic worth, their penetrating thought, and severe classic style; and partly because of their profound influence upon the writers of the present age. The most noted of his prose works are his six volumes of Imaginary Conversations (1824-1846).

For these conversations Landor brings together, sometimes in groups, sometimes in couples, well-known characters, or rather shadows, from the four corners of the earth and from the remotest ages of recorded history. Thus Diogenes talks with Plato, AEsop with a young slave girl in Egypt, Henry VIII with Anne Boleyn in prison, Dante with Beatrice, Leofric with Lady Godiva,--all these and many others, from Epictetus to Cromwell, are brought together and speak of life and love and death, each from his own view point.

Occasionally, as in the meeting of Henry and Anne Boleyn, the situation is tense and dramatic; but as a rule the characters simply meet and converse in the same quiet strain, which becomes, after much reading, somewhat monotonous. On the other hand, one who reads the Imaginary Conversations is lifted at once into a calm and noble atmosphere which braces and inspires him, making him forget petty things, like a view from a hilltop. By its combination of lofty thought and severely classic style the book has won, and deserves, a very high place among our literary records.

The same criticism applies to Pericles and Aspasia, which is a series of imaginary letters, telling the experiences of Aspasia, a young lady from Asia Minor, who visits Athens at the summit of its fame and glory, in the great age of Pericles. This is, in our judgment, the best worth reading of all Landor's works. One gets from it not only Landor's classic style, but--what is well worth while--a better picture of Greece in the days of its greatness than can be obtained from many historical volumes.

SUMMARY OF THE AGE OF ROMANTICISM

This period extends from the war with the colonies, following the Declaration of Independence, in 1776, to the accession of Victoria in 1837, both limits being very indefinite, as will be seen by a glance at the Chronology following. During the first part of the period especially, England was in a continual turmoil, produced by political and economic agitation at home, and by the long wars that covered two continents and the wide sea between them.

The mighty changes resulting from these two causes have given this period the name of the Age of Revolution. The storm center of all the turmoil at home and abroad was the French Revolution, which had a profound influence on the life and literature of all Europe. On the Continent the overthrow of Napoleon at Waterloo (1815) apparently checked the progress of liberty, which had started with the French Revolution,] but in England the case was reversed.

The agitation for popular liberty, which at one time threatened a revolution, went steadily forward till it resulted in the final triumph of democracy, in the Reform Bill of 1832, and in a number of exceedingly important reforms, such as the extension of manhood suffrage, the removal of the last unjust restrictions against Catholics, the establishment of a national system of schools, followed by a rapid increase in popular education, and the abolition of slavery in all English colonies (1833).

To this we must add the changes produced by the discovery of steam and the invention of machinery, which rapidly changed England from an agricultural to a manufacturing nation, introduced the factory system, and caused this period to be known as the Age of Industrial Revolution.

The literature of the age is largely poetical in form, and almost entirely romantic in spirit. For, as we have noted, the triumph of democracy in government is generally accompanied by the triumph of romanticism in literature. At first the literature, as shown especially in the early work of Wordsworth, Byron, and Shelley, reflected the turmoil of the age and the wild hopes of an ideal democracy occasioned by the French Revolution.

Later the extravagant enthusiasm subsided, and English writers produced so much excellent literature that the age is often called the Second Creative period, the first being the Age of Elizabeth.

The six chief characteristics of the age are: the prevalence of romantic poetry; the creation of the historical novel by Scott; the first appearance of women novelists, such as Mrs. Anne Radcliffe, Jane Porter, Maria Edgeworth, and Jane Austen; the development of literary criticism, in the work of Lamb, De Quincey, Coleridge, and Hazlitt; the practical and economic bent of philosophy, as shown in the work of Malthus, James Mill, and Adam Smith; and the establishment of great literary magazines, like the Edinburgh Review, the Quarterly, Blackwood's, and the Athenaeum.

In our study we have noted (1) the Poets of Romanticism: the importance of the Lyrical Ballads of 1798; the life and work of Wordsworth, Coleridge, Scott, Byron, Shelley, and Keats; (2) the Prose Writers: the novels of Scott; the development of literary criticism; the life and work of the essayists, Lamb, De Quincey, Landor, and of the novelist Jane Austen.

2

The Victorian Age (1850-1900)

THE MODERN PERIOD OF PROGRESS AND UNREST

When Victoria became queen, in 1837, English literature seemed to have entered upon a period of lean years, in marked contrast with the poetic fruitfulness of the romantic age which we have just studied. Coleridge, Shelley, Keats, Byron, and Scott had passed away, and it seemed as if there were no writers in England to fill their places. Wordsworth had written, in 1835,

Like clouds that rake, the mountain summits,
Or waves that own no curbing hand,
How fast has brother followed brother,
From sunshine to the sunless land!

In these lines is reflected the sorrowful spirit of a literary man of the early nineteenth century who remembered the glory that had passed away from the earth. But the leanness of these first years is more apparent than real. Keats and Shelley were dead, it is true, but already there had appeared three disciples of these poets who were destined to be far more widely, read than were their masters. Tennyson had been publishing poetry since 1827, his first poems appearing almost simultaneously with the last work of Byron, Shelley, and Keats; but it was not until 1842, with the publication of his collected poems, in two volumes, that England recognized in him one of her great literary leaders. So also

Elizabeth Barrett had been writing since 1820, but not till twenty years later did her poems become deservedly popular; and Browning had published his Pauline in 1833, but it was not until 1846, when he published the last of the series called Bells and Pomegranates, that the reading public began to appreciate his power and originality. Moreover, even as romanticism seemed passing away, a group of great prose writers--Dickens, Thackeray, Carlyle, and Ruskin--had already begun to proclaim the literary glory of a new age, which now seems to rank only just below the Elizabethan and the Romantic periods.

HISTORICAL SUMMARY

Amid the multitude of social and political forces of this great age, four things stand out clearly. First, the long struggle of the Anglo-Saxons for personal liberty is definitely settled, and democracy becomes the established order of the day. The king, who appeared in an age of popular weakness and ignorance, and the peers, who came with the Normans in triumph, are both stripped of their power and left as figureheads of a past civilization. The last vestige of personal government and of the divine right of rulers disappears; the House of Commons becomes the ruling power in England; and a series of new reform bills rapidly extend the suffrage, until the whole body of English people choose for themselves the men who shall represent them.

Second, because it is an age of democracy, it is an age of popular education, of religious tolerance, of growing brotherhood, and of profound social unrest. The slaves had been freed in 1833; but in the middle of the century England awoke to the fact that slaves are not necessarily negroes, stolen in Africa to be sold like cattle in the market place, but that multitudes of men, women, and little children in the mines and factories were victims of a more terrible industrial and social slavery. To free these slaves also, the unwilling victims of our unnatural competitive methods, has been the growing purpose of the Victorian Age until the present day.

Third, because it is an age of democracy and education, it is an age of comparative peace. England begins to think less of the pomp and false glitter of fighting, and more of its moral evils, as the nation realizes that it is the common people who bear the burden and the sorrow and the poverty of war, while the privileged classes reap most of the financial and political rewards. Moreover, with the growth of trade and of friendly foreign relations, it becomes evident that the social equality for which England was contending at home belongs to the whole race of men; that brotherhood is universal, not insular; that a question of justice is never settled by fighting; and that war is generally unmitigated horror and barbarism. Tennyson, who came of age when the great Reform Bill occupied attention, expresses the ideals of the Liberals of his day who proposed to spread the gospel of peace,

> *Till the war-drum throbb'd no longer, and the battle-flags were furled*
>
> *In the Parliament of Man, the Federation of the world.*

Fourth, the Victorian Age is especially remarkable because of its rapid progress in all the arts and sciences and in mechanical inventions. A glance at any record of the industrial achievements of the nineteenth century will show how vast they are, and it is unnecessary to repeat here the list of the inventions, from spinning looms to steamboats, and from matches to electric lights. All these material things, as well as the growth of education, have their influence upon the life of a people, and it is inevitable that they should react upon its prose and poetry; though as yet we are too much absorbed in our sciences and mechanics to determine accurately their influence upon literature. When these new things shall by long use have became familiar as country roads, or have been replaced by newer and better things, then they also will have their associations and memories, and a poem on the railroads may be as suggestive as Wordsworth's sonnet on Westminster Bridge; and the busy, practical workingmen who to-day throng our streets and factories may seem, to a future and greater age, as quaint and poetical as to us seem the slow toilers of the Middle Ages.

LITERARY CHARACTERISTICS

When one is interested enough to trace the genealogy of Victoria he finds, to his surprise, that in her veins flowed the blood both of William the Conqueror and of Cerdic, the first Saxon king of England; and this seems to be symbolic of the literature of her age, which embraces the whole realm of Saxon and Norman life,--the strength and ideals of the one, and the culture and refinement of the other. The romantic revival had done its work, and England entered upon a new free period, in which every form of literature, from pure romance to gross realism, struggled for expression. At this day it is obviously impossible to judge the age as a whole; but we are getting far enough away from the early half of it to notice certain definite characteristics. First, though the age produced many poets, and two who deserve to rank among the greatest, nevertheless this is emphatically an age of prose. And since the number of readers has increased a thousandfold with the spread of popular education, it is the age of the newspaper, the magazine, and the modern novel,--the first two being the story of the world's daily life, and the last our pleasantest form of literary entertainment, as well as our most successful method of presenting modern problems and modern ideals. The novel in this age fills a place which the drama held in the days of Elizabeth; and never before, in any age or language, has the novel appeared in such numbers and in such perfection.

[Moral Purpose] The second marked characteristic of the age is that literature, both in prose and in poetry, seems to depart from the purely artistic standard, of art for art's sake, and to be actuated by a definite moral purpose Tennyson, Browning, Carlyle, Ruskin,--who and what were these men if not the teachers of England, not vaguely but definitely, with superb faith in their message, and with the conscious moral purpose to uplift and to instruct? Even the novel breaks away from Scott's romantic influence, and first studies life as it is, and then points out what life may and ought to be. Whether we read the fun and sentiment of Dickens, the social miniatures of Thackeray, or the psychological studies of George Eliot, we find in almost every case a definite purpose to sweep away error and to reveal the underlying truth of human life.

So the novel sought to do for society in this age precisely what Lyell and Darwin sought to do for science, that is, to find the truth, and to show how it might be used to uplift humanity. Perhaps for this reason the Victorian Age is emphatically an age of realism rather than of romance,--not the realism of Zola and Ibsen, but a deeper realism which strives to tell the whole truth, showing moral and physical diseases as they are, but holding up health and hope as the normal conditions of humanity.

It is somewhat customary to speak of this age as an age of doubt and pessimism, following the new conception of man and of the universe which was formulated by science under the name of involution. It is spoken of also as a prosaic age, lacking in great ideals. Both these criticisms seem to be the result of judging a large thing when we are too close to it to get its true proportions, just as Cologne Cathedral, one of the world's most perfect structures, seems to be a shapeless pile of stone when we stand too close beneath its mighty walls and buttresses. Tennyson's immature work, like that of the minor poets, is sometimes in a doubtful or despairing strain; but his In Memoriam is like the rainbow after storm; and Browning seems better to express the spirit of his age in the strong, manly faith of "Rabbi Ben Ezra," and in the courageous optimism of all his poetry. Stedman's Victorian

Anthology is, on the whole, a most inspiring book of poetry. It would be hard to collect more varied cheer from any age. And the great essayists, like Macaulay, Carlyle, Ruskin, and the great novelists, like Dickens, Thackeray, George Eliot, generally leave us with a larger charity and with a deeper faith in our humanity.

So also the judgment that this age is too practical for great ideals may be only a description of the husk that hides a very full ear of corn. It is well to remember that Spenser and Sidney judged their own age (which we now consider to be the greatest in our literary history) to be altogether given over to materialism, and to be incapable of literary greatness. Just as time has made us smile at their blindness, so the next century may correct our judgment of this as a material age, and looking upon the enormous growth of charity and brotherhood among us, and at the literature which expresses our faith in men, may judge the Victorian Age to be, on the whole, the noblest and most inspiring in the history of the world.

I. THE POETS OF THE VICTORIAN AGE

ALFRED TENNYSON (1809-1892)

O young Mariner,
You from the haven
Under the sea-cliff,
You that are watching
The gray Magician
With eyes of wonder,
I am Merlin,
And I am dying,
I am Merlin
Who follow The Gleam.

O young Mariner,
Down to the haven
Call your companions,
Launch your vessel,
And crowd your canvas,
And, ere it vanishes
Over the margin,
After it, follow it,
Follow The Gleam.

One who reads this haunting poem of "Merlin and The Gleam" finds in it a suggestion of the spirit of the poet's whole life,--his devotion to the ideal as expressed in poetry, his early romantic impressions, his struggles, doubts, triumphs, and his thrilling message to his race. Throughout the entire Victorian period Tennyson stood at the summit of poetry in England. Not in vain was he appointed laureate at the death of Wordsworth, in 1850; for, almost alone among those who have held the office, he felt the importance of his place, and filled and honored it.

For nearly half a century Tennyson was not only a man and a poet; he was a voice, the voice of a whole people, expressing in exquisite melody their doubts and their faith, their griefs and their triumphs. In the wonderful variety of his verse he suggests all the qualities of England's greatest poets. The dreaminess of Spenser, the majesty of Milton, the natural simplicity of Wordsworth, the fantasy of Blake and Coleridge, the melody of Keats and Shelley, the narrative vigor of Scott and Byron,--all these striking qualities are evident on successive pages of Tennyson's poetry.

The only thing lacking is the dramatic power of the Elizabethans. In reflecting the restless spirit of this progressive age Tennyson is as remarkable as Pope was in voicing the artificiality of the early eighteenth century. As a poet, therefore, who expresses not so much a personal as a national spirit, he is probably the most representative literary man of the Victorian era.

Life

Tennyson's life is a remarkable one in this respect, that from beginning to end he seems to have been dominated by a single impulse, the impulse of poetry. He had no large or remarkable experiences, no wild oats to sow, no great successes or reverses, no business cares or public offices. For sixty-six years, from the appearance of the Poems by Two Brothers, in 1827, until his death in 1892, he studied and practiced his art continually and exclusively. Only Browning, his fellow-worker, resembles him in this; but the differences in the two men are world-wide. Tennyson was naturally shy, retiring, indifferent to men, hating noise and publicity, loving to be alone with nature, like Wordsworth. Browning was sociable, delighting in applause, in society, in travel, in the noise and bustle of the big world.

Tennyson was born in the rectory of Somersby, Lincolnshire, in 1809. The sweet influences of his early natural surroundings can be better understood from his early poems than from any biography. He was one of the twelve children of the Rev. George Clayton Tennyson, a scholarly clergyman, and his wife Elizabeth Fytche, a gentle, lovable woman, "not learned, save in gracious household ways," to whom the poet pays a son's loyal tribute near the close of The Princess. It is interesting to note that most of these children were poetically inclined, and that two of the brothers, Charles and Frederick, gave far greater promise than did Alfred.

When seven years old the boy went to his grandmother's house at Louth, in order to attend a famous grammar school at that place. Not even a man's memory, which generally makes light of hardship and glorifies early experiences, could ever soften Tennyson's hatred of school life. His complaint was not so much at the roughness of the boys, which had so frightened Cowper, as at the brutality of the teachers, who put over the school door a wretched Latin inscription translating Solomon's barbarous advice about the rod and the child. In these psychologic days, when the child is more important than the curriculum, and when we teach girls and boys rather than Latin and arithmetic, we read with wonder Carlyle's description of his own schoolmaster, evidently a type of his kind, who "knew of the human soul thus much, that it had a faculty called memory, and could be acted on through the muscular integument by appliance of birch rods." After four years of most unsatisfactory school life, Tennyson returned home, and was fitted for the university by his scholarly father. With his brothers he wrote many verses, and his first efforts appeared in a little volume called Poems by Two Brothers, in 1827. The next year he entered Trinity College, Cambridge, where he became the center of a brilliant circle of friends, chief of whom was the young poet Arthur Henry Hallam.

At the university Tennyson soon became known for his poetical ability, and two years after his entrance he gained the prize of the Chancellor's Medal for a poem called "Timbuctoo," the subject, needless to say, being chosen by the chancellor. Soon after winning this honor Tennyson published his first signed work, called Poems Chiefly Lyrical (1830), which, though it seems somewhat crude and disappointing to us now, nevertheless contained the germ of all his later poetry.

One of the most noticeable things in this volume is the influence which Byron evidently exerted over the poet in his early days; and it was perhaps due largely to the same romantic influence that Tennyson and his friend Hallam presently sailed away to Spain, with the idea of joining the army of insurgents against King Ferdinand. Considered purely as a revolutionary venture, this was something of a fiasco, suggesting the noble Duke of York and his ten thousand men,--"he marched them up a hill, one day; and he marched them down again." From a literary view point, however, the experience was not without its value. The deep impression which the wild beauty of the Pyrenees made upon the young poet's mind is reflected clearly in the poem "Oenone."

In 1831 Tennyson left the university without taking his degree. The reasons for this step are not clear; but the family was poor, and poverty may have played a large part in his determination. His father died a few months later; but, by a generous arrangement with the new rector, the family retained the rectory at Somersby, and here, for nearly six years, Tennyson lived in a retirement which strongly suggests Milton at Horton. He read and studied widely, cultivated an intimate acquaintance with nature, thought deeply on the problems suggested by the Reform Bill which was then agitating England, and during his leisure hours wrote poetry. The first fruits of this retirement appeared, late in 1832, in a wonderful little volume bearing the simple name Poems. As the work of a youth only twenty-three, this book is remarkable for the variety and melody of its verse. Among its treasures we still read with delight "The Lotos Eaters," "Palace of Art," "A Dream of Fair Women," "The Miller's Daughter," "Oenone," and "The Lady of Shalott"; but the critics of the Quarterly, who had brutally condemned his earlier work, were again unmercifully severe. The effect of this harsh criticism upon a sensitive nature was most unfortunate; and when his friend Hallam died, in 1833, Tennyson was plunged into a period of gloom and sorrow. The sorrow may be read in the exquisite little poem beginning, "Break, break, break, On thy cold gray stones, O Sea!" which was his first published elegy for his friend; and the depressing influence of the harsh and unjust criticism is suggested in "Merlin and The Gleam," which the reader will understand only after he has read Tennyson's biography.

For nearly ten years after Hallam's death Tennyson published nothing, and his movements are hard to trace as the family went here and there, seeking peace and a home in various parts of England. But though silent, he continued to write poetry, and it was in these sad wandering days that he began his immortal In Memoriam and his Idylls of the King. In 1842 his friends persuaded him to give his work to the world, and with some hesitation he published his Poems. The success of this work was almost instantaneous, and we can appreciate the favor with which it was received when we read the noble blank verse of "Ulysses" and "Morte d'Arthur," the perfect little song of grief for Hallam which we have already mentioned, and the exquisite idyls like "Dora" and "The Gardener's Daughter," which aroused even Wordsworth's enthusiasm and brought from him a letter saying that he had been trying all his life to write such an English pastoral as "Dora" and had failed. From this time forward Tennyson, with increasing confidence in himself and his message, steadily maintained his place as the best known and best loved poet in England.

The year 1850 was a happy one for Tennyson. He was appointed poet laureate, to succeed Wordsworth; and he married Emily Sellwood,

Her whose gentle will has changed my fate

And made my life a perfumed altar flame,

whom he had loved for thirteen years, but whom his poverty had prevented him from marrying. The year is made further remarkable by the publication of In Memoriam, probably the most enduring of his poems, upon which he had worked at intervals for sixteen years. Three years later, with the money that his work now brought him, he leased the house Farringford, in the Isle of Wight, and settled in the first permanent home he had known since he left the rectory at Somersby.

For the remaining forty years of his life he lived, like Wordsworth, "in the stillness of a great peace," writing steadily, and enjoying the friendship of a large number of people, some distinguished, some obscure, from the kindly and sympathetic Victoria to the servants on his own farm. All of these he called with equal sincerity his friends, and to each one he was the same man, simple, strong, kindly, and noble. Carlyle describes him as "a fine, large-featured, dim-eyed, bronze-colored, shaggy-headed man,... most restful, brotherly, solid-hearted." Loving solitude and hating publicity as he did, the numerous tourists from both sides of the ocean, who sought him out in his retreat and insisted upon seeing him, made his life at times intolerable. Influenced partly by the desire to escape such popularity, he bought land and built for himself a new house, Aldworth, in Surrey, though he made his home in Farringford for the greater part of the year.

His labor during these years and his marvelous freshness and youthfulness of feeling are best understood by a glance at the contents of his complete works. Inferior poems, like The Princess, which was written in the first flush of his success, and his dramas, which were written against the advice of his best friends, may easily be criticised; but the bulk of his verse shows an astonishing originality and vigor to the very end. He died very quietly at Aldworth, with his family about him in the moonlight, and beside him a volume of Shakespeare, open at the dirge in Cymbeline:

Fear no more the heat o' the sun,

Nor the furious winter's rages;

Thou thy worldly task hast done,

Home art gone, and ta'en thy wages.

The strong and noble spirit of his life is reflected in one of his best known poems, "Crossing the Bar," which was written in his eighty-first year, and which he desired should be placed at the end of his collected works:

Sunset and evening star,

And one clear call for me!

And may there be no moaning of the bar,

When I put out to sea,
But such a tide as, moving, seems asleep,
Too full for sound and foam,
When that which drew from out the boundless deep
Turns again home.
Twilight and evening bell,
And after that the dark!
And may there be no sadness of farewell,
When I embark;
For tho' from out our bourne of Time and Place
The flood may bear me far,
I hope to see my Pilot face to face
When I have crost the bar.

Works

At the outset of our study of Tennyson's works it may be well to record two things, by way of suggestion. First, Tennyson's poetry is not so much to be studied as to be read and appreciated; he is a poet to have open on one's table, and to enjoy as one enjoys his daily exercise. And second, we should by all means begin to get acquainted with Tennyson in the days of our youth. Unlike Browning, who is generally appreciated by more mature minds, Tennyson is for enjoyment, for inspiration, rather than for instruction. Only youth can fully appreciate him; and youth, unfortunately, except in a few rare, beautiful cases, is something which does not dwell with us long after our school days. The secret of poetry, especially of Tennyson's poetry, is to be eternally young, and, like Adam in Paradise, to find every morning a new world, fresh, wonderful, inspiring, as if just from the hands of God.

Except by the student, eager to understand the whoje range of poetry in this age, Tennyson's earlier poems and his later dramas may well be omitted. Opinions vary about both; but the general judgment seems to be that the earlier poems show too much of Byron's influence, and their crudeness suffers by comparison with the exquisitely finished work of Tennyson's middle life. Of dramatic works he wrote seven, his great ambition being to present a large part of the history of England in a series of dramas. Becket was one of the best of these works and met with considerable favor on the stage; but, like all the others, it indicates that Tennyson lacked the dramatic power and the humor necessary for a successful playwright.

Among the remaining poems there is such a wide variety that every reader must be left largely to follow his own delightful choice. Of the Poems of 1842 we have already mentioned those best worth reading. The Princess, a Medley (1847), a long poem of over three thousand lines of blank verse, is Tennyson's answer to the question of woman's rights and woman's sphere, which was then, as in our own day, strongly agitating the public mind. In this poem a baby finally solves the problem which philosophers have pondered ever since men began to think connectedly about human society. A few exquisite songs, like "Tears, Idle Tears," "Bugle Song," and "Sweet and Low," form the most delightful part of this poem, which in general is hardly up to the standard of the poet's later work.

Maud (1855) is what is called in literature a monodrama, telling the story of a lover who passes from morbidness to ecstasy, then to anger and murder, followed by insanity and recovery. This was Tennyson's favorite, and among his friends he read aloud from it more than from any other poem. Perhaps if we could hear Tennyson read it, we should appreciate it better; but, on the whole, it seems overwrought and melodramatic. Even its lyrics, like "Come into the Garden, Maud," which make this work a favorite with young lovers, are characterized by "prettiness" rather than by beauty or strength.

Perhaps the most loved of all Tennyson's works is In Memoriam, which, on account of both its theme and its exquisite workmanship, is "one of the few immortal names that were not born to die." The immediate occasion of this remarkable poem was Tennyson's profound personal grief at the death of his friend Hallam. As he wrote lyric after lyric, inspired by this sad subject, the poet's grief became less personal, and the greater grief of humanity mourning for its dead and questioning its immortality took possession of him. Gradually the poem became an expression, first, of universal doubt, and then of universal faith, a faith which rests ultimately not on reason or philosophy but on the soul's instinct for immortality. The immortality of human love is the theme of the poem, which is made up of over one hundred different lyrics. The movement takes us through three years, rising slowly from poignant sorrow and doubt to a calm peace and hope, and ending with a noble hymn of courage and faith,--a modest courage and a humble faith, love-inspired,--which will be a favorite as long as saddened men turn to literature for consolation. Though Darwin's greatest books had not yet been written, science had already overturned many old conceptions of life; and Tennyson, who lived apart and thought deeply on all the problems of his day, gave this poem to the world as his own answer to the doubts and questionings of men. This universal human interest, together with its exquisite form and melody, makes the poem, in popular favor at least, the supreme threnody, or elegiac poem, of our literature; though Milton's Lycidas is, from the critical view point, undoubtedly a more artistic work.

The Idylls of the King ranks among the greatest of Tennyson's later works. Its general subject is the Celtic legends of King Arthur and his knights of the Round Table, and the chief source of its material is Malory's Morte d'Arthur. Here, in this mass of beautiful legends, is certainly the subject of a great national epic; yet after four hundred years, during which many poets have used the material, the great epic is still unwritten. Milton and Spenser, as we have already noted, considered this material carefully; and Milton alone, of all English writers, had perhaps the power to use it in a great epic. Tennyson began to use these legends in his Morte d'Arthur (1842); but the epic idea probably occurred to him later, in 1856, when he began "Geraint and Enid," and he added the stories of "Vivien," "Elaine," "Guinevere," and other heroes and heroines at intervals, until "Balin," the last of the Idylls, appeared in 1885. Later these works were gathered together and arranged with an attempt at unity. The result is in no sense an epic poem, but rather a series of single poems loosely connected by a thread of interest in Arthur, the central personage, and in his unsuccessful attempt to found an ideal kingdom.

Entirely different in spirit is another collection of poems called English Idyls, which began in the Poems of 1842, and which Tennyson intended should reflect the ideals of widely different types of English life. Of these varied poems, "Dora," "The Gardener's Daughter," "Ulysses," "Locksley Hall" and "Sir Galahad" are the best; but all are worthy of study. One of the most famous of this series is "Enoch Arden" (1864), in which Tennyson turns from mediaeval knights, from lords, heroes, and fair ladies, to find the material for true poetry among the lowly people that make up the bulk of English life. Its rare melody, its sympathy for common life, and its revelation of the beauty and heroism which hide in humble men and women everywhere, made this work an instant favorite. Judged by its sales alone, it was the most popular of his works during the poet's lifetime.

Tennyson's later volumes, like the Ballads (1880) and Demeter (1889), should not be overlooked, since they contain some of his best work. The former contains stirring war songs, like "The Defence of Lucknow," and pictures of wild passionate grief, like "Rizpah"; the latter is notable for "Romney's Remorse," a wonderful piece of work; "Merlin and The Gleam," which expresses the poet's lifelong ideal; and several exquisite little songs, like "The Throstle," and "The Oak," which show how marvelously the aged poet retained his youthful freshness and inspiration. Here certainly is variety enough to give us long years of literary enjoyment; and we need hardly mention miscellaneous poems, like "The Brook" and "The Charge of the Light Brigade," which are known to every schoolboy; and "Wages" and "The Higher Pantheism," which should be read by every man who thinks about the old, old problem of life and death.

CHARACTERISTICS OF TENNYSON'S POETRY

If we attempt to sum up the quality of Tennyson, as shown in all these works, the task is a difficult one; but three things stand out more or less plainly. First, Tennyson is essentially the artist. No other in his age studied the art of poetry so constantly or with such singleness of purpose; and only Swinburne rivals him in melody and the perfect finish of his verse. Second, like all the great writers of his age, he is emphatically a teacher, often a leader. In the preceding age, as the result of the turmoil produced by the French Revolution, lawlessness was more or less common, and individuality was the rule in literature. Tennyson's theme, so characteristic of his age, is the reign of order,--of law in the physical world, producing evolution, and of law in the spiritual world, working out the perfect man. In Memoriam, Idylls of the King, The Princess,-here are three widely different poems; yet the theme of each, so far as poetry is a kind of spiritual philosophy and weighs its words before it utters them, is the orderly development of law in the natural and in the spiritual world.

This certainly is a new doctrine in poetry, but the message does not end here. Law implies a source, a method, an object. Tennyson, after facing his doubts honestly and manfully, finds law even in the sorrows and losses of humanity. He gives this law an infinite and personal source, and finds the supreme purpose of all law to be a revelation of divine love.

All earthly love, therefore, becomes an image of the heavenly. What first perhaps attracted readers to Tennyson, as to Shakespeare, was the character of his women,--pure, gentle, refined beings, whom we must revere as our Anglo-Saxon forefathers revered the women they loved. Like Browning, the poet had loved one good woman supremely, and her love made clear the meaning of all life. The message goes one step farther. Because law and love are in the world, faith is the only reasonable attitude toward life and death, even though we understand them not. Such, in a few words, seems to be Tennyson's whole message and philosophy.

If we attempt now to fix Tennyson's permanent place in literature, as the result of his life and work, we must apply to him the same test that we applied to Milton and Wordsworth, and, indeed, to all our great poets, and ask with the German critics, "What new thing has he said to the world or even to his own country?" The answer is, frankly, that we do not yet know surely; that we are still too near Tennyson to judge him impersonally. This much, however, is clear. In a marvelously complex age, and amid a hundred great men, he was regarded as a leader. For a full half century he was the voice of England, loved and honored as a man and a poet, not simply by a few discerning critics, but by a whole people that do not easily give their allegiance to any one man. And that, for the present, is Tennyson's sufficient eulogy.

ROBERT BROWNING (1812-1889)

How good is man's life, the mere living! how fit to employ, All the heart and the soul and the senses for ever in joy!

In this new song of David, from Browning's Saul, we have a suggestion of the astonishing vigor and hope that characterize all the works of Browning, the one poet of the age who, after thirty years of continuous work, was finally recognized and placed beside Tennyson, and whom future ages may judge to be a greater poet,--perhaps, even, the greatest in our literature since Shakespeare. The chief difficulty in reading Browning is the obscurity of his style, which the critics of half a century ago held up to ridicule. Their attitude towards the poet's early work may be inferred from Tennyson's humorous criticism of Sordello. It may be remembered that the first line of this obscure poem is, "Who will may hear Sordello's story told"; and that the last line is, "Who would has heard Sordello's story told." Tennyson remarked that these were the only lines in the whole poem that he understood, and that they were evidently both lies. If we attempt to explain this obscurity, which puzzled Tennyson and many less friendly critics, we find that it has many sources.

First, the poet's thought is often obscure, or else so extremely subtle that language expresses it imperfectly,--

Thoughts hardly to be packed

Into a narrow act,

Fancies that broke through language and escaped.

Second, Browning is led from one thing to another by his own mental associations, and forgets that the reader's associations may be of an entirely different kind.

Third, Browning is careless in his English, and frequently clips his speech, giving us a series of ejaculations. As we do not quite understand his processes of thought, we must stop between the ejaculations to trace out the connections.

Fourth, Browning's, allusions are often far-fetched, referring to some odd scrap of information which he has picked up in his wide reading, and the ordinary reader finds it difficult to trace and understand them.

Finally, Browning wrote too much and revised too Little. The time which he should have given to making one thought clear was used in expressing other thoughts that flitted through his head like a flock of swallows. His field was the individual soul, never exactly alike in any two men, and he sought to express the hidden motives and principles which govern individual action. In this field he is like a miner delving-underground, sending up masses of mingled earth and ore; and the reader must sift all this material to separate the gold from the dross.

Here, certainly, are sufficient reasons for Browning's obscurity; and we must add the word that the fault seems unpardonable, for the simple reason that Browning shows himself capable, at times, of writing directly, melodiously, and with noble simplicity.

So much for the faults, which must be faced and overlooked before one finds the treasure that is hidden in Browning's poetry. Of all the poets in our literature, no other is so completely, so consciously, so magnificently a teacher of men. He feels his mission of faith and courage in a world of doubt and timidity. For thirty years he faced indifference or ridicule, working bravely and cheerfully the while, until he made the world recognize and follow him. The spirit of his whole life is well expressed in his Paracelsus, written when he was only twenty-two years old:

I see my way as birds their trackless way.

I shall arrive,--what time, what circuit first,

I ask not; but unless God send his hail

Or blinding fire-balls, sleet or stifling snow,

In some time, his good time, I shall arrive;

He guides me and the bird. In his good time.

He is not, like so many others, an entertaining poet. One cannot read him after dinner, or when settled in a comfortable easy-chair. One must sit up, and think, and be alert when he reads Browning. If we accept these conditions, we shall probably find that Browning is the most stimulating poet in our language. His influence upon our life is positive and tremendous. His strength, his joy of life, his robust faith, and his invincible optimism enter into us, making us different and better men after reading him. And perhaps the best thing he can say of Browning is that his thought is slowly but surely taking possession of all well-educated men and women.

Life

Browning's father was outwardly a business man, a clerk for fifty years in the Bank of England; inwardly he was an interesting combination of the scholar and the artist, with the best tastes of both. His mother was a sensitive, musical woman, evidently very lovely in character, the daughter of a German shipowner and merchant who had settled in Scotland. She was of Celtic descent, and Carlyle describes her as the true type of a Scottish gentlewoman. From his neck down, Browning was the typical Briton,--short, stocky, large-chested, robust; but even in the lifeless portrait his face changes as we view it from different angles. Now it is like an English business man, now like a German scientist, and now it has a curious suggestion of Uncle Remus,--these being, no doubt, so many different reflections of his mixed and unremembered ancestors.

He was born in Camberwell, on the outskirts of London, in 1812. From his home and from his first school, at Peckham, he could see London; and the city lights by night and the smoky chimneys by day had the same powerful fascination for the child that the woods and fields and the beautiful country had for his friend Tennyson. His schooling was short and desultory, his education being attended to by private tutors and by his father, who left the boy largely to follow his own inclination.

Like the young Milton, Browning was fond of music, and in many of his poems, especially in "Abt Vogler" and "A Toccata of Galuppi's," he interprets the musical temperament better, perhaps, than any other writer in our literature. But unlike Milton, through whose poetry there runs a great melody, music seems to have had no consistent effect upon his verse, which is often so jarring that one must wonder how a musical ear could have endured it.

Like Tennyson, this boy found his work very early, and for fifty years hardly a week passed that he did not write poetry. He began at six to produce verses, in imitation of Byron; but fortunately this early work has been lost. Then he fell under the influence of Shelley, and his first known work, Pauline (1833), must be considered as a tribute to Shelley and his poetry. Tennyson's earliest work, Poems by Two Brothers, had been published and well paid for, five years before; but Browning could find no publisher who would even consider Pauline, and the work was published by means of money furnished by an indulgent relative. This poem received scant notice from the reviewers, who had pounced like hawks on a dovecote upon Tennyson's first two modest volumes. Two years later appeared Paracelsus, and then his tragedy Strafford was put upon the stage; but not till Sordello was published, in 1840, did he attract attention enough to be denounced for the obscurity and vagaries of his style. Six years later, in 1846, he suddenly became famous, not because he finished in that year his Bells and Pomegranates (which is Browning's symbolic name for "poetry and thought" or "singing and sermonizing"), but because he eloped with the best known literary woman in England, Elizabeth Barrett, whose fame was for many years, both before and after her marriage, much greater than Browning's, and who was at first considered superior to Tennyson.

Thereafter, until his own work compelled attention, he was known chiefly as the man who married Elizabeth Barrett. For years this lady had been an almost helpless invalid, and it seemed a quixotic thing when Browning, having failed to gain her family's consent to the marriage, carried her off romantically. Love and Italy proved better than her physicians, and for fifteen years Browning and his wife lived an ideally happy life in Pisa and in Florence. The exquisite romance of their love is preserved in Mrs. Browning's Sonnets from the Portuguese, and in the volume of Letters recently published,--wonderful letters, but so tender and intimate that it seems almost a sacrilege for inquisitive eyes to read them.

Mrs. Browning died in Florence in 1861. The loss seemed at first too much to bear, and Browning fled with his son to England. For the remainder of his life he lived alternately in London and in various parts of Italy, especially at the Palazzo Rezzonico, in Venice, which is now an object of pilgrimage to almost every tourist who visits the beautiful city. Wherever he went he mingled with men and women, sociable, well dressed, courteous, loving crowds and popular applause, the very reverse of his friend Tennyson. His earlier work had been much better appreciated in America than in England; but with the publication of The Ring and the Book, in 1868, he was at last recognized by his countrymen as one of the greatest of English poets. He died in Venice, on December 12, 1889, the same day that saw the publication of his last work, Asolando. Though Italy offered him an honored resting place, England claimed him for her own, and he lies buried beside Tennyson in Westminster Abbey. The spirit of his whole life is magnificently expressed in his own lines, in the Epilogue of his last book:

One who never turned his back, but marched breast forward,

Never doubted clouds would break,

Never dreamed, tho' right were worsted, wrong would triumph,

Held we fall to rise, are baffled to fight better,

Sleep to wake.

Works

A glance at even the titles which Browning gave to his best known volumes--Dramatic Lyrics (1842), Dramatic Romances and Lyrics (1845), Men and Women (1853),

Dramatis Persona (1864)--will suggest how strong the dramatic element is in all his work. Indeed, all his poems may be divided into three classes,--pure dramas, like Strafford and A Blot in the 'Scutcheon; dramatic narratives, like Pippa Passes, which are dramatic in form, but were not meant to be acted; and dramatic lyrics, like The Last Ride Together, which are short poems expressing some strong personal emotion, or describing some dramatic episode in human life, and in which the hero himself generally tells the story.

Though Browning is often compared with Shakespeare, the reader will understand that he has very little of Shakespeare's dramatic talent. He cannot bring a group of people together and let the actions and words of his characters show us the comedy and tragedy of human life. Neither can the author be disinterested, satisfied, as Shakespeare was, with life itself, without drawing any moral conclusions. Browning has always a moral ready, and insists upon giving us his own views of life, which Shakespeare never does. His dramatic power lies in depicting what he himself calls the history of a soul. Sometimes, as in Paracelsus, he endeavors to trace the progress of the human spirit.

More often he takes some dramatic moment in life, some crisis in the ceaseless struggle between good and evil, and describes with wonderful insight the hero's own thoughts and feelings; but he almost invariably tells us how, at such and such a point, the good or the evil in his hero must inevitably have triumphed. And generally, as in "My Last Duchess," the speaker adds a word here and there, aside from the story, which unconsciously shows the kind of man he is. It is this power of revealing the soul from within that causes Browning to fascinate those who study him long enough. His range is enormous, and brings all sorts and conditions of men under analysis. The musician in "Abt Vogler," the artist in "Andrea del Sarto," the early Christian in "A Death in the Desert," the Arab horseman in "Muteykeh," the sailor in "Herve Kiel," the mediaeval knight in "Childe

Roland," the Hebrew in "Saul," the Greek in "Balaustion's Adventure," the monster in "Caliban," the immortal dead in "Karshish,"--all these and a hundred more histories of the soul show Browning's marvelous versatility. It is this great range of sympathy with many different types of life that constitutes Browning's chief likeness to Shakespeare, though otherwise there is no comparison between the two men.

If we separate all these dramatic poems into three main periods,--the early, from 1833 to 1841; the middle, from 1841 to 1868; and the late, from 1868 to 1889,--the work of the beginner will be much more easily designated. Of his early soul studies, Pauline (1833), Paracelsus (1835), and Sordello (1840), little need be said here, except perhaps this: that if we begin with these works, we shall probably never read anything else by Browning. And that were a pity. It is better to leave these obscure works until his better poems have so attracted us to Browning that we will cheerfully endure his worst faults for the sake of his undoubted virtues. The same criticism applies, though in less degree, to his first drama, Strafford (1837), which belongs to the early period of his work.

The merciless criticism which greeted Sordello had a wholesome effect on Browning, as is shown in the better work of his second period. Moreover, his new power was developing rapidly, as may be seen by comparing the eight numbers of his famous Bells and Pomegranates series (1841-1846) with his earlier work. Thus, the first number of this wonderful series, published in 1841, contains Pippa Passes, which is, on the whole, the most perfect of his longer poems; and another number contains A Blot in the 'Scutcheon, which is the most readable of his dramas. Even a beginner must be thrilled by the beauty and the power of these two works. Two other noteworthy dramas of the period are Colombe's Birthday (1844) and In a Balcony (1855), which, however, met with scant appreciation on the stage, having too much subtle analysis and too little action to satisfy the public.

Nearly all his best lyrics, dramas, and dramatic poems belong to this middle period of labor; and when The Ring and the Book appeared, in 1868, he had given to the world the noblest expression of his poetic genius.

In the third period, beginning when Browning was nearly sixty years old, he wrote even more industriously than before, and published on an average nearly a volume of poetry a year. Such volumes as Fifine at the Fair, Red Cotton Night-Cap Country, The Inn Album, Jocoseria, and many others, show how Browning gains steadily in the power of revealing the hidden springs of human action; but he often rambles most tiresomely, and in general his work loses in sustained interest. It is perhaps significant that most of his best work was done under Mrs. Browning's influence.

Of the short miscellaneous poems there is such an unusual variety that one must hesitate a little in suggesting this or that to the beginner's attention. "My Star," "Evelyn Hope," "Wanting is--What?" "Home Thoughts from Abroad," "Meeting at Night," "One Word More" (an exquisite tribute to his dead wife), "Prospice" (Look Forward); songs from Pippa Passes; various love poems like "By the Fireside" and "The Last Ride Together"; the inimitable "Pied Piper," and the ballads like "Herve Riel" and "How They Brought the Good News,"-- these are a mere suggestion, expressing only the writer's personal preference; but a glance at the contents of Browning's volumes will reveal scores of other poems, which another writer might recommend as being better in themselves or more characteristic of Browning.

Among Browning's dramatic soul studies there is also a very wide choice. "Andrea del Sarto" is one of the best, revealing as it does the strength and the weakness of "the perfect painter," whose love for a soulless woman with a pretty face saddens his life and hampers his best work. Next in importance to "Andrea" stands "An Epistle," reciting the experiences of Karshish, an Arab physician, which is one of the best examples of Browning's peculiar method of presentin the truth. The half-scoffing, half-earnest, and wholly bewildered state of this Oriental scientist's mind is clearly indicated between the lines of his letter to his old master. His description of Lazarus, whom he meets by chance, and of the state of mind of one who, having seen the glories of immortality, must live again in the midst of the jumble of trivial and stupendous things which constitute our life, forms one of the most original and suggestive poems in our literature. "My Last Duchess" is a short but very keen analysis of the soul of a selfish man, who reveals his character unconsciously by his words of praise concerning his dead wife's picture.

In "The Bishop Orders his Tomb" we have another extraordinarily interesting revelation of the mind of a vain and worldly man, this time a churchman, whose words tell you far more than he dreams about his own character. "Abt Vogler," undoubtedly one of Browning's finest poems, is the study of a musician's soul. "Muleykeh" gives us the soul of an Arab, vain and proud of his fast horse, which was never beaten in a race. A rival steals the horse and rides away upon her back; but, used as she is to her master's touch, she will not show her best pace to the stranger. Muleykeh rides up furiously; but instead of striking the thief from his saddle, he boasts about his peerless mare, saying that if a certain spot on her neck were touched with the rein, she could never be overtaken. Instantly the robber touches the spot, and the mare answers with a burst of speed that makes pursuit hopeless. Muleykeh has lost his mare; but he has kept his pride in the unbeaten one, and is satisfied. "Rabbi Ben Ezra," which refuses analysis, and which must be read entire to be appreciated, is perhaps the most quoted of all Browning's works, and contains the best expression of his own faith in life, both here and hereafter.

All these wonderful poems are, again, merely a suggestion. They indicate simply the works to which one reader turns when he feels mentally vigorous enough to pick up Browning.

Another list of soul studies, citing "A Toccata of Galuppi's," "A Grammarian's Funeral," "Fra Lippo Lippi," "Saul," "Cleon," "A Death in the Desert," and "Soliloquy of the Spanish Cloister," might, in another's judgment, be more interesting and suggestive.

[Pippa Passes] Among Browning's longer poems there are two, at least, that well deserve our study. Pippa Passes, aside from its rare poetical qualities, is a study of unconscious influence. The idea of the poem was suggested to Browning while listening to a gypsy girl singing in the woods near his home; but he transfers the scene of the action to the little mountain town of Asolo, in Italy. Pippa is a little silk weaver, who goes out in the morning to enjoy her one holiday of the whole year. As she thinks of her own happiness she is vaguely wishing that she might share it, and do some good. Then, with her childish imagination, she begins to weave a little romance in which she shares in the happiness of the four greatest and happiest people in Asolo. It never occurs to her that perhaps there is more of misery than of happiness in the four great ones of whom she dreams; and so she goes on her way singing,

The year's at the spring
And day's at the morn;
Morning's at seven;
The hillside's dew-pearled;
The lark's on the wing;
The snail's on the thorn:
God's in his heaven--
All's right with the world!

Fate wills it that the words and music of her little songs should come to the ears of four different groups of people at the moment when they are facing the greatest crises of their lives, and turn the scale from evil to good. But Pippa knows nothing of this. She enjoys her holiday, and goes to bed still singing, entirely ignorant of the good she has done in the world. With one exception, it is the most perfect of all Browning's works. At best it is not easy, nor merely entertaining reading; but it richly repays whatever hours we spend in studying it.

The Ring and the Book is Browning's masterpiece. It is an immense poem, twice as long as Paradise Lost, and longer by some two thousand lines than the Iliad; and before we begin the undoubted task of reading it, we must understand that there is no interesting story or dramatic development to carry us along. In the beginning we have an outline of the story, such as it is--a horrible story of Count Guido's murder of his beautiful young wife; and Browning tells us in detail just when and how he found a book containing the record of the crime and the trial. There the story element ends, and the symbolism of the book begins. The title of the poem is explained by the habit of the old Etruscan goldsmiths who, in making one of their elaborately chased rings, would mix the pure gold with an alloy, in order to harden it. When the ring was finished, acid was poured upon it; and the acid ate out the alloy, leaving the beautiful design in pure gold. Browning purposes to follow the same plan with his literary material, which consists simply of the evidence given at the trial of Guido in Rome, in 1698. He intends to mix a poet's fancy with the crude facts, and create a beautiful and artistic work.

The result of Browning's purpose is a series of monologues, in which the same story is retold nine different times by the different actors in the drama. The count, the young wife, the suspected priest, the lawyers, the Pope who presides at the trial,--each tells the story, and each unconsciously reveals the depths of his own nature in the recital. The most interesting of the characters are Guido, the husband, who changes from bold defiance to abject fear; Caponsacchi, the young priest, who aids the wife in her flight from her brutal husband, and is unjustly accused of false motives; Pompilia, the young wife, one of the noblest characters in literature, fit in all respects to rank with Shakespeare's great heroines; and the Pope, a splendid figure, the strongest of all Browning's masculine characters. When we have read the story, as told by these four different actors, we have the best of the poet's work, and of the most original poem in our language.

Browning's Place and Message

Browning's place in our literature will be better appreciated by comparison with his friend Tennyson, whom we have just studied. In one respect, at least, these poets are in perfect accord. Each finds in love the supreme purpose and meaning of life. In other respects, especially in their methods of approaching the truth, the two men are the exact opposites. Tennyson is first the artist and then the teacher; but with Browning the message is always the important thing, and he is careless, too careless, of the form in which it is expressed. Again, Tennyson is under the influence of the romantic revival, and chooses his subjects daintily; but "all's fish" that comes to Browning's net. He takes comely and ugly subjects with equal pleasure, and aims to show that truth lies hidden in both the evil and the good. This contrast is all the more striking when we remember that Browning's essentially scientific attitude was taken by a man who refused to study science. Tennyson, whose work is always artistic, never studied art, but was devoted to the sciences; while Browning, whose work is seldom artistic in form, thought that art was the most suitable subject for a man's study.

The two poets differ even more widely in their respective messages. Tennyson's message reflects the growing order of the age, and is summed up in the word "law." in his view, the individual will must be suppressed; the self must always be subordinate. His resignation is at times almost Oriental in its fatalism, and occasionally it suggests Schopenhauer in its mixture of fate and pessimism. Browning's message, on the other hand, is the triumph of the individual will over all obstacles; the self is not subordinate but supreme. There is nothing Oriental, nothing doubtful, nothing pessimistic in the whole range of his poetry. His is the voice of the Anglo-Saxon, standing up in the face of all obstacles and saying, "I can and I will." He is, therefore, far more radically English than is Tennyson; and it may be for this reason that he is the more studied, and that, while youth delights in Tennyson, manhood is better satisfied with Browning. Because of his invincible will and optimism, Browning is at present regarded as the poet who has spoken the strongest word of faith to an age of doubt. His energy, his cheerful courage, his faith in life and in the development that awaits us beyond the portals of death, are like a bugle-call to good living. This sums up his present influence upon the minds of those who have learned to appreciate him. Of the future we can only say that, both at home and abroad, he seems to be gaining steadily in appreciation as the years go by.

MINOR POETS OF THE VISTORIAN AGE

Elizabeth Barrett

Among the minor poets of the past century Elizabeth Barrett (Mrs. Browning) occupies perhaps the highest place in popular favor. She was born at Coxhoe Hall, near Durham, in 1806; but her childhood and early youth were spent in Herefordshire, among the Malvern Hills made famous by Piers Plowman. In 1835 the Barrett family moved to London, where Elizabeth gained a literary reputation by the publication of The Seraphim and Other Poems (1838). Then illness and the shock caused by the tragic death of her brother, in 1840, placed her frail life in danger, and for six years she was confined to her own room. The innate strength and beauty of her spirit here showed itself strongly in her daily study, her poetry, and especially in her interest in the social problems which sooner or later occupied all the Victorian writers. "My mind to me a kingdom is" might well have been written over the door of the room where this delicate invalid worked and suffered in loneliness and in silence.

In 1844 Miss Barrett published her Poems, which, though somewhat impulsive and overwrought, met with remarkable public favor. Such poems as "The Cry of the Children," which voices the protest of humanity against child labor, appealed tremendously to the readers of the age, and this young woman's fame as a poet temporarily overshadowed that of Tennyson and Browning. Indeed, as late as 1850, when Wordsworth died, she was seriously considered for the position of poet laureate, which was finally given to Tennyson. A reference to Browning, in "Lady Geraldine's Courtship," is supposed to have first led the poet to write to Miss Barrett in 1845. Soon afterwards he visited the invalid; they fell in love almost at first sight, and the following year, against the wishes of her father,--who was evidently a selfish old tyrant,--Browning carried her off and married her. The exquisite romance of their love is reflected in Mrs. Browning's Sonnets from the Portuguese (1850). This is a noble and inspiring book of love poems; and Stedman regards the opening sonnet, "I thought once how Theocritus had sung," as equal to any in our language. For fifteen years the Brownings lived an ideally happy life at Pisa, and at Casa Guidi, Florence, sharing the same poetical ambitions. And love was the greatest thing in the world,--

How do I love thee? Let me count the ways.

I love thee to the depth and breadth and height

My soul can reach, when feeling out of sight

For the ends of Being and ideal Grace.

I love thee to the level of everyday's

Most quiet need, by sun and candlelight.

I love thee freely, as men strive for Right;

I love thee purely, as they turn from Praise;

I love thee with the passion put to use

In my old griefs, and with my childhood's faith;

I love thee with a love I seemed to lose

With my lost saints--I love thee with the breath,

Smiles, tears, of all my life!--and, if God choose,

I shall but love thee better after death.

Mrs. Browning entered with whole-souled enthusiasm into the aspirations of Italy in its struggle against the tyranny of Austria; and her Casa Guidi Windows (1851) is a combination of poetry and politics, both, it must be confessed, a little too emotional. In 1856 she published Aurora Leigh, a novel in verse, having for its hero a young social reformer, and for its heroine a young woman, poetical and enthusiastic, who strongly suggests Elizabeth Barrett herself. It emphasizes in verse precisely the same moral and social ideals which Dickens and George Eliot were proclaiming in all their novels. Her last two volumes were Poems before Congress (1860), and Last Poems, published after her death. She died suddenly in 1861 and was buried in Florence. Browning's famous line, "O lyric love, half angel and half bird," may well apply to her frail life and aerial spirit.

Rossetti

Dante Gabriel Rossetti (1828-1882), the son of an exiled Italian painter and scholar, was distinguished both as a painter and as a poet. He was a leader in the Pre-Raphaelite movement and published in the first numbers of The Germ his "Hand and Soul," a delicate prose study, and his famous "The Blessed Damozel," beginning,

The blessed damozel leaned out

From the gold bar of Heaven;

Her eyes were deeper than the depth

Of waters stilled at even;

She had three lilies in her hand,

And the stars in her hair were seven.

These two early works, especially "The Blessed Damozel," with its simplicity and exquisite spiritual quality, are characteristic of the ideals of the Pre-Raphaelites.

In 1860, after a long engagement, Rossetti married Elizabeth Siddal, a delicate, beautiful English girl, whom he has immortalized both in his pictures and in his poetry. She died two years later, and Rossetti never entirely recovered from the shock. At her burial he placed in her coffin the manuscripts of all his unpublished poems, and only at the persistent demands of his friends did he allow them to be exhumed and printed in 1870. The publication of this volume of love poems created a sensation in literary circles, and Rossetti was hailed as one of the greatest of living poets. In 1881 he published his Ballads and Sonnets, a remarkable volume containing, among other poems, "The Confession," modeled after Browning; "The Ballad of Sister Helen," founded on a mediaeval superstition; "The King's Tragedy," a masterpiece of dramatic narrative; and "The House of Life," a collection of one hundred and one sonnets reflecting the poet's love and loss. This last collection deserves to rank with Mrs. Browning's Sonnets from the Portuguese and with Shakespeare's Sonnets, as one of the three great cycles of love poems in our language. It has been well said that both Rossetti and Morris paint pictures as well in their poems as on their canvases, and this pictorial quality of their verse is its chief characteristic.

Morris

William Morris (1834-1896) is a most interesting combination of literary man and artist. In the latter capacity, as architect, designer, and manufacturer of furniture, carpets, and wall paper, and as founder of the Kelmscott Press for artistic printing and bookbinding, he has laid us all under an immense debt of gratitude. From boyhood he had steeped himself in the legends and ideals of the Middle Ages, and his best literary work is wholly mediaeval in spirit. The

Earthly Paradise (1868-1870) is generally regarded as his masterpiece. This delightful collection of stories in verse tells of a roving band of Vikings, who are wrecked on the fabled island of Atlantis, and who discover there a superior race of men having the characteristics of ideal Greeks. The Vikings remain for a year, telling stories of their own Northland, and listening to the classic and Oriental tales of their hosts. Morris's interest in Icelandic literature is further shown by his Sigurd the Volsung, an epic founded upon one of the old sagas, and by his prose romances, The House of the Wolfings, The Story of the Glittering Plain, and The Roots of the Mountains. Later in life he became deeply interested in socialism, and two other romances, The Dream of John Ball and News from Nowhere, are interesting as modern attempts at depicting an ideal society governed by the principles of More's Utopia.

Swinburne

Algernon Charles Swinburne (1837-1909) is, chronologically, the last of the Victorian poets. As an artist in technique--having perfect command of all old English verse forms and a remarkable faculty for inventing new--he seems at the present time to rank among the best in our literature. Indeed, as Stedman says, "before his advent we did not realize the full scope of English verse." This refers to the melodious and constantly changing form rather than to the content of Swinburne's poetry. At the death of Tennyson, in 1892, he was undoubtedly the greatest living poet, and only his liberal opinions, his scorn of royalty and of conventions, and the prejudice aroused by the pagan spirit of his early work prevented his appointment as poet laureate. He has written a very large number of poems, dramas, and essays in literary criticism; but we are still too near to judge of the permanence of his work or of his place in literature. Those who would read and estimate his work for themselves will do well to begin with a volume of selected poems, especially those which show his love of the sea and his exquisite appreciation of child life. His Atalanta in Calydon (1864), a beautiful lyric drama modeled on the Greek tragedy, is generally regarded as his masterpiece. In all his work Swinburne carries Tennyson's love of melody to an extreme, and often sacrifices sense to sound. His poetry is always musical, and, like music, appeals almost exclusively to the emotions.

We have chosen, somewhat arbitrarily, these four writers--Mrs. Browning, D. G. Rossetti, Morris, and Swinburne--as representative of the minor poets of the age; but there are many others who are worthy of study,--Arthur Hugh Clough and Matthew Arnold, who are often called the poets of skepticism, but who in reality represent a reverent seeking for truth through reason and human experience; Frederick William Faber, the Catholic mystic, author of some exquisite hymns; and the scholarly John Keble, author of The Christian Year, our best known book of devotional verse; and among the women poets, Adelaide Procter, Jean Ingelow, and Christina Rossetti, each of whom had a large, admiring circle of readers. It would be a hopeless task at the present time to inquire into the relative merits of all these minor poets. We note only their careful workmanship and exquisite melody, their wide range of thought and feeling, their eager search for truth, each in his own way, and especially the note of freshness and vitality which they have given to English poetry.

THE NOVELISTS OF THE VICTORIAN AGE

Charles Dickens (1812-1870)

When we consider Dickens's life and work, in comparison with that of the two great poets we have been studying, the contrast is startling. While Tennyson and Browning were being educated for the life of literature, and shielded most tenderly from the hardships of the world, Dickens, a poor, obscure, and suffering child, was helping to support a shiftless family by pasting labels on blacking bottles, sleeping under a counter like a homeless cat, and once a week timidly approaching the big prison where his father was confined for debt. In 1836 his Pickwick was published, and life was changed as if a magician had waved his wand over him. While the two great poets were slowly struggling for recognition, Dickens, with plenty of money and too much fame, was the acknowledged literary hero of England, the idol of immense audiences which gathered to applaud him wherever he appeared. And there is also this striking contrast between the novelist and the poets,--that while the whole tendency of the age was toward realism, away from the extremes of the romanticists and from the oddities and absurdities of the early novel writers, it was precisely by emphasizing oddities and absurdities, by making caricatures rather than characters, that Dickens first achieved his popularity.

Life

In Dickens's early life we see a stern but unrecognized preparation for the work that he was to do. Never was there a better illustration of the fact that a boy's early hardship and suffering are sometimes only divine messengers disguised, and that circumstances which seem only evil are often the source of a man's strength and of the influence which he is to wield in the world. He was the second of eight poor children, and was born at Landport in 1812. His father, who is supposed to be the original of Mr. Micawber, was a clerk in a navy office. He could never make both ends meet, and after struggling with debts in his native town for many years, moved to London when Dickens was nine years old. The debts still pursued him, and after two years of grandiloquent misfortune he was thrown into the poor-debtors' prison. His wife, the original of Mrs. Micawber, then set up the famous Boarding Establishment for Young Ladies; but, in Dickens's words, no young ladies ever came. The only visitors were creditors, and they were quite ferocious. In the picture of the Micawber family, with its tears and smiles and general shiftlessness, we have a suggestion of Dickens's own family life.

At eleven years of age the boy was taken out of school and went to work in the cellar of a blacking factory. At this time he was, in his own words, a "queer small boy," who suffered as he worked; and we can appreciate the boy and the suffering more when we find both reflected in the character of David Copperfield. It is a heart-rending picture, this sensitive child working from dawn till dark for a few pennies, and associating with toughs and waifs in his brief intervals of labor; but we can see in it the sources of that intimate knowledge of the hearts of the poor and outcast which was soon to be reflected in literature and to startle all England by its appeal for sympathy. A small legacy ended this wretchedness, bringing the father from the prison and sending the boy to Wellington House Academy,--a worthless and brutal school, evidently, whose head master was, in Dickens's words, a most ignorant fellow and a tyrant. He learned little at this place, being interested chiefly in stories, and in acting out the heroic parts which appealed to his imagination; but again his personal experience was of immense value, and resulted in his famous picture of Dotheboys Hall, in Nicholas Nickleby, which helped largely to mitigate the evils of private schools in England. Wherever he went, Dickens was a marvelously keen observer, with an active imagination which made stories out of incidents and characters that ordinary men would have hardly noticed. Moreover he was a born actor, and was at one time the leading spirit of a band of amateurs who gave entertainments for charity all over England. These three things, his keen observation, his active imagination, and the actor's spirit which animated him, furnish a key to his life and writings.

When only fifteen years old, he left the school and again went to work, this time as clerk in a lawyer's office. By night he studied shorthand, in order to fit himself to be a reporter,--this in imitation of his father, who was now engaged by a newspaper to report the speeches in Parliament. Everything that Dickens attempted seems to have been done with vigor and intensity, and within two years we find him reporting important speeches, and writing out his notes as the heavy coach lurched and rolled through the mud of country roads on its dark way to London town.

It was largely during this period that he gained his extraordinary knowledge of inns and stables and "horsey" persons, which is reflected in his novels. He also grew ambitious, and began to write on his own account. At the age of twenty-one he dropped his first little sketch "stealthily, with fear and trembling, into a dark letter-box, in a dark office up a dark court in Fleet Street." The name of this first sketch was "Mr. Minns and his Cousin," and it appeared with other stories in his first book, Sketches by Boz, in 1835. One who reads these sketches now, with their intimate knowledge of the hidden life of London, can understand Dickens's first newspaper success perfectly. His best known work, Pickwick, was published serially in 1836-1837, and Dickens's fame and fortune were made. Never before had a novel appeared so full of vitality and merriment. Though crude in design, a mere jumble of exaggerated characters and incidents, it fairly bubbled over with the kind of humor in which the British public delights, and it still remains, after three quarters of a century, one of our most care-dispelling books.

The remainder of Dickens's life is largely a record of personal triumphs. Pickwick was followed rapidly by Oliver Twist, Nicholas Nickleby, Old Curiosity Shop, and by many other works which seemed to indicate that there was no limit to the new author's invention of odd, grotesque, uproarious, and sentimental characters. In the intervals of his novel writing he attempted several times to edit a weekly paper; but his power lay in other directions, and with the exception of Household Words, his journalistic ventures were not a marked success. Again the actor came to the surface, and after managing a company of amateur actors successfully, Dickens began to give dramatic readings from his own works. As he was already the most popular writer in the English language, these readings were very successful. Crowds thronged to hear him, and his journeys became a continuous ovation. Money poured into his pockets from his novels and from his readings, and he bought for himself a home, Gadshill Place, which he had always desired, and which is forever associated with his memory. Though he spent the greater part of his time and strength in travel at this period, nothing is more characteristic of the man than the intense energy with which he turned from his lecturing to his novels, and then, for relaxation, gave himself up to what he called the magic lantern of the London streets.

In 1842, while still a young man, Dickens was invited to visit the United States and Canada, where his works were even better known than in England, and where he was received as the guest of the nation and treated with every mark of honor and appreciation. At this time America was, to most Europeans, a kind of huge fairyland, where money sprang out of the earth, and life was happy as a long holiday. Dickens evidently shared this rosy view, and his romantic expectations were naturally disappointed. The crude, unfinished look of the big country seems to have roused a strong prejudice in his mind, which was not overcome at the time of his second visit, twenty-five years later, and which brought forth the harsh criticism of his American Notes (1842) and of Martin Chuzzlewit (1843-1844).

These two unkind books struck a false note, and Dickens began to lose something of his great popularity. In addition he had spent money beyond his income. His domestic life, which had been at first very happy, became more and more irritating, until he separated from his wife in 1858. To get inspiration, which seemed for a time to have failed, he journeyed to Italy, but was disappointed. Then he turned back to the London streets, and in the five years from 1848 to 1853 appeared Dombey and Son, David Copperfield, and Bleak House,--three remarkable novels, which indicate that he had rediscovered his own power and genius. Later he resumed the public readings, with their public triumph and applause, which soon came to be a necessity to one who craved popularity as a hungry man craves bread. These excitements exhausted Dickens, physically and spiritually, and death was the inevitable result. He died in 1870, over his unfinished Edwin Drood, and was buried in Westminster Abbey.

Dickens's Work in View of His Life

A glance through even this unsatisfactory biography gives us certain illuminating suggestions in regard to all of Dickens's work.

First, as a child, poor and lonely, longing for love and for society, he laid the foundation for those heartrending pictures of children, which have moved so many readers to unaccustomed tears.

Second, as clerk in a lawyer's office and in the courts, he gained his knowledge of an entirely different side of human life. Here he learned to understand both the enemies and the victims of society, between whom the harsh laws of that day frequently made no distinction.

Third, as a reporter, and afterwards as manager of various newspapers, he learned the trick of racy writing, and of knowing to a nicety what would suit the popular taste.

Fourth, as an actor, always an actor in spirit, he seized upon every dramatic possibility, every tense situation, every peculiarity of voice and gesture in the people whom he met, and reproduced these things in his novels, exaggerating them in the way that most pleased his audience.

When we turn from his outward training to his inner disposition we find two strongly marked elements. The first is his excessive imagination, which made good stories out of incidents that ordinarily pass unnoticed, and which described the commonest things--a street, a shop, a fog, a lamp-post, a stagecoach--with a wealth of detail and of romantic suggestion that makes many of his descriptions like lyric poems. The second element is his extreme sensibility, which finds relief only in laughter and tears. Like shadow and sunshine these follow one another closely throughout all his books.

Remembering these two things, his training and disposition, we can easily foresee the kind of novel he must produce. He will be sentimental, especially over children and outcasts; he will excuse the individual in view of the faults of society; he will be dramatic or melodramatic; and his sensibility will keep him always close to the public, studying its tastes and playing with its smiles and tears. If pleasing the public be in itself an art, then Dickens is one of our greatest artists. And it is well to remember that in pleasing his public there was nothing of the hypocrite or demagogue in his máke-up. He was essentially a part of the great drifting panoramic crowd that he loved. His sympathetic soul made all their joys and griefs his own. He fought against injustice; he championed the weak against the strong; he gave courage to the faint, and hope to the weary in heart; and in the love which the public gave him in return he found his best reward. Here is the secret of Dickens's unprecedented popular success, and we may note here a very significant parallel with Shakespeare. The great different in the genius and work of the two men does not change the fact that each won success largely because he studied and pleased his public.

General Plan of Dickens's Novels

An interesting suggestion comes to us from a study of the conditions which led to Dickens's first three novels. Pickwick was written, at the suggestion of an editor, for serial publication. Each chapter was to be accompanied by a cartoon by Seymor (a comic artist of the day), and the object was to amuse the public, and, incidentally, to sell the paper. The result was a series of characters and scenes and incidents which for vigor and boundless fun have never been equaled in our language. Thereafter, no matter what he wrote, Dickins was lbeled a humorist. Like a certain American writer of our own generation, everything he said, whether for a feast or a funeral, was spposed to contain a laugh. In a word, he was the victim of his own book. Dickens was keen enough to understand his danger, and his next novel, Oliver Twist, had the serious purpose of mitigating the evils under which the poor were suffering. Its hero was a poor child, the unfortunate victim of society; and, in order to draw attention to the real need, Dickens exaggerated the woeful condition of the poor, and filled his pages with sentiment which easily slipped over into sentimentality. This also was a popular success, and in his third novel, Nicholas Nickleby, and indeed in most of his remaining works, Dickens combined the principles of his first two books, giving us mirth on the one hand, injustice and suffering on the other; mingling humor and pathos, tears and laughter, as we find them in life itself. And in order to increase the lights and shadows in his scenes, and to give greater dramatic effect to his narrative, he introduced odious and lothsome characters, and made vice more hateful by contrasting it with innocence and virtue.

We find, therefore, in most of Dickens's novels three or four widely different types of character: first, the innocent little child, like Oliver, Joe, Paul, Tiny Tim, and Little Nell, appealing powerfully to the child love in every human heart; scond, the horrible or grotesque foil, like Sqeers, Fagin, Quilp, Uriah Heep, and Bill Sykes; third, the grandiloquent or broadly humorous fellow, the fun maker, like Micawber and Sam Weller; and fourth, a tenderly or powerfully drawn figure, like Lady Deadlock of Bleak House, and Sydney Carton of A Tale of Two Cities, which rise to the dignity of true characters. We note also that most of Dickens's novels belong decidely to the class of purpose or problem novels. Thus Bleak House attacks "the law's delays"; Little Dorrit, the injustice which persecutes poor debtors; Nicholas Nickleby, the abuses of charity schools and brutal schoolmasters; and Oliver Twist, the unnecessary degradation and suffering of the poor in English workhouses. Dickens's serious purpose was to make the novel the instrument of morality and justice, and whatver we may think of the exaggeration of his characters, it is certain that his stories did more to correct the general selfishness and injustice of society toward the poor than all the works of other literary men of his age combined.

The Limitations of Dickens

Any severe criticism of Dickens as a novelist must seem, at first glance, unkind an unnecessary. In almost every house he is a welcome guest, a personal friend who has beguiled many an hour with his stories, and who has furnished us much good laughter and a few good tears. Moreover, he has always a cheery message. He emphasizes the fact that this is an excellant world; that some errors have crept into it, due largely to thoughtlessness, but that they can be easily remedied by a little human sympathy. That is a most welcome creed to an age overburdened with social problems; and to criticise our cheery companion seems as discourteous as to speak unkindly of a guest who has just left our home. But we must consider Dickens not merely as a friend, but as a novelist, and apply to his work the same standards of art which we apply to other writers; and when we do this we are sometimes a little disappointed. We must confess that his novels, while they contain many realistic details, seldom give the impression of reality. His characters, though we laugh or weep or shudder at them, are sometimes only caricatures, each one an exaggeration of some peculiarity, which suggest Ben Jonson's Every Man in His Humour. It is Dickens's art to give his heroes sufficient reality to make them suggest certain types of men and women whom we know; but in reading him we find ourselves often in the mental state of a man who is watching through a microscope the swarming life of a water drop. Here are lively, bustling, extraordinary creatures, some beautiful, some grotesque. but all far apart from the life that we know in daily experience. It is certainly not the reality of these characters, but rather the genius of the author in managing them, which interests us and holds our attention. Notwithstanding this criticism, which we would gladly have omitted, Dickens is excellent reading, and his novels will continue to be popular just so long as men enjoy a wholesome and absorbing story.

What to Read

Aside from the reforms in schools and prisons and workhouses which Dickens accomplished, he has laid us all, rich and poor alike, under a debt of gratitude. After the year 1843 the one literary work which he never neglected was to furnish a Christmas story for his readers; and it is due in some measure to the help of these stories, brimming over with good cheer, that Christmas has become in all English-speaking countries a season of gladness, of gift giving at home, and of remembering those less fortunate than ourselves, who are still members of a common brotherhood.

If we read nothing else of Dickens, once a year, at Christmas time, we should remember him and renew our youth by reading one of his holiday stories,--The Cricket on the Hearth, The Chimes, and above all the unrivaled Christmas Carol. The latter especially will be read and loved as long as men are moved by the spirit of Christmas.

Of the novels, David Copperfield is regarded by many as Dickens's masterpiece. It is well to begin with this novel, not simply for the unusual interest of the story, but also for the glimpse it gives us of the author's own boyhood and family. For pure fun and hilarity Pickwick will always be a favorite; but for artistic finish, and for the portrayal of one great character, Sydney Carton, nothing else that Dickens wrote is comparable to A Tale of Two Cities. Here is an absorbing story, with a carefully constructed plot, and the action moves swiftly to its thrilling, inevitable conclusion. Usually Dickens introduces several pathetic or grotesque or laughable characters besides the main actors, and records various unnecessary dramatic episodes for their own sake; but in A Tale of Two Cities everything has its place in the development of the main story.

There are, as usual, many characters,--Sydney Carton, the outcast, who lays down his life for the happiness of one whom he loves; Charles Darnay, an exiled young French noble; Dr. Manette, who has been "recalled to life" from a frightful imprisonment, and his gentle daughter Lucie, the heroine; Jarvis Lorry, a lovable, old-fashioned clerk in the big banking house; the terrible Madame Defarge, knitting calmly at the door of her wine shop and recording, with the ferocity of a tiger licking its chops, the names of all those who are marked for vengeance; and a dozen others, each well drawn, who play minor parts in the tragedy. The scene is laid in London and Paris, at the time of the French Revolution; and, though careless of historical details, Dickens reproduces the spirit of the Reign of Terror so well that A Tale of Two Cities is an excellent supplement to the history of the period. It is written in Dickens's usual picturesque style, and reveals his usual imaginative outlook on life and his fondness for fine sentiments and dramatic episodes. Indeed, all his qualities are here shown, not brilliantly or garishly, as in other novels, but subdued and softened, like a shaded light, for artistic effect.

Those who are interested in Dickens's growth and methods can hardly do better than to read in succession his first three novels, Pickwick, Oliver Twist, and Nicholas Nickleby, which, as we have indicated, show clearly how he passed from fun to serious purpose, and which furnish in combination the general plan of all his later works. For the rest, we can only indicate those which, in our personal judgment, seem best worth reading,--Bleak House, Dombey and Son, Our Mutual Friend, and Old Curiosity Shop,--but we are not yet far enough away from the first popular success of these works to determine their permanent value and influence.

William Makepeace Thackeray (1811-1863)

As the two most successful novelists of their day, it is natural for us, as it was for their personal friends and admirers, to compare Dickens and Thackeray with respect to their life and work, and their attitude toward the world in which they lived.

Dickens, after a desperately hard struggle in his boyhood, without friends or higher education, comes into manhood cheery, self-confident, energetic, filled with the joy of his work; and in the world, which had at first treated him so harshly, he finds good everywhere, even in the jails and in the slums, simply because he is looking for it. Thackeray, after a boyhood spent in the best of English schools, with money, friends, and comforts of every kind, faces life timidly, distrustfully, and dislikes the literary work which makes him famous. He has a gracious and lovable personality, is kind of heart, and reveres all that is pure and good in life; yet he is almost cynical toward the world which uses him so well, and finds shams, deceptions, vanities everywhere, because he looks for them. One finds what one seeks in this world, but it is perhaps significant that Dickens sought his golden fleece among plain people, and Thackeray in high society.

The chief difference between the two novelists, however, is not one of environment but of temperament. Put Thackeray in a workhouse, and he will still find material for another Book of Snobs; put Dickens in society, and he cannot help finding undreamed-of possibilities among bewigged and bepowdered high lords and ladies. For Dickens is romantic and emotional, and interprets the world largely through his imagination; Thackeray is the realist and moralist, who judges solely by observation and reflection. He aims to give us a true picture of the society of his day, and as he finds it pervaded by intrigues and snobbery he proceeds to satirize it and point out its moral evils. In his novels he is influenced by Swift and Fielding, but he is entirely free from the bitterness of the one and the coarseness of the other, and his satire is generally softened by a noble tenderness. Taken together, the novels of Dickens and Thackeray give us a remarkable picture of all classes of English society in the middle of the nineteenth century.

Life

Thackeray was born in 1811, in Calcutta, where his father held a civil position under the Indian government. When the boy was five years old his father died, and the mother returned with her child to England. Presently she married again, and Thackeray was sent to the famous Charterhouse school, of which he has given us a vivid picture in The Newcomes. Such a school would have been a veritable heaven to Dickens, who at this time was tossed about between poverty and ambition; but Thackeray detested it for its rude manners, and occasionally referred to it as the "Slaughterhouse." Writing to his mother he says: "There are three hundred and seventy boys in the school. I wish, there were only three hundred and sixty-nine."

In 1829 Thackeray entered Trinity College, Cambridge, but left after less than two years, without taking a degree, and went to Germany and France where he studied with the idea of becoming an artist. When he became of age, in 1832, he came into possession of a comfortable fortune, returned to England, and settled down in the Temple to study law. Soon he began to dislike the profession intensely, and we have in Pendennis a reflection of his mental attitude toward the law and the young men who studied it. He soon lost his fortune, partly by gambling and speculation, partly by unsuccessful attempts at running a newspaper, and at twenty-two began for the first time to earn his own living, as an artist and illustrator. An interesting meeting between Thackeray and Dickens at this time (1836) suggests the relative importance of the two writers. Seymour, who was illustrating the Pickwick Papers, had just died, and Thackeray called upon Dickens with a few drawings and asked to be allowed to continue the illustrations. Dickens was at this time at the beginning of his great popularity. The better literary artist, whose drawings were refused, was almost unknown, and had to work hard for more than ten years before he received recognition. Disappointed by his failure as an illustrator, he began his literary career by writing satires on society for Fraser's Magazine. This was the beginning of his success; but though the Yellowplush Papers, The Great Hoggarty Diamond, Catherine, The Fitz Boodlers, The Book of Snobs, Barry Lyndon, and various other immature works made him known to a few readers of Punch and of Fraser's Magazine, it was not till the publication of Vanity Fair (1847-1848) that he began to be recognized as one of the great novelists of his day. All his earlier works are satires, some upon society, others upon the popular novelists,--Bulwer, Disraeli, and especially Dickens,--with whose sentimental heroes and heroines he had no patience whatever. He had married, meanwhile, in 1836, and for a few years was very happy in his home. Then disease and insanity fastened upon his young wife, and she was placed in an asylum. The whole after life of our novelist was darkened by this loss worse than death. He became a man of the clubs, rather than of his own home, and though his wit and kindness made him the most welcome of clubmen, there was an undercurrent of sadness in all that he wrote. Long afterwards he said that, though his marriage ended in shipwreck, he "would do it over again; for behold Love is the crown and completion of all earthly good."

After the moderate success of Vanity Fair, Thackeray wrote the three novels of his middle life upon which his fame chiefly rests,--Pendennis in 1850, Henry Esmond in 1852, and The Newcomes in 1855. Dickens's great popular success as a lecturer and dramatic reader had led to a general desire on the part of the public to see and to hear literary men, and Thackeray, to increase his income, gave two remarkable courses of lectures, the first being English Humorists of the Eighteenth Century, and the second The Four Georges,--both courses being delivered with gratifying success in England and especially in America. Dickens, as we have seen, was disappointed in America and vented his displeasure in outrageous criticism; but Thackeray, with his usual good breeding, saw only the best side of his generous entertainers, and in both his public and private utterances emphasized the virtues of the new land, whose restless energy seemed to fascinate him. Unlike Dickens, he had no confidence in himself when he faced an audience, and like most literary men he disliked lecturing, and soon gave it up. In 1860 he became editor of the Cornhill Magazine, which prospered in his hands, and with a comfortable income he seemed just ready to do his best work for the world (which has always believed that he was capable of even better things than he ever wrote) when he died suddenly in 1863. His body lies buried in Kensal Green, and only a bust does honor to his memory in Westminster Abbey.

Works of Thackeray

The beginner will do well to omit the earlier satires of Thackeray, written while he was struggling to earn a living from the magazines, and open Henry Esmond (1852), his most perfect novel, though not the most widely known and read. The fine historical and literary, flavor of this story is one of its most marked characteristics, and only one who knows something of the history and literature of the eighteenth century can appreciate its value. The hero, Colonel Esmond; relates his own story, carrying the reader through the courts and camps of Queen Anne's reign, and giving the most complete and accurate picture of a past age that has ever appeared in a novel. Thackeray is, as we have said, a realist, and he begins his story by adopting the style and manner of a scholarly gentleman of the period he is describing. He has an extraordinary knowledge of eighteenth-century literature, and he reproduces its style in detail, going so far as to insert in his narrative an alleged essay from the Tatler. And so perfectly is it done that it is impossible to say wherein it differs from the style of Addison and Steele.

In his matter also Thackeray is realistic, reflecting not the pride and pomp of war, which are largely delusions, but its brutality and barbarism, which are all too real; painting generals and leaders, not as the newspaper heroes to whom we are accustomed, but as moved by intrigues, petty jealousies, and selfish ambitions; showing us the great Duke of Marlborough not as the military hero, the idol of war-crazed multitudes, but as without personal honor, and governed by despicable avarice. In a word, Thackeray gives us the "back stairs" view of war, which is, as a rule, totally neglected in our histories. When he deals with the literary men of the period, he uses the same frank realism, showing us Steele and Addison and other leaders, not with halos about their heads, as popular authors, but in slippers and dressing gowns, smoking a pipe in their own rooms, or else growing tipsy and hilarious in the taverns,--just as they appeared in daily life. Both in style and in matter, therefore, Esmond deserves to rank as probably the best historical novel in our language.

The plot of the story is, like most of Thackeray's plots, very slight, but perfectly suited to the novelist's purpose. The plans of his characters fail; their ideals grow dim; there is a general disappearance of youthful ambitions. There is a love story at the center; but the element of romance, which furnishes the light and music and fragrance of love, is inconspicuous. The hero, after ten years of devotion to a young woman, a paragon of beauty, finally marries her mother, and ends with a few pious observations concerning Heaven's mercy and his own happy lot. Such an ending seems disappointing, almost bizarre, in view of the romantic novels to which we are accustomed; but we must remember that Thackeray's purpose was to paint life as he saw it, and that in life men and things often take a different way from that described in romances. As we grow acquainted with Thackeray's characters, we realize that no other ending was possible to his story, and conclude that his plot, like his style, is perhaps as near perfection as a realistic novelist can ever come.

Vanity Fair (1847--1848) is the best known of Thackeray's novels. It was his first great work, and was intended to express his own views of the social life about him, and to protest against the overdrawn heroes of popular novels. He takes for his subject that Vanity Fair to which Christian and Faithful were conducted on their way to the Heavenly City, as recorded in Pilgrim's Progress. In this fair there are many different booths, given over to the sale of "all sorts of vanities," and as we go from one to another we come in contact with "juggling, cheats, games, plays, fools, apes, knaves, rogues, and that of every kind." Evidently this is a picture of one side of social life; but the difference between Bunyan and Thackeray is simply this,--that Bunyan made Vanity Fair a small incident in a long journey, a place through which most of us pass on our way to better things; while Thackeray, describing high society in his own day, makes it a place of long sojourn, wherein his characters spend the greater part of their lives. Thackeray styles this work "a novel without a hero." The whole action of the story, which is without plot or development, revolves about two women,--Amelia, a meek creature of the milk-and-water type, and Becky Sharp, a keen, unprincipled intriguer, who lets nothing stand in the way of her selfish desire to get the most out of the fools who largely constitute society. On the whole, it is the most powerful but not the most wholesome of Thackeray's works.

In his second important novel, Pendennis (1849-1850), we have a continuation of the satire on society begun in Vanity Fair. This novel, which the beginner should read after Esmond, is interesting to us for two reasons,--because it reflects more of the details of Thackeray's life than all his other writings, and because it contains one powerfully drawn character who is a perpetual reminder of the danger of selfishness. The hero is "neither angel nor imp," in Thackeray's words, but the typical young man of society, whom he knows thoroughly, and whom he paints exactly as he is,--a careless, good-natured but essentially selfish person, who goes through life intent on his own interests. Pendennis is a profound moral study, and the most powerful arraignment of well-meaning selfishness in our literature, not even excepting George Eliot's Romola, which it suggests.

Two other novels, The Newcomes (1855) and The Virginians (1859), complete the list of Thackeray's great works of fiction. The former is a sequel to Pendennis, and the latter to Henry Esmond; and both share the general fate of sequels in not being quite equal in power or interest to their predecessors. The Newcomes, however, deserves a very high place,--some critics, indeed, placing it at the head of the author's works. Like all Thackeray's novels, it is a story of human frailty; but here the author's innate gentleness and kindness are seen at their best, and the hero is perhaps the most genuine and lovable of all his characters.

Thackeray is known in English literature as an essayist as well as a novelist. His English Humorists and The Four Georges are among the finest essays of the nineteenth century. In the former especially, Thackeray shows not only a wide knowledge but an extraordinary understanding of his subject. Apparently this nineteenth-century writer knows Addison, Fielding, Swift, Smollett, and other great writers of the past century almost as intimately as one knows his nearest friend; and he gives us the fine flavor of their humor in a way which no other writer, save perhaps Larnb, has ever rivaled. The Four Georges is in a vein of delicate satire, and presents a rather unflattering picture of four of England's rulers and of the courts in which they moved. Both these works are remarkable for their exquisite style, their gentle humor, their keen literary criticisms, and for the intimate knowledge and sympathy which makes the' people of a-past age live once more in the written pages.

General Characteristics

In treating of Thackeray's view of life, as reflected in his novels, critics vary greatly, and the following summary must be taken not as a positive judgment but only as an attempt to express the general impression of his works on an uncritical reader. He is first of a realist, who paints life as he sees it. As he says himself, "I have no brains above my eyes; I describe what I see.". His pictures of certain types, notably the weak and vicious elements of society, are accurate and true to life, but they seem to play too large a part in his books, and have perhaps too greatly influenced his general judgment of humanity. An excessive sensibility, or the capacity for fine feelings and emotions, is a marked characteristic of Thackeray, as it is of Dickens and Carlyle. He is easily offended, as they are, by the shams of society; but he cannot find an outlet, as Dickens does, in laughter and tears, and he is too gentle to follow Carlyle in violent denunciations and prophecies. He turns to satire,--influenced, doubtless, by eighteenth-century literature which he knew so well, and in which satire played too large a part. His satire is never personal, like Pope's, or brutal, like Swift's, and is tempered by kindness and humor; but it is used too freely, and generally lays too much emphasis on faults and foibles to be considered a true picture of any large class of English society.

Besides being a realist and satirist, Thackeray is essentially a moralist, like Addison, aiming definitely in all his work at producing a moral impression. So much does he revere goodness, and so determined is he that his Pendennis or his Becky Sharp shall be judged at their true value, that he is not content, like Shakespeare, to be simply an artist, to tell an artistic tale and let it speak its own message; he must explain and emphasize the moral significance of his work. There is no need to consult our own conscience over the actions of Thackeray's characters; the beauty of virtue and the ugliness of vice are evident on every page.

Whatever we may think of Thackeray's matter, there is one point in which critics are agreed,--that he is master of a pure and simple English style. Whether his thought be sad or humorous, commonplace or profound, he expresses it perfectly, without effort or affectation. In all his work there is a subtle charm, impossible to describe, which gives the impression that we are listening to a gentleman. And it is the ease, the refinement, the exquisite naturalness of Thackeray's style that furnishes a large part of our pleasure in reading him.

Mary Ann Evans, George Eliot (1819-1880)

In nearly all the writers of the Victorian Age we note, on the one hand, a strong intellectual tendency to analyze the problems of life, and on the other a tendency to teach, that is, to explain to men the method by which these problems may be solved. The novels especially seem to lose sight of the purely artistic ideal of writing, and to aim definitely at moral instruction. In George Eliot both these tendencies reach a climax. She is more obviously, more consciously a preacher and moralizer than any of her great contemporaries. Though profoundly religious at heart, she was largely occupied by the scientific spirit of the age; and finding no religious creed or political system satisfactory, she fell back upon duty as the supreme law of life. All her novels aim, first, to show in individuals the play of universal moral forces, and second, to establish the moral law as the basis of human society. Aside from this moral teaching, we look to George Eliot for the reflection of country life in England, just as we look to Dickens for pictures of the city streets, and to Thackeray for the vanities of society. Of all the women writer's who have helped and are still helping to place our English novels at the head of the world's fiction, she holds at present unquestionably the highest rank.

Life

Mary Ann (or Marian) Evans, known to us by her pen name of George Eliot, began to write late in life, when nearly forty years of age, and attained the leading position among living English novelists in the ten years between 1870 and 1880, after Thackeray and Dickens had passed away. She was born at Arbury Farm, Warwickshire, some twenty miles from Stratford-on-Avon, in 1819. Her parents were plain, honest folk, of the farmer class, who brought her up in the somewhat strict religious manner of those days. Her father seems to have been a man of sterling integrity and of practical English sense,--one of those essentially noble characters who do the world's work silently and well, and who by their solid worth obtain a position of influence among their fellow-men.

A few months after George Eliot's birth the family moved to another home, in the parish of Griff, where her childhood was largely passed. The scenery of the Midland counties and many details of her own family life are reflected in her earlier novels. Thus we find her and her brother, as Maggie and Tom Tulliver, in The Mill on the Floss; her aunt, as Dinah Morris, and her mother, as Mrs. Poyser, in Adam Bede. We have a suggestion of her father in the hero of the latter novel, but the picture is more fully drawn as Caleb Garth, in Middlemarch. For a few years she studied at two private schools for young ladies, at Nuneaton and Coventry; but the death of her mother called her, at seventeen years of age, to take entire charge of the household. Thereafter her education was gained wholly by miscellaneous reading. We have a suggestion of her method in one of her early letters, in which she says: "My mind presents an assemblage of disjointed specimens of history, ancient and modern; scraps of poetry picked up from Shakespeare, Cowper, Wordsworth, and Milton; newspaper topics, morsels of Addison and Bacon, Latin verbs, geometry, entomology, and chemistry; reviews and metaphysics, all arrested and petrified and smothered by the fast-thickening everyday accession of actual events, relative anxieties, and household cares and vexations."

When Mary was twenty-one years old the family again moved, this time to Foleshill Road, near Coventry. Here she became acquainted with the family of Charles Bray, a prosperous ribbon manufacturer, whose house was a gathering place for the freethinkers of the neighborhood. The effect of this liberal atmosphere upon Miss Evans, brought up in a narrow way, with no knowledge of the world, was to unsettle many of her youthful convictions. From a narrow, intense dogmatism, she went to the other extreme of radicalism; then (about 1860) she lost all sympathy with the freethinkers, and, being instinctively religious, seemed to be groping after a definite faith while following the ideal of duty. This spiritual struggle, which suggests that of Carlyle, is undoubtedly the cause of that gloom and depression which hang, like an English fog, over much of her work; though her biographer, Cross, tells us that she was not by any means a sad or gloomy woman.

In 1849 Miss Evans's father died, and the Brays took her abroad for a tour of the continent. On her return to England she wrote several liberal articles for the Westminster Review, and presently was made assistant editor of that magazine. Her residence in London at this time marks a turning point in her career and the real beginning of her literary life. She made strong friendships with Spencer, Mill, and other scientists of the day, and through Spencer met George Henry Lewes, a miscellaneous writer, whom she afterwards married.

Under his sympathetic influence she began to write fiction for the magazines, her first story being "Amos Barton" (1857), which was later included in the Scenes of Clerical Life (1858). Her first long novel, Adam Bede, appeared early in 1859 and met with such popular favor that to the end of her life she despaired of ever again repeating her triumph. But the unexpected success proved to be an inspiration, and she completed The Mill on the Floss and began Silas Marner during the following year. Not until the great success of these works led to an insistent demand to know the author did the English public learn that it was a woman, and not an English clergyman, as they supposed, who had suddenly jumped to the front rank of living writers.

Up to this point George Eliot had confined herself to English country life, but now she suddenly abandoned the scenes and the people with whom she was most familiar in order to write an historical novel. It was in 1860, while traveling in Italy, that she formed "the great project" of Romola,--a mingling of fiction and moral philosophy, against the background of the mighty Renaissance movement. In this she was writing of things of which she had no personal knowledge, and the book cost her many months of hard and depressing labor. She said herself that she was a young woman when she began the work, and an old woman when she finished it. Romola (1862--1863) was not successful with the public, and the same may be said of Felix Holt the Radical (1866) and The Spanish Gypsy (1868).

The last-named work was the result of the author's ambition to write a dramatic poem which should duplicate the lesson of Romola; and for the purpose of gathering material she visited Spain, which she had decided upon as the scene of her poetical effort. With the publication of Middlemarch (1871-1872) George Eliot came back again into popular favor, though this work is less spontaneous, and more labored and pedantic, than her earlier novels.

The fault of too much analysis and moralizing was even more conspicuous in Daniei Deronda (1876), which she regarded as her greatest book. Her life during all this time was singularly uneventful, and the chief milestones along the road mark the publication of her successive novels.

During all the years of her literary success her husband Lewes had been a most sympathetic friend and critic, and when he died, in 1878, the loss seemed-to be more than she could bear. Her letters of this period are touching in their loneliness and their craving for sympathy. Later she astonished everybody by marrying John Walter Cross, much younger than herself, who is known as her biographer. "Deep down below there is a river of sadness, but... I am able to enjoy my newly re-opened life," writes this woman of sixty, who, ever since she was the girl whom we know as Maggie Tulliver, must always have some one to love and to depend upon. Her new interest in life lasted but a few months, for she died in December of the same year (1880). One of the best indications of her strength and her limitations is her portrait, with its strong masculine features, suggesting both by resemblance and by contrast that wonderful portrait of Savonarola which hangs over his old desk in the monastery at Florence.

Works of George Eliot

These are conveniently divided into three groups, corresponding to the three periods of her life. The first group includes all her early essays and miscellaneous work, from her translation of Strauss's Leben Jesu, in 1846, to her union with Lewes in 1854. The second group includes Scenes of Clerical Life, Adam Bede, Mill on the Floss, and Silas Marner, all published between 1858 and 1861.

These four novels of the middle period are founded on the author's own life and experience; their scenes are laid in the country, and their characters are taken from the stolid people of the Midlands, with whom George Eliot had been familiar since childhood. They are probably the author's most enduring works. They have a naturalness, a spontaneity, at times a flash of real humor, which are lacking in her later novels; and they show a rapid development of literary power which reaches a climax in Silas Marner.

The novel of Italian life, Romola (1862-1863), marks a transition to the third group, which includes three more novels,--Felix Holt (1866), Middlemarch (1871-1872), Daniel Deronda (1876), the ambitious dramatic poem The Spanish Gypsy (1868), and a collection of miscellaneous essays called The Impressions of Theophrastus Such (1879). The general impression, of these works is not so favorable as that produced by the novels of the middle period. They are more labored and less interesting; they contain much deep reflection and analysis of character, but less observation, less delight in picturing country life as it is, and very little of what we call inspiration. We must add, however, that this does not express a unanimous literary judgment, for critics are not wanting who assert that Daniel Deronda is the highest expression of the author's genius.

The general character of all these novels may be described, in the author's own term, as psychologic realism. This means that George Eliot sought to do in her novels what Browning attempted in his poetry; that is, to represent the inner struggle of a soul, and to reveal the motives, impulses, and hereditary influences which govern human action. Browning generally stops when he tells his story, and either lets you draw your own conclusion or else gives you his in a few striking lines. But George Eliot is not content until she has minutely explained the motives of her characters and the moral lesson to be learned from them.

Moreover, it is the development of a soul, the slow growth or decline of moral power, which chiefly interests her. Her heroes and heroines differ radically from those of Dickens and Thackeray in this respect,--that when we meet the men and women of the latter novelists, their characters are already formed, and we are reasonably sure what they will do under given circumstances. In George Eliot's novels the characters develop gradually as we come to know them. They go from weakness to strength, or from strength to weakness, according to the works that they do and the thoughts that they cherish.

In Romola, for instance, Tito, as we first meet him, may be either good or bad, and we know not whether he will finally turn to the right hand or to the left. As time passes, we see him degenerate steadily because he follows his selfish impulses, while Romola, whose character is at first only faintly indicated, grows into beauty and strength with every act of self-renunciation.

In these two characters, Tito and Romola, we have an epitome of our author's moral teaching. The principle of law was in the air during the Victorian era, and we have already noted how deeply Tennyson was influenced by it. With George Eliot law is like fate; it overwhelms personal freedom and inclination. Moral law was to her as inevitable, as automatic, as gravitation. Tito's degeneration, and the sad failure of Dorothea and Lydgate in Middlemarch, may be explained as simply as the fall of an apple, or as a bruised knee when a man loses his balance. A certain act produces a definite moral effect on the individual; and character is the added sum of all, the acts of a man's; life,--just as the weight of a body is the sum of the weights of many different atoms which constitute it. The matter of rewards and punishments, therefore, needs no final judge or judgment, since these things take care of themselves automatically in a world of inviolable moral law.

Perhaps one thing more should be added to the general characteristics of George Eliot's novels,--they are all rather depressing. The gladsomeness of life, the sunshine of smiles and laughter, is denied her. It is said that once, when her husband remarked that her novels were all essentially sad, she wept, and answered that she must describe life as she had found it.

What to Read

George Eliot's first stories are in some respects her best, though her literary power increases during her second period, culminating in Silas Marner, and her psychological analysis is more evident in Daniel Deronda. On the whole, it is an excellent way to begin with the freshness and inspiration of the Scenes of Clerical Life and read her books in the order in which they were written. In the first group of novels Adam Bede is the most natural, and probably interests more readers than all the others combined. The Mill on the Floss has a larger personal interest, because it reflects much of George Eliot's history and the scenes and the friends of her early life. The lack of proportion in this story, which gives rather too much space to the girl-and-boy experiences, is naturally explained by the tendency in every man and woman to linger over early memories.

Silas Marner is artistically the most perfect of George Eliot's novels, and we venture to analyze it as typical of her ideals and methods. We note first the style, which is heavy and a little self-conscious, lacking the vigor and picturesqueness of Dickens, and the grace and naturalness of Thackeray. The characters are the common people of the Midlands, the hero being a linen weaver, a lonely outcast who hoards and gloats over his hard-earned money, is robbed, thrown into utter despair, and brought back to life and happiness by the coming of an abandoned child to his fire.

In the development of her story the author shows herself, first, a realist, by the naturalness of her characters and the minute accuracy with which she reproduces their ways and even the accents of their speech; second, a psychologist, by the continual analysis and explanation of motives; third, a moralist, by showing in each individual the action and reaction of universal moral forces, and especially by making every evil act bring inevitable punishment to the man who does it. Tragedy, therefore, plays a large part in the story; for, according to George Eliot, tragedy and suffering walk close behind us, or lurk at every turn in the road of life. Like all her novels, Silas Marner is depressing. We turn away from even the wedding of Eppie--which is just as it should be--with a sense of sadness and incompleteness. Finally, as we close the book, we are conscious of a powerful and enduring impression of reality. Silas, the poor weaver; Godfrey Cass, the well-meaning, selfish man; Mr. Macey, the garrulous, and observant parish clerk; Dolly Winthrop, the kind-hearted countrywoman who cannot understand the mysteries of religion and so interprets God in terms of human love,--these are real people, whom having once met we can never forget.

Romola has the same general moral theme as the English novels; but the scenes are entirely different, and opinion is divided as to the comparative merit of the work. It is a study, a very profound study of moral development in one character and of moral degeneracy in another. Its characters and its scenes are both Italian, and the action takes place during a critical period of the Renaissance movement, when Savonarola was at the height of his power in Florence. Here is a magnificent theme and a superb background for a great novel, and George Eliot read and studied till she felt sure that she understood the place, the time, and the people of her story. Romola is therefore interesting reading, in many respects the most interesting of her works.

It has been called one of our greatest historical novels; but as such it has one grievous fault. It is not quite true to the people or even to the locality which it endeavors to represent. One who reads it here, in a new and different land, thinks only of the story and of the novelist's power; but one who reads it on the spot which it describes, and amidst the life which it pictures, is continually haunted by the suggestion that George Eliot understood neither Italy nor the Italians.

It is this lack of harmony with Italian life itself which caused Morris and Rossetti and even Browning, with all his admiration for the author, to lay aside the book, unable to read it with pleasure or profit. In a word, Romola is a great moral study and a very interesting book; but the characters are not Italian, and the novel as a whole lacks the strong reality which marks George Eliot's English studies.

MINOR NOVELISTS OF THE VICTORIAN AGE

In the three great novelists just considered we have an epitome of the fiction of the age, Dickens using the novel to solve social problems, Thackeray to paint the life of society as he saw it, and George Eliot to teach the fundamental principles of morality.

The influence of these three writers is reflected in all the minor novelists of the Victorian Age. Thus, Dickens is reflected in Charles Reade, Thackeray in Anthony Trollope and the Bronte sisters, and George Eliot's psychology finds artistic expression in George Meredith. To these social and moral and realistic studies we should add the element of romance, from which few of our modern novelist's can long escape. The nineteenth century, which began with the romanticism of Walter Scott, returns to its first love, like a man glad to be home, in its delight over Blackmore's Lorna Doone and the romances of Robert Louis Stevenson.

Charles Reade

In his fondness for stage effects, for picturing the romantic side of common life, and for using the novel as the instrument of social reform, there is a strong suggestion of Dickens in the work of Charles Reade (1814-1884). Thus his Peg Woffington is a study of stage life from behind the scenes; A Terrible Temptation is a study of social reforms and reformers; and Put yourself in his Place is the picture of a workingman who struggles against the injustice of the trades unions. His masterpiece, The Cloister and the Hearth (1861), one of our best historical novels, is a somewhat laborious study of student and vagabond life in Europe in the days of the German Renaissance.

It has small resemblance to George Eliot's Romola, whose scene is laid in Italy during the same period; but the two works may well be read in succession, as the efforts of two very different novelists of the same period to restore the life of an age long past.

Anthony Trollope

In his realism, and especially in his conception of the novel as the entertainment of an idle hour, Trollope (1815-1882) is a reflection of Thackeray. It would be hard to find a better duplicate of Becky Sharp, the heroine of Vanity Fair, for instance, than is found in Lizzie Eustace, the heroine of The Eustace Diamonds. Trollope was the most industrious and systematic of modern novelists, writing a definite amount each day, and the wide range of his characters suggests the Human Comedy of Balzac. His masterpiece is Barchester Towers (1857). This is a study of life in a cathedral town, and is remarkable for its minute pictures of bishops and clergymen, with their families and dependents. It would be well to read this novel in connection with The Warden (1855), The Last Chronicle of Barset (1867), and other novels of the same series, since the scenes and characters are the same in all these books, and they are undoubtedly the best expression of the author's genius. Hawthorne says of his novels: "They precisely suit my taste,--solid and substantial, and... just as real as if some giant had hewn a great lump out of the earth and put it under a glass case, with all the inhabitants going about their daily business and not suspecting that they were being made a show of."

Charlotte Bronte

We have another suggestion of Thackeray in the work of Charlotte Bronte (1816-1855). She aimed to make her novels a realistic picture of society, but she added to Thackeray's realism the element of passionate and somewhat unbalanced romanticism. The latter element was partly the expression of Miss Bronte's own nature, and partly the result of her lonely and grief-stricken life, which was darkened by a succession of family tragedies. It will help us to understand her work if we remember that both Charlotte Bronte and her sister Emily turned to literature because they found their work as governess and teacher unendurable, and sought to relieve the loneliness and sadness of their own lot by creating a new world of the imagination. In this new world, however, the sadness of the old remains, and all the Bronte novels have behind them an aching heart. Charlotte Bronte's best known work is Jane Eyre (1847), which, with all its faults, is a powerful and fascinating study of elemental love and hate, reminding us vaguely of one of Marlowe's tragedies. This work won instant favor with the public, and the author was placed in the front rank of living novelists. Aside from its value as a novel, it is interesting, in many of its early passages, as the reflection of the author's own life and experience. Shirley (1849) and Villette (1853) make up the trio of novels by which this gifted woman is generally remembered.

Bulwer Lytton

Edward Bulwer Lytton (1803-1873) was an extremely versatile writer, who tried almost every kind of novel known to the nineteenth century. In his early life he wrote poems and dramas, under the influence of Byron; but his first notable work, Pelham (1828), one of the best of his novels, was a kind of burlesque on the Byronic type of gentleman. As a study of contemporary manners in high society, Pelham has a suggestion of Thackeray, and the resemblance is more noticeable in other novels of the same type, such as Ernest Maltravers (1837), The Caxtons (1848-1849), My Novel (1853), and Kenelm Chillingly (1873). We have a suggestion of Dickens in at least two of Lytton's novels, Paul Clifford and Eugene Aram, the heroes of which are criminals, pictured as the victims rather than as the oppressors of society. Lytton essayed also, with considerable popular success, the romantic novel in The Pilgrims of the Rhine and Zanoni, and tried the ghost story in The Haunted and the Haunters. His fame at the present day rests largely upon his historical novels, in imitation of Walter Scott, The Last Days of Pompeii (1834), Riettza (1835), and Harold (1848), the last being his most ambitious attempt to make the novel the supplement of history. In all his novels Lytton is inclined to sentimentalism and sensationalism, and his works, though generally interesting, seem hardly worthy of a high place in the history of fiction.

Kingsley

Entirely different in spirit are the novels of the scholarly clergyman, Charles Kingsley (1819-1875). His works naturally divide themselves into three classes. In the first are his social studies and problem novels, such as Alton Locke (1850), having for its hero a London tailor and poet, and Yeast (1848), which deals with the problem of the agricultural laborer. In the second class are his historical novels, Hereward the Wake, Hypatia, and Westward Ho! Hypatia is a dramatic story of Christianity in contact with paganism, having its scene laid in Alexandria at the beginning of the fifth century. Westward Ho! (1855), his best known work, is a stirring tale of English conquest by land and sea in the days of Elizabeth. In the third class are his various miscellaneous works, not the least of which is Water-Babies, a fascinating story of a chimney sweep, which mothers read to their children at bedtime,--to the great delight of the round-eyed little listeners under the counterpane.

Mrs. Gaskell

Mrs. Elizabeth Gaskell (1810-1865) began, like Kingsley, with the idea of making the novel the instrument of social reform. As the wife of a clergyman in Manchester, she had come in close contact with the struggles and ideals of the industrial poor of a great city, and she reflected her sympathy as well as her observation in Mary Barton (1848) and in North and South (1855).

Between these two problem novels she published her masterpiece, Cranford, in 1853. The original of this country village, which is given over to spinsters, is undoubtedly Knutsford, in Cheshire, where Mrs. Gaskell had spent her childhood. The sympathy, the keen observation, and the gentle humor with which the small affairs of a country village are described make Cranford one of the most delightful stories in the English language. We are indebted to Mrs. Gaskell also for the Life of Charlotte Bronte, which is one of our best biographies.

Blackmore

Richard Doddridge Blackrhore (1825--1900) was a prolific writer, but he owes his fame almost entirely to one splendid novel, Lorna Doone, which was published in 1869. The scene of this fascinating romance is laid in Exmoor in the seventeenth century. The story abounds in romantic scenes and incidents; its descriptions of natural scenery are unsurpassed; the rhythmic language is at times almost equal to poetry; and the whole tone of the book is wholesome and refreshing.

Altogether it would be hard to find a more delightful romance in any language, and it well deserves the place it has won as one of the classics of our literature. Other works of Blackmore which will repay the reader are Clara Vaughan (1864), his first novel, The Maid of Sker (1872), Springhaven (1887), Perlycross (1894), and Tales from the Telling House (1896); but none of these, though he counted them his best work, has met with the same favor as Lorna Doone.

Meredith

So much does George Meredith (1828-1909) belong to our own day that it is difficult to think of him as one of the Victorian novelists. His first notable work, The Ordeal of Richard Feverel, was published in 1859, the same year as George Eliot's Adam Bede; but it was not till the publication of Diana of the Crossways in 1885, that his power as a novelist was widely recognized. He resembles Browning not only in his condensed style, packed with thought, but also in this respect,--that he labored for years in obscurity, and after much of his best work was published and apparently forgotten he slowly won the leading place in English fiction. We are still too near him to speak of the permanence of his work, but a casual reading of any of his novels suggests a comparison and a contrast with George Eliot.

Like her, he is a realist and a psychologist; but while George Eliot uses tragedy to teach a moral lesson, Meredith depends more upon comedy, making vice not terrible but ridiculous. For the hero or heroine of her novel George Eliot invariably takes an individual, and shows in each one the play of universal moral forces.

Meredith constructs a type-man as a hero, and makes this type express his purpose and meaning. So his characters seldom speak naturally, as George Eliot's do; they are more like Browning's characters in packing a whole paragraph into a single sentence or an exclamation. On account of his enigmatic style and his psychology, Meredith will never be popular; but by thoughtful men and women he will probably be ranked among our greatest writers of fiction.

The simplest and easiest of his novels for a beginner is The Adventures of Henry Richmond (1871). Among the best of his works, besides the two mentioned above, are Beauchamp's Career (1876) and The Egoist (1879). The latter is, in our personal judgment, one of the strongest and most convincing novels of the Victorian Age.

Hardy

Thomas Hardy (1840-) seems, like Meredith, to belong to the present rather than to a past age, and an interesting comparison may be drawn between these two novelists. In style, Meredith is obscure and difficult, while Hardy is direct and simple, aiming at realism in all things. Meredith makes man the most important phenomenon in the universe; and the struggles of men are brightened by the hope of victory. Hardy makes man an insignificant part of the world, struggling against powers greater than himself,--sometimes against systems which he cannot reach or influence, sometimes against a kind of grim world-spirit who delights in making human affairs go wrong. He is, therefore, hardly a realist, but rather a man blinded by pessimism; and his novels, though generally powerful and sometimes fascinating, are not pleasant or wholesome reading. From the reader's view point some of his earlier works, like the idyllic love story Under the Greenwood Tree (1872) and A Pair of Blue Eyes (1873), are the most interesting. Hardy became noted, however, when he published Far from the Madding Crowd, a book which, when it appeared anonymously in the Cornhill Magazine (1874), was generally attributed to George Eliot, for the simple reason that no other novelist was supposed to be capable of writing it. The Return of the Native (1878) and The Woodlanders are generally regarded as Hardy's masterpieces; but two novels of our own day, Tess of the D'Ubervilles (1891) and Jude the Obscure (1895), are better expressions of Hardy's literary art and of his gloomy philosophy.

Stevenson

In pleasing contrast with Hardy is Robert Louis Stevenson (1850-1894), a brave, cheery, wholesome spirit, who has made us all braver and cheerier by what he has written. Aside from their intrinsic value, Stevenson's novels are interesting in this respect,--that they mark a return to the pure romanticism of Walter Scott. The novel of the nineteenth century had, as we have shown, a very definite purpose. It aimed not only to represent life but to correct it, and to offer a solution to pressing moral and social problems. At the end of the century Hardy's gloom in the face of modern social conditions became oppressive, and Stevenson broke away from it into that land of delightful romance in which youth finds an answer to all its questions. Problems differ, but youth is ever the same, and therefore Stevenson will probably be regarded by future generations as one of our most enduring writers. To his life, with its "heroically happy" struggle, first against poverty, then against physical illness, it is impossible to do justice in a short article. Even a longer biography is inadequate, for Stevenson's spirit, not the incidents of his life, is the important thing; and the spirit has no biographer. Though he had written much better work earlier, he first gained fame by his Treasure Island (1883), an absorbing story of pirates and of a hunt for buried gold. Dr. Jekyll and Mr. Hyde (1886) is a profound ethical parable, in which, however, Stevenson leaves the psychology and the minute analysis of character to his readers, and makes the story the chief thing in his novel. Kidnapped (1886), The Master of Ballantrae (1889), and David Balfour (1893) are novels of adventure, giving us vivid pictures of Scotch life. Two romances left unfinished by his early death in Samoa are The Weir of Hermiston and St. Ives. The latter was finished by Quiller-Couch in 1897; the former is happily just as Stevenson left it, and though unfinished is generally regarded as his masterpiece. In addition to these novels, Stevenson wrote a large number of essays, the best of which are collected in Virginibus Puerisque, Familiar Studies of Men and Books, and Memories and Portraits. Delightful sketches of his travels are found in An Inland Voyage (1878), Travels with a Donkey (1879), Across the Plains (1892), and The Amateur Emigrant (1894). Underwoods (1887) is an exquisite little volume of poetry, and A Child's Garden of Verses is one of the books that mothers will always keep to read to their children.

In all his books Stevenson gives the impression of a man at play rather than at work, and the reader soon shares in the happy spirit of the author. Because of his beautiful personality, and because of the love and admiration he awakened for himself in multitudes of readers, we are naturally inclined to exaggerate his importance as a writer. However that may be, a study of his works shows him to be a consummate literary artist. His style is always simple, often perfect, and both in his manner and in his matter he exercises a profound influence, on the writers of the present generation.

ESSAYISTS OF THE VICTORIAN AGE

Thomas Babington Macaulay (1800-1859)

Macaulay is one of the most typical figures of the nineteenth century. Though not a great writer, if we compare him with Browning or Thackeray, he was more closely associated than any of his literary contemporaries with the social and political struggles of the age. While Carlyle was proclaiming the gospel of labor, and Dickens writing novels to better the condition of the poor, Macaulay went vigorously to work on what he thought to be the most important task of the hour, and by his brilliant speeches did perhaps more than any other single man to force the passage of the famous Reform Bill. Like many of the Elizabethans, he was a practical man of affairs rather than a literary man, and though we miss in his writings the imagination and the spiritual insight which stamp the literary genius, we have the impression always of a keen, practical, honest mind, which looks at present problems in the light of past experience. Moreover, the man himself, with his marvelous mind, his happy spirit, and his absolute integrity of character, is an inspiration to better living.

Life

Macaulay was born at Rothley Temple, Leicestershire, in 1800. His father, of Scotch descent, was at one time governor of the Sierra Leone colony for liberated negroes, and devoted a large part of his life to the abolition of the slave trade. His mother, of Quaker parentage, was a brilliant, sensitive woman, whose character is reflected in that of her son. The influence of these two, and the son's loyal devotion to his family, can best be read in Trevelyan's interesting biography.

As a child, Macaulay is strongly suggestive of Coleridge. At three years of age he began to read eagerly; at five he "talked like a book"; at ten he had written a compendium of universal history, besides various hymns, verse romances, arguments for Christianity, and one ambitious epic poem. The habit of rapid reading, begun in childhood, continued throughout his life, and the number and vari ety of books which he read is almost incredible. His memory was phenomenal. He could repeat long poems and essays after a single reading; he could quote not only passages but the greater part of many books,. including Pilgrim's Progress, Paradise Lost, and various novels like Clarissa. Once, to test his memory, he recited two newspaper poems which he had read in a coffeehouse forty years before, and which he had never thought of in the interval.

At twelve years of age this remarkable boy was sent to a private school at Little Shelford, and at eighteen he eqgered Trinity College, Cambridge. Here he made a reputation as a classical scholar and a brilliant talker, but made a failure of his mathematics. In a letter to his mother he wrote: "Oh for words to express my abomination of that science.... Discipline of the mind! Say rather starvation, confinement, torture, annihilation!" We quote this as a commentary on Macaulay's later writings, which are frequently lacking in the exactness and the logical sequence of the science which he detested.

After his college course Macaulay studied law, was admitted to the bar, devoted himself largely to politics, entered Parliament in 1830, and almost immediately won a reputation as the best debater and the most eloquent speaker, of the Liberal or Whig party. Gladstone says of him: "Whenever he arose to speak it was a summons like a trumpet call to fill the benches." At the time of his election he was poor, and the loss of his father's property threw upon him the support of his brothers and sisters; but he took up the burden with cheerful courage, and by his own efforts soon placed himself and his family in comfort. His political progress was rapid, and was due not to favoritism or intrigue, but to his ability, his hard work, and his sterling character. He was several times elected to Parliament, was legal adviser to the Supreme

Council of India, was a member of the cabinet, and declined many offices for which other men labor a lifetime. In 1857 his great ability and services to his country were recognized by his being raised to the peerage with the title of Baron Macaulay of Rothley.

Macaulay's literary work began in college with the contribution of various ballads and essays to the magazines. In his later life practical affairs claimed the greater part of his time, and his brilliant essays were written in the early morning or late at night. His famous Essay on Milton appeared in the Edinburgh Review in 1825. It created a sensation, and Macaulay, having gained the ear of the public, never once lost it during the twenty years in which he was a contributor to the magazines. His Lays of Ancient Rome appeared in 1842, and in the following year three volumes of his collected Essays.

In 1847 he lost his seat in Parliament, temporarily, through his zealous efforts in behalf of religious toleration; and the loss was most fortunate, since it gave him opportunity to begin his History of England,--a monumental work which he had been planning for many years. The first two volumes appeared in 1848, and their success can be compared only to that of the most popular novels. The third and fourth volumes of the History (1855) were even more successful, and Macaulay was hard at work on the remaining volumes when he died, quite suddenly, in 1859. He was buried, near Addison, in the Poets' Corner of Westminster Abbey. A paragraph from one of his letters, written at the height of his fame and influence, may give us an insight into his life and work:

I can truly say that I have not, for many years, been so happy as I am at present.... I am free. I am independent. I am in Parliament, as honorably seated as man can be. My family is comfortably off. I have leisure for literature, yet I am not reduced to the necessity of writing for money. If I had to choose a lot from all that there are in human life, I am not sure that I should prefer any to that which has fallen to me. I am sincerely and thoroughly contented.

Works of Macaulay

Macaulay is famous in literature for his essays, for his martial ballads, and for his History of England. His first important work, the Essay on Milton (1825), is worthy of study not only for itself, as a critical estimate of the Puritan poet, but as a key to all Macaulay's writings. Here, first of all, is an interesting work, which, however much we differ from the author's opinion, holds our attention and generally makes us regret that the end comes so soon. The second thing to note is the historical flavor of the essay. We study not only Milton, but also the times in which he lived, and the great movements of which he was a part. History and literature properly belong together, and Macaulay was one of the first writers to explain the historical conditions which partly account for a writer's work and influence.

The third thing to note is Macaulay's enthusiasm for his subject,--an enthusiasm which is often partisan, but which we gladly share for the moment as we follow the breathless narrative. Macaulay generally makes a hero of his man, shows him battling against odds, and the heroic side of our own nature awakens and responds to the author's plea. The fourth, and perhaps most characteristic thing in the essay is the style, which is remarkably clear, forceful, and convincing.

Jeffrey, the editor of the Edinburgh Review, wrote enthusiastically when he received the manuscript, "The more I think, the less I can conceive where you picked up that style." We still share in the editor's wonder; but the more we think, the less we conceive that such a style could be picked up. It was partly the result of a well-stored mind, partly of unconscious imitation of other writers, and partly of that natural talent for clear speaking and writing which is manifest in all Macaulay's work.

In the remaining essays we find the same general qualities which characterize Macaulay's first attempt. They cover a wide range of subjects, but they may be divided into two general classes, the literary or critical, and the historical. Of the literary essays the best are those on Milton, Addison, Goldsmith, Byron, Dryden, Leigh Hunt, Bunyan, Bacon, and Johnson. Among the best known of the historical essays are those on Lord Clive, Chatham, Warren Hastings, Hallam's Constitutional History, Von Ranke's History of the Papacy, Frederick the Great, Horace Walpole, William Pitt, Sir William Temple, Machiavelli, and Mirabeau. Most of these were produced in the vigor of young manhood, between 1825 and 1845, while the writer was busy with practical affairs of state. They are often one-sided and inaccurate, but always interesting, and from them a large number of busy people have derived their first knowledge of history and literature.

The best of Macaulay's poetical work is found in the Lays of Ancient Rome (1842), a collection of ballads in the style of Scott, which sing of the old heroic days of the Rome Roman republic. The ballad does not require much thought or emotion. It demands clearness, vigor, enthusiasm, action; and it suited Macaulay's genius perfectly. He was, however, much more careful than other ballad writers in making his narrative true to tradition. The stirring martial spirit of these ballads, their fine workmanship, and their appeal to courage and patriotism made them instantly popular. Even to-day, after more than fifty years, such ballads as those on Virginius and Horatius at the Bridge are favorite pieces in many school readers.

The History of England, Macaulay's masterpiece, is still one of the most popular historical works in the English language. Originally it was intended to cover the period from the accession of James II, in 1685, to the death of George IV, in 1830. Only five volumes of the work were finished, and so thoroughly did Macaulay go into details that these five volumes cover only sixteen years. It has been estimated that to complete the work on the same scale would require some fifty volumes and the labor of one man for over a century.

In his historical method Macaulay suggests Gibbon. His own knowledge of history was very great, but before writing he read numberless pages, consulted original documents, and visited the scenes which he intended to describe. Thackeray's remark, that "Macaulay reads twenty books to write a sentence and travels one hundred miles to make a line of description," is, in view of his industry, a well-warranted exaggeration.

As in his literary essays, he is fond of making heroes, and he throws himself so heartily into the spirit of the scene he is describing that his word pictures almost startle us by their vivid reality. The story of Monmouth's rebellion, for instance, or the trial of the seven bishops, is as fascinating as the best chapters of Scott's historical novels.

While Macaulay's search for original sources of information suggests the scientific historian, his use of his material is much more like that of a novelist or playwright. In his essay on Machiavelli he writes: "The best portraits are perhaps those in which there is a slight mixture of caricature, and we are not certain that the best histories are not those in which a little of the exaggeration of fictitious narrative is judiciously employed. Something is lost in accuracy, but much is gained in effect." Whether this estimate of historical writing be true or false, Macaulay employed it in his own work and made his narrative as absorbing as a novel. To all his characters he gives the reality of flesh and blood, and in his own words he "shows us over their houses and seats us at their tables." All that is excellent, but it has its disadvantages. In his admiration for heroism, Macaulay makes some of his characters too good and others too bad. In his zeal for details he misses the importance of great movements, and of great leaders who are accustomed to ignore details; and in his joy of describing events he often loses sight of underlying causes. In a word, he is without historical insight, and his work, though fascinating, is seldom placed among the reliable histories of England.

General Characteristics

To the reader who studies Macaulay's brilliant essays and a few chosen chapters of his History, three things soon become manifest. First, Macaulay's art is that of a public speaker rather than that of a literary man. He has a wonderful command of language, and he makes his meaning clear by striking phrases, vigorous antitheses, anecdotes, and illustrations. His style is so clear that "he who runs may read," and from beginning to end he never loses the attention of his readers. Second, Macaulay's good spirits and enthusiasm are contagious. As he said himself, he wrote "out of a full head," chiefly for his own pleasure or recreation; and one who writes joyously generally awakens a sense of pleasure in his readers. Third, Macaulay has "the defect of his qualities." He reads and remembers so much that he has no time to think or to form settled opinions. As Gladstone said, Macaulay is "always conversing or recollecting or reading or composing, but reflecting never." So he wrote his brilliant Essay on Milton, which took all England by storm, and said of it afterward that it contained "scarcely a paragraph which his mature judgment approved." Whether he speaks or writes, he has always before him an eager audience, and he feels within him the born orator's power to hold and fascinate. So he gives loose rein to his enthusiasm, quotes from a hundred books, and in his delight at entertaining us forgets that the first quality of a critical or historical work is to be accurate, and the second to be interesting.

THOMAS CARLYLE (1795-1881)

In marked contrast with Macaulay, the brilliant and cheerful essayist, is Thomas Carlyle, the prophet and censor of the nineteenth century. Macaulay is the practical man of affairs, helping and rejoicing in the progress of his beloved

England. Carlyle lives apart from all practical interests, looks with distrust on the progress of his age, and tells men that truth, justice, and immortality are the only worthy objects of human endeavor. Macaulay is delighted with material comforts; he is most at home in brilliant and fashionable company; and he writes, even when ill and suffering, with unfailing hopefulness and good nature. Carlyle is like a Hebrew prophet just in from the desert, and the burden of his message is, "Woe to them that are at ease in Zion!" Both men are, in different ways, typical of the century, and somewhere between the two extremes--the practical, helpful activity of Macaulay and the spiritual agony and conflict of Carlyle--we shall find the measure of an age which has left the deepest impress upon our own.

Life of Carlyle

Carlyle was born at Ecclefechan, Dumfriesshire, in 1795, a few months before Burns's death, and before Scott had published his first work. Like Burns, he came of peasant stock,--strong, simple, God-fearing folk, whose influence in Carlyle's later life is beyond calculation. Of his mother he says, "She was too mild and peaceful for the planet she lived in"; and of his father, a stone mason, he writes, "Could I write my books as he built his houses, walk my way so manfully through this shadow world, and leave it with so little blame, it were more than all my hopes."

Of Carlyle's early school life we have some interesting glimpses in Sartor Resartus. At nine years he entered the Annan grammar school, where he was bullied by the older boys, who nicknamed him Tom the Tearful. For the teachers of those days he has only ridicule, calling them "hide-bound pedants," and he calls the school by the suggestive German name of Hinterschlag Gymnasium. At the wish of his parents, who intended Carlyle for the ministry, he endured this hateful school life till 1809, when he entered Edinburgh University. There he spent five miserable years, of which his own record is: "I was without friends, experience, or connection in the sphere of human business, was of sly humor, proud enough and to spare, and had begun my long curriculum of dyspepsia." This nagging illness was the cause of much of that irritability of temper which frequently led him to scold the public, and for which he has been harshly handled by unfriendly critics.

The period following his university course was one of storm and stress for Carlyle. Much to the grief of the father whom he loved, he had given up the idea of entering the ministry. Wherever he turned, doubts like a thick fog surrounded him,--doubts of God, of his fellow-men, of human progress, of himself. He was poor, and to earn an honest living was his first problem. He tried successively teaching school, tutoring, the study of law, and writing miscellaneous articles for the Edinburgh Encyclopedia. All the while he was fighting his doubts, living, as he says, "in a continual, indefinite, pining fear." After six or seven years of mental agony, which has at times a suggestion of Bunyan's spiritual struggle, the crisis came in 1821, when Carlyle suddenly shook off his doubts and found himself. "All at once," he says in Sartor, "there arose a thought in me, and I asked myself: 'What Art thou afraid of? Wherefore like a coward dost thou forever pip and whimper, and go cowering and trembling? Despicable biped! What is the sum total of the worst that lies before thee? Death? Well, Death; and say the pangs of Tophet too, and all that the Devil and Man may, will, or can do against thee! Hast thou not a heart; canst thou not suffer whatsoever it be; and, as a Child of Freedom, though outcast, trample Tophet itself under thy feet, while it consumes thee?

Let it come then; I will meet it and defy it!' And as I so thought, there rushed like a stream of fire over my whole soul; and I shook base Fear away from me forever." This struggle between fear and faith, and the triumph of the latter, is recorded in two remarkable chapters, "The Everlasting No" and "The Everlasting Yea," of Sartor Resartus.

Carlyle now definitely resolved on a literary life, and began with any work that offered a bare livelihood. He translated Legendre's Geometry from the French, wrote numerous essays for the magazines, and continued his study of German while making translations from that language. His translation of Goethe's Wilhelm Meister Appeared in 1824, his Life of Schiller in 1825, and his Specimens of German Romance in 1827.

He began at this time a correspondence with Goethe, his literary hero, which lasted till the German poet's death in 1832. While still busy with "hack work," Carlyle, in 1826, married Jane Welsh, a brilliant and beautiful woman, whose literary genius almost equaled that of her husband. Soon afterwards, influenced chiefly by poverty, the Carlyles retired to a farm, at Craigen-puttoch (Hawks' Hill), a dreary and lonely spot, far from friends and even neighbors.

They remained here six years, during which time Carlyle wrote many of his best essays, and Sartor Resartus, his most original work. The latter went begging among publishers for two years, and was finally published serially in Fraser's Magazine, in 1833-1834. By this time Carlyle had begun to attract attention as a writer, and, thinking that one who made his living by the magazines should be in close touch with the editors, took his wife's advice and moved to London "to seek work and bread." He settled in Cheyne Row, Chelsea,--a place made famous by More, Erasmus, Bolingbroke, Smollett, Leigh Hunt, and many lesser lights of literature,--and began to enjoy the first real peace he had known since childhood.

In 1837 appeared The French Revolution, which first made Carlyle famous; and in the same year, led by the necessity of earning money, he began the series of lectures--German. Literature (1837), Periods of European Culture (1838), Revolutions of Modern Europe (1839), Heroes and Hero Worship (1841)--which created a sensation in London. "It was," says Leigh Hunt, "as if some Puritan had come to life again, liberalized by German philosophy and his own intense reflection and experience."

Though Carlyle set himself against the spirit of his age, calling the famous Reform Bill a "progress into darkness," and democracy "the rule of the worst rather than the best," his rough sincerity was unquestioned, and his remarks were more quoted than those of any other living man. He was supported, moreover, by a rare circle of friends,--Edward Irving, Southey, Sterling, Landor, Leigh Hunt, Dickens, Mill, Tennyson, Browning, and, most helpful of all, Emerson, who had visited Carlyle at Craigenputtoch in 1833. It was due largely to Emerson's influence that Carlyle's works were better appreciated, and brought better financial rewards, in America than in England.

Carlyle's fame reached its climax in the monumental History of Frederick the Great (1858-1865), published after thirteen years of solitary toil, which, in his own words, "made entire devastation of home life and happiness." The proudest moment of his life was when he was elected to succeed Gladstone as lord rector of Edinburgh University, in 1865, the year in which Frederick the Great was finished. In the midst of his triumph, and while he was in Scotland to deliver his inaugural address, his happiness was suddenly destroyed by the death of his wife,--a terrible blow, from which he never recovered. He lived on for fifteen years, shorn of his strength and interest in life; and his closing hours were like the dull sunset of a November day. Only as we remember his grief and remorse at the death of the companion who had shared his toil but not his triumph, can we understand the sorrow that pervades the pages of his Reminiscences. He died in 1881, and at his own wish was buried, not in Westminster Abbey, but among his humble kinsfolk in Ecclefechan. However much we may differ from his philosophy or regret the harshness of his minor works, we shall probably all agree in this sentiment from one of his own letters,--that the object of all his struggle and writing was "that men should find out and believe the truth, and match their lives to it."

Works of Carlyle

There are two widely different judgments of Carlyle as a man and a writer. The first, which is founded largely on his minor writings, like Chartism, Latter-Day Pamphlets, and Shooting Niagara, declares that he is a misanthrope and dyspeptic with a barbarous style of writing; that he denounces progress, democracy, science, America, Darwin,--everybody and everything that he does not understand; that his literary opinions are largely prejudices; that he began as a prophet and ended as a scold; and that in denouncing shams of every sort he was something of a sham himself, since his practice was not in accord with his own preaching. The second judgment, which is founded upon Heroes and Hero Worship, Cromwell, and Sartor Resartus, declares that these works are the supreme manifestation of genius; that their rugged, picturesque style makes others look feeble or colorless by comparison; and that the author is the greatest teacher, leader, and prophet of the nineteenth century.

Somewhere between these two extremes will be found the truth about Carlyle. We only note here that, while there are some grounds for the first unfavorable criticism, we are to judge an author by his best rather than by his worst work; and that a man's aims as well as his accomplishments must be taken into consideration. As it is written, "Whereas it was in thine heart to build an house unto my name, thou didst well that it was in thine heart." Whatever the defects of Carlyle and his work, in his heart he was always planning a house or temple to the God of truth and justice.

Carlyle's important works may be divided into three general classes,--critical and literary essays, historical works, and Sartor Resartus, the last being in a class by itself, since there is nothing like it in literature. To these should be added a biography, the admirable Life of John Sterling, and

Carlyle's Letters and Reminiscences, which are more interesting and suggestive than some of his better known works. We omit here all consideration of translations, and his intemperate denunciations of men and institutions in Chartism, Latter-Day Pamphlets, and other essays, which add nothing to the author's fame or influence.

Of the essays, which are all characterized by Carlyle's zeal to get at the heart of things, and to reveal the soul rather than the works of a writer, the best are those on "Burns," "Scott," "Novalis," "Goethe," "Characteristics," "Signs of the Times," and "Boswell's Life of Johnson." In the famous Essay on Burns, which is generally selected for special study, we note four significant things:

(1) Carlyle is peculiarly well fitted for his task, having many points in common with his hero.

(2) In most of his work Carlyle, by his style and mannerisms and positive opinions, generally attracts our attention away from his subject; but in this essay he shows himself capable of forgetting himself for a moment. To an unusual extent he sticks to his subject, and makes us think of Burns rather than of Carlyle. The style, though unpolished, is fairly simple and readable, and is free from the breaks, crudities, ejaculations, and general "nodulosities" which disfigure much of his work.

(3) Carlyle has an original and interesting theory of biography and criticism. The object of criticism is to show the man himself, his aims, ideals, and outlook on the universe; the object of biography is "to show what and how produced was the effect of society upon him; what and how produced was his effect on society."

(4) Carlyle is often severe, even harsh, in his estimates of other men, but in this case the tragedy of Burns's "life of fragments" attracts and softens him. He grows enthusiastic and--a rare thing for Carlyle--apologizes

for his enthusiasm in the striking sentence, "We love Burns, and we pity him; and love and pity are prone to magnify."-So he gives us the most tender and appreciative of his essays, and one of the most illuminating criticisms of Burns that has appeared in our language.

The central idea of Carlyle's historical works is found in his Heroes and Hero Worship (1841), his most widely read book. "Universal history," he says, "is at bottom the history of the great men who have worked here." To get at the truth of history we must study not movements but men, and read not state papers but the biographies of heroes. His summary of history as presented in this work has six divisions:

(1) The Hero as Divinity, having for its general subject Odin, the "type Norseman," who, Carlyle thinks, was some old heroic chief, afterwards deified by his countrymen;

(2) The Hero as Prophet, treating of Mahomet and the rise of Islam;

(3) The Hero as Poet, in which Dante and Shakespeare are taken as types;

(4) The Hero as Priest, or religious leader, in which Luther appears as the hero of the Reformation, and Knox as the hero of Puritanism;

(5) The Hero as Man of Letters, in which we have the curious choice of Johnson, Rousseau, and Burns;

(6) The Hero as King, in which Cromwell and Napoleon appear as the heroes of reform by revolution.

It is needless to say that Heroes is not a book of history; neither is it scientifically written in the manner of Gibbon. With science in any form Carlyle had no patience; and he miscalculated the value of that patient search for facts and evidence which science undertakes before building any theories, either of kings or cabbages. The book, therefore, abounds in errors; but they are the errors of carelessness and are perhaps of small consequence. His misconception of history, however, is more serious. With the modern idea of history, as the growth of freedom among all classes, he has no sympathy. The progress of democracy was to him an evil thing, a "turning of the face towards darkness and anarchy." At certain periods, according to Carlyle, God sends us geniuses, sometimes as priests or poets, sometimes as soldiers or statesmen; but in whatever guise they appear, these are our real rulers. He shows, moreover, that whenever such men appear, multitudes follow them, and that a man's following is a sure index of his heroism and kingship.

Whether we agree with Carlyle or not, we must accept for the moment his peculiar view of history, else Heroes can never open its treasures to us. The book abounds in startling ideas, expressed with originality and power, and is pervaded throughout by an atmosphere of intense moral earnestness. The more we read it, the more we find to admire and to remember.

Carlyle's French Revolution (1837) is to be taken more seriously as a historical work; but here again his hero worship comes to the front, and his book is a series of flashlights thrown upon men in dramatic situations, rather than a tracing of causes to their consequences. The very titles of his chapters--"Astraea Redux," "Windbags," "Broglie the War God"--do violence to our conception of history, and are more suggestive of Carlyle's individualism than of French history. He is here the preacher rather than the historian; his text is the eternal justice; and his message is that all wrongdoing is inevitably followed by vengeance. His method is intensely dramatic. From a mass of historical details he selects a few picturesque incidents and striking figures, and his vivid pictures of the storming of the Bastille, the rush of the mob to Versailles, the death of Louis XVI, and the Reign of Terror, seem like the work of an eyewitness describing some terrible catastrophe. At times, as it portrays Danton,

Robespierre, and the great characters of the tragedy, Carlyle's work is suggestive of an historical play of Shakespeare; and again, as it describes the rush and riot of men led by elemental passion, it is more like a great prose epic. Though not a reliable history in any sense, it is one of the most dramatic and stirring narratives in our language.

Two other historical works deserve at least a passing notice. The History of Frederick the Great (1858-1865), in six volumes, is a colossal picture of the life and times of the hero of the Prussian Empire. Oliver Cromwell's Letters and Speeches is, in our personal judgment, Carlyle's best historical work. His idea is to present the very soul of the great Puritan leader. He gives us, as of first importance, Cromwell's own words, and connects them by a commentary in which other men and events are described with vigor and vividness. Cromwell was one of Carlyle's greatest heroes, and in this case he is most careful to present the facts which occasion his own enthusiasm. The result is, on the whole, the most lifelike picture of a great historical character that we possess. Other historians had heaped calumny upon Cromwell till the English public regarded him with prejudice and horror; and it is an indication of Carlyle's power that by a single book he revolutionized England's opinion of one of her greatest men.

Carlyle's Sartor Resartus (1834), his only creative work, is a mixture of philosophy and romance, of wisdom and nonsense,--a chaotic jumble of the author's thoughts, feelings, and experiences during the first thirty-five years of his life. The title, which means "The Tailor Patched-up," is taken from an old Scotch song. The hero is Diogenes Teufelsdroeckh, a German professor at the University of Weissnichtwo (don't know where); the narrative concerns this queer professor's life and opinions; and the central thought of the book is the philosophy of clothes, which are considered symbolically as the outward expression of spirit. Thus, man's body is the outward garment of his soul, and the universe is the visible garment of the invisible God. The arrangement of Sartor is clumsy and hard to follow. In order to leave himself free to bring in everything he thought about, Carlyle assumed the position of one who was translating and editing the old professor's manuscripts, which are supposed to consist of numerous sheets stuffed into twelve paper bags, each labeled with a sign of the zodiac. The editor pretends to make order out of this chaos; but he is free to jump from one subject to another and to state the most startling opinion by simply using quotation marks and adding a note that he is not responsible for Teufelsdroeckh's crazy notions,--which are in reality Carlyle's own dreams and ideals. Partly because of the matter, which is sometimes incoherent, partly because of the style, which, though picturesque, is sometimes confused and ungrammatical, Sartor is not easy reading; but it amply repays whatever time and study we give to it. Many of its passages are more like poetry than prose; and one cannot read such chapters as "The Everlasting No," "The Everlasting Yea," "Reminiscences," and "Natural Supernaturalism," and be quite the same man afterwards; for Carlyle's thought has entered into him, and he walks henceforth more gently, more reverently through the world, as in the presence of the Eternal.

General Characteristics

Concerning Carlyle's style there are almost as many opinions as there are readers. This is partly because he impresses different people in widely different ways, and partly because his expression varies greatly. At times he is calm, persuasive, grimly humorous, as if conversing; at other times, wildly exclamatory, as if he were shouting and waving his arms at the reader. We have spoken of Macaulay's style as that of the finished orator, and we might reasonably speak of Carlyle's as that of the exhorter, who cares little for methods so long as he makes a strong impression on his hearers. "Every sentence is alive to its finger tips," writes a modern critic; and though Carlyle often violates the rules of grammar and rhetoric, we can well afford to let an original genius express his own intense conviction in his own vivid and picturesque way.

Carlyle's message may be summed up in two imperatives,--labor, and be sincere. He lectured and wrote chiefly for the upper classes who had begun to think, somewhat sentimentally, of the conditions of the laboring men of the world; and he demanded for the latter, not charity or pity, but justice and honor. All labor, whether of head or hand, is divine; and labor alone justifies a man as a son of earth and heaven. To society, which Carlyle thought to be occupied wholly with conventional affairs, he came with the stamp of sincerity, calling upon men to lay aside hypocrisy and to think and speak and live the truth. He had none of Addison's delicate satire and humor, and in his fury at what he thought was false he was generally unsympathetic and often harsh; but we must not forget that Thackeray--who knew society much better than did Carlyle--gave a very unflattering picture of it in Vanity Fair and The Book of Snobs. Apparently the age needed plain speaking, and Carlyle furnished it in scripture measure. Harriet Martineau, who knew the world for which Carlyle wrote, summed up his influence when she said that he had "infused into the mind of the English nation... sincerity, earnestness, healthfulness, and courage." If we add to the above message Carlyle's conceptions of the world as governed by a God of justice who never forgets, and of human history as "an inarticulate Bible," slowly revealing the divine purpose, we shall understand better the force of his ethical appeal and the profound influence he exercised on the moral and intellectual life of the past century.

JOHN RUSKIN (1819-1900)

In approaching the study of Ruskin we are to remember, first of all, that we are dealing with a great and good man, who is himself more inspiring than any of his books. In some respects he is like his friend Carlyle, whose disciple he acknowledged himself to be; but he is broader in his sympathies, and in every way more hopeful, helpful, and humane. Thus, in the face of the drudgery and poverty of the competitive system, Carlyle proposed, with the grim satire of Swift's "Modest Proposal," to organize an annual hunt in which successful people should shoot the unfortunate, and to use the game for the support of the army and navy. Ruskin, facing the same problem, wrote: "I will endure it no longer quietly; but henceforward, with any few or many who will help, do my best to abate this misery." Then, leaving the field of art criticism, where he was the acknowledged leader, he begins to write of labor and justice; gives his fortune in charity, in establishing schools and libraries; and founds his St. George's Guild of workingmen, to put in practice the principles of brotherhood and cooperation for which he and Carlyle contended. Though his style marks him as one of the masters of English prose, he is generally studied not as a literary man but as an ethical teacher, and we shall hardly appreciate his works unless we see behind every book the figure of the heroically sincere man who wrote it.

Life

Ruskin was born in London, in 1819. His father was a prosperous wine merchant who gained a fortune in trade, and who spent his leisure hours in the company of good books and pictures. On his tombstone one may still read this inscription written by Ruskin: "He was an entirely honest merchant and his memory is to all who keep it dear and helpful. His son, whom he loved to the uttermost and taught to speak truth, says this of him." Ruskin's mother, a devout and somewhat austere woman, brought her son up with Puritanical strictness, not forgetting Solomon's injunction that "the rod and reproof give wisdom."

Of Ruskin's early years at Herne Hill, on the outskirts of London, it is better to read his own interesting record in Praeterita. It was in some respects a cramped and lonely childhood, but certain things which strongly molded his character are worthy of mention. First, he was taught by word and example in all things to speak the truth, and he never forgot the lesson. Second, he had few toys, and spent much time in studying the leaves, the flowers, the grass, the clouds, even the figures and colors of the carpet, and so laid the foundation for that minute and accurate observation which is manifest in all his writings. Third, he was educated first by his mother, then by private tutors, and so missed the discipline of the public schools. The influence of this lonely training is evident in all his work. Like Carlyle, he is often too positive and dogmatic,--the result of failing to test his work by the standards of other men of his age. Fourth, he was obliged to read the Bible every day and to learn long passages verbatim. The result of this training was, he says, "to make every word of the Scriptures familiar to my ear in habitual music." We can hardly read a page of his later work without finding some reflection of the noble simplicity or vivid imagery of the sacred records. Fifth, he traveled much with his father and mother, and his innate love of nature was intensified by what he saw on his leisurely journeys through the most beautiful parts of England and the Continent.

Ruskin entered Christ Church College, Oxford, in 1836, when only seventeen years old. He was at this time a shy, sensitive boy, a lover of nature and of every art which reflects nature, but almost entirely ignorant of the ways of boys and men. An attack of consumption, with which he had long been threatened, caused him to leave Oxford in 1840, and for nearly two years he wandered over Italy searching for health and cheerfulness, and gathering materials for the first volume of Modern Painters, the book that made him famous.

Ruskin's literary work began in childhood, when he was encouraged to write freely in prose and poetry. A volume of poems illustrated by his own drawings was published in 1859, after he had won fame as a prose writer, but, save for the drawings, it is of small importance. The first volume of Modern Painters (1843) was begun as a heated defense of the artist Turner, but it developed into an essay on art as a true picture of nature, "not only in her outward aspect but in her inward spirit." The work, which was signed simply "Oxford Graduate," aroused a storm of mingled approval and protest; but however much critics warred over its theories of art, all were agreed that the unknown author was a master of descriptive prose. Ruskin now made frequent trips to the art galleries of the Continent, and produced four more volumes of Modern Painters during the next seventeen years. Meanwhile he wrote other books,--Seven Lamps of Architecture (1849), Stones of Venice (1851-1853), Pre-Raphaelitism, and numerous lectures and essays, which gave him a place in the world of art similar to that held by Matthew Arnold in the world of letters. In 1869 he was appointed professor of art at Oxford, a position which greatly increased his prestige and influence, not only among students but among a great variety of people who heard his lectures and read his published works. Lectures on Art, Aratra Pentelici (lectures on sculpture), Ariadne Florentina (lectures on engraving), Michael Angela and Tintoret, The Art of England, Val d'Arno (lectures on Tuscan art), St. Mark's Rest (a history of Venice), Mornings in Florence (studies in Christian art, now much used as a guidebook to the picture galleries of Florence), The Laws of Fiesole (a treatise on drawing and painting for schools), Academy of Fine Arts in Venice, Pleasures of England,--all these works on art show Ruskin's literary industry. And we must also record Love's Meinie (a study of birds), Proserpina (a study of flowers), Deucalion (a study of waves and stones), besides various essays on political economy which indicate that Ruskin, like Arnold, had begun to consider the practical problems of his age.

At the height of his fame, in 1860, Ruskin turned for a time from art, to consider questions of wealth and labor,--terms which were used glibly by the economists of the age without much thought for their fundamental meaning. "There is no wealth but life," announced Ruskin,--"life, including all its powers of love, of joy, and of admiration. That country is the richest which nourishes the greatest number of noble and happy human beings." Such a doctrine, proclaimed by Goldsmith in his Deserted Village, was regarded as a pretty sentiment, but coming from one of the greatest leaders and teachers of England it was like a bombshell. Ruskin wrote four essays establishing this doctrine and pleading for a more socialistic form of government in which reform might be possible.

The essays were published in the Cornhill Magazine, of which Thackeray was editor, and they aroused such a storm that the publication was discontinued. Ruskin then published the essays in book form, with the title Unto This Last, in 1862. Munera Pulveris (1862) was another work in which the principles of capital and labor and the evils of the competitive system were discussed in such a way that the author was denounced as a visionary or a madman. Other works of this practical period are Time and Tide, Fors Clavigera, Sesame and Lilies, and the Crown of Wild Olive.

The latter part of Ruskin's life was a time of increasing sadness, due partly to the failure of his plans, and partly to public attacks upon his motives or upon his sanity. He grew bitter at first, as his critics ridiculed or denounced his principles, and at times his voice is as querulous as that of Carlyle. We are to remember, however, the conditions under which he struggled. His health had been shattered by successive attacks of disease; he had been disappointed in love; his marriage was unhappy; and his work seemed a failure. He had given nearly all his fortune in charity, and the poor were more numerous than ever before. His famous St. George's Guild was not successful, and the tyranny of the competitive system seemed too deeply rooted to be overthrown. On the death of his mother he left London and, in 1879, retired to Brantwood, on Coniston Lake, in the beautiful region beloved of Wordsworth. Here he passed the last quiet years of his life under the care of his cousin, Mrs. Severn, the "angel of the house," and wrote, at Professor Norton's suggestion, Praeterita, one of his most interesting books, in which he describes the events of his youth from his own view point. He died quietly in 1900, and was buried, as he wished, without funeral pomp or public ceremony, in the little churchyard at Coniston.

Works of Ruskin

There are three little books which, in popular favor, stand first on the list of Ruskin's numerous works,--Ethics-of-the-Dust, a series of Lectures to Little Housewives, which appeals most to women; Crown of Wild Olive, three lectures on Work, Traffic, and War, which appeals to thoughtful men facing the problems of work and duty; and Sesame and Lilies, which appeals to men and women alike. The last is the most widely known of Ruskin's works and the best with which to begin our reading.

The first thing we notice in Sesame and Lilies is the symbolical title. "Sesame," taken from the story of the robbers' cave in the Arabian Nights, means a secret word or talisman which unlocks a treasure house. It was intended, no doubt, to introduce the first part of the work, called "Of Kings' Treasuries," which treats of books and reading. "Lilies," taken from Isaiah as a symbol of beauty, purity, and peace, introduces the second lecture, "Of Queens' Gardens," which is an exquisite study of woman's life and education. These two lectures properly constitute the book, but a third is added, on "The Mystery of Life." The last begins in a monologue upon his own failures in life, and is pervaded by an atmosphere of sadness, sometimes of pessimism, quite different from the spirit of the other two lectures.

Though the theme of the first lecture is books, Ruskin manages to present to his audience his whole philosophy of life. He gives us, with a wealth of detail, a description of what constitutes a real book; he looks into the meaning of words, and teaches us how to read, using a selection from Milton's Lycidas as an illustration. This study of words gives us the key with which we are to unlock "Kings' Treasuries," that is, the books which contain the precious thoughts of the kingly minds of all ages. He shows the real meaning and end of education, the value of labor and of a purpose in life; he treats of nature, science, art, literature, religion; he defines the purpose of government, showing that soul-life, not money or trade, is the measure of national greatness; and he criticises the general injustice of his age, quoting a heartrending story of toil and suffering from the newspapers to show how close his theory is to daily needs. Here is an astonishing variety in a small compass; but there is no confusion. Ruskin's mind was wonderfully analytical, and one subject develops naturally from the other.

In the second lecture, "Of Queens' Gardens," he considers the question of woman's place and education, which Tennyson had attempted to answer in The Princess. Ruskin's theory is that the purpose of all education is to acquire power to bless and to redeem human society; and that in this noble work woman must always play the leading part. He searches all literature for illustrations, and his description of literary heroines, especially of Shakespeare's perfect women, is unrivaled. Ruskin is always at his best in writing of women or for women, and the lofty idealism of this essay, together with its rare beauty of expression, makes it, on the whole, the most delightful and inspiring of his works.

Among Ruskin's practical works the reader will find in Fors Clavigera, a series of letters to workingmen, and Unto This Last, four essays on the principles of political economy, the substance of his economic teachings. In the latter work, starting with the proposition that our present competitive system centers about the idea of wealth, Ruskin tries to find out what wealth is; and the pith of his teaching is this,--that men are of more account than money; that a man's real wealth is found in his soul; not in his pocket; and that the prime object of life and labor is "the producing of as many as possible full-breathed, bright-eyed, and happy-hearted human creatures." To make this ideal practical, Ruskin makes four suggestions:

(1) that training schools be established to teach young men and women three things,--the laws and practice of health, habits of gentleness and justice, and the trade or calling by which they are to live;

(2) that the government establish farms and workshops for the production of all the necessaries of life, where only good and honest work shall be tolerated and where a standard of work and wages shall be maintained;

(3) that any person out of employment shall be received at the nearest government school: if ignorant he shall be educated, and if competent to do any work he shall have the opportunity to do it;

(4) that comfortable homes be provided for the sick and for the aged, and that this be done in justice, not in charity. A laborer serves his country as truly as does a soldier or a statesman, and a pension should be no more disgraceful in one case than in the other.

Among Ruskin's numerous books treating of art, we recommend the Seven Lamps of Architecture (1849), Stones of Venice (1851-1853), and the first two volumes of Modern Painters (1843-1846). With Ruskin's art theories, which, as Sydney Smith prophesied, "worked a complete revolution in the world of taste," we need not concern ourselves here.

We simply point out four principles that are manifest in all his work: (1) that the object of art, as of every other human endeavor, is to find and to express the truth; (2) that art, in order to be true, must break away from conventionalities and copy nature; (3) that morality is closely allied with art, and that a careful study of any art reveals the moral strength or weakness of the people that produced it; (4) that the main purpose of art is not to delight a few cultured people but to serve the daily uses of common life. "The giving brightness to pictures is much," he says, "but the giving brightness to life is more." In this attempt to make art serve the practical ends of life, Ruskin is allied with all the great writers of the period, who use literature as the instrument of human progress.

General Characteristics

One who reads Ruskin is in a state of mind analogous to that of a man who goes through a picture gallery, pausing now to admire a face or a landscape for its own sake, and again to marvel at the technical skill of the artist, without regard to his subject. For Ruskin is a great literary artist and a great ethical teacher, and we admire one page for its style, and the next for its message to humanity. The best of his prose, which one may find in the descriptive passages of Praeterita and Modern Painters, is written in a richly ornate style, with a wealth of figures and allusions, and at times a rhythmic, melodious quality which makes it almost equal to poetry. Ruskin had a rare sensitiveness to beauty in every form, and more, perhaps, than any other writer in our language, he has helped us to see and appreciate the beauty of the world around us.

As for Ruskin's ethical teaching, it appears in so many forms and in so many different works that any summary must appear inadequate. For a full half century he was "the apostle of beauty" in England, and the beauty for which he pleaded was never sensuous or pagan, as in the Renaissance, but always spiritual, appealing to the soul of man rather than to his eyes, leading to better work and better living. In his economic essays Ruskin is even more directly and positively ethical. To mitigate the evils of the unreasonable competitive system under which we labor and sorrow; to bring master and man together in mutual trust and helpfulness; to seek beauty, truth, goodness as the chief ends of life, and, having found them, to make our characters correspond; to share the best treasures of art and literature with rich and poor alike; to labor always, and, whether we work with hand or head, to do our work in praise of something that we love,--this sums up Ruskin's purpose and message. And the best of it is that, like Chaucer's country parson, he practiced his doctrine before he preached it.

MATTHEW ARNOLD (1822-1888)

In the world of literature Arnold has occupied for many years an authoritative position as critic and teacher, similar to that held by Ruskin in the world of art. In his literary work two very different moods are manifest. In his poetry he reflects the doubt of an age which witnessed the conflict between science and revealed religion. Apparently he never passed through any such decisive personal struggle as is recorded in Sartor Resartus, and he has no positive conviction such as is voiced in "The Everlasting Yea." He is beset by doubts which he never settles, and his poems generally express sorrow or regret or resignation. In his prose he shows the cavalier spirit,--aggressive, light-hearted, self-confident. Like Carlyle, he dislikes shams, and protests against what he calls the barbarisms of society; but he writes with a light touch, using satire and banter as the better part of his argument. Carlyle denounces with the zeal of a Hebrew prophet, and lets you know that you are hopelessly lost if you reject his message. Arnold is more like the cultivated Greek; his voice is soft, his speech suave, but he leaves the impression, if you happen to differ with him, that you must be deficient in culture. Both these men, so different in spirit and methods, confronted the same problems, sought the same ends, and were dominated by the same moral sincerity.

Life

Arnold was born in Laleham, in the valley of the Thames, in 1822. His father was Dr. Thomas Arnold, head master of

Rugby, with whom many of us have grown familiar by reading Tom Brown's School Days.

After fitting for the university at Winchester and at Rugby, Arnold entered Balliol College, Oxford, where he was distinguished by winning prizes in poetry and by general excellence in the classics. More than any other poet Arnold reflects the spirit of his university. "The Scholar-Gipsy" and "Thyrsis" contain many references to Oxford and the surrounding country, but they are more noticeable for their spirit of aloofness,--as if Oxford men were too much occupied with classic dreams and ideals to concern themselves with the practical affairs of life.

After leaving the university Arnold first taught the classics at Rugby; then, in 1847, he became private secretary to Lord Lansdowne, who appointed the young poet to the position of inspector of schools under the government. In this position Arnold worked patiently for the next thirty-five years, traveling about the country, examining teachers, and correcting endless examination papers. For ten years (1857-1867) he was professor of poetry at Oxford, where his famous lectures On Translating Homer were given. He made numerous reports on English and foreign schools, and was three times sent abroad to study educational methods on the Continent. From this it will be seen that Arnold led a busy, often a laborious life, and we can appreciate his statement that all his best literary work was done late at night, after a day of drudgery.

It is well to remember that, while Carlyle was preaching about labor, Arnold labored daily; that his work was cheerfully and patiently done; and that after the day's work he hurried away, like Lamb, to the Elysian fields of literature. He was happily married, loved his home, and especially loved children, was free from all bitterness and envy, and, notwithstanding his cold manner, was at heart sincere, generous, and true. We shall appreciate his work better if we can see the man himself behind all that he has written.

Arnold's literary work divides itself into three periods, which we may call the poetical, the critical, and the practical. He had written poetry since his school days, and his first volume, The Strayed Reveller and Other Poems, appeared anonymously in 1849. Three years later he published Empedocles on Etna and other Poems; but only a few copies of these volumes were sold, and presently both were withdrawn from circulation. In 1853-1855 he published his signed Poems, and twelve years later appeared his last volume of poetry. Compared with the early work of Tennyson, these works met with little favor, and Arnold practically abandoned poetry in favor of critical writing.

The chief works of his critical period are the lectures On Translating Homer (1861) and the two volumes of Essays in Criticism (1865-1888), which made Arnold one of the best known literary men in England. Then, like Ruskin, he turned to practical questions, and his Friendship's Garland (1871) was intended to satirize and perhaps reform the great middle class of England, whom he called the Philistines. Culture and Anarchy, the most characteristic work of his practical period, appeared in 1869. These were followed by four books on religious subjects,--St. Paul and Protestantism (1870), Literature and Dogma (1873), God and the Bible (1875), and Last Essays on Church and Religion (1877). The Discourses in America (1885) completes the list of his important works. At the height of his fame and influence he died suddenly, in 1888, and was buried in the churchyard at Laleham. The spirit of his whole life is well expressed in a few lines of one of his own early sonnets:

One lesson, Nature, let me learn of thee,

One lesson which in every wind is blown,

One lesson of two duties kept at one

Though the loud world proclaim their enmity--

Of toil unsever'd from tranquillity;

Of labour, that in lasting fruit outgrows

Far noisier schemes, accomplish'd in repose,
Too great for haste, too high for rivalry.

Works of Matthew Arnold

We shall better appreciate Arnold's poetry if we remember two things: First, he had been taught in his home a simple and devout faith in revealed religion, and in college he was thrown into a world of doubt and questioning. He faced these doubts honestly, reverently,--in his heart longing to accept the faith of his fathers, but in his head demanding proof and scientific exactness.

The same struggle between head and heart, between reason and intuition, goes on to-day, and that is one reason why Arnold's poetry, which wavers on the borderland between doubt and faith, is a favorite with many readers. Second, Arnold, as shown in his essay on The Study of Poetry, regarded poetry as "a criticism of life under the conditions fixed for such criticism by the laws of poetic truth and poetic beauty." Naturally, one who regards poetry as a "criticism" will write very differently from one who regards poetry as the natural language of the soul. He will write for the head rather than for the heart, and will be cold and critical rather than enthusiastic.

According to Arnold, each poem should be a unit, and he protested against the tendency of English poets to use brilliant phrases and figures of speech which only detract attention from the poem as a whole. For his models he went to Greek poetry, which he regarded as "the only sure guidance to what is sound and true in poetical art." Arnold is, however, more indebted than he thinks to English masters, especially to Wordsworth and Milton, whose influence is noticeable in a large part of his poetry.

Of Arnold's narrative poems the two best known are Balder Dead (1855), an incursion into the field of Norse mythology which is suggestive of Gray, and Sohrab and

Rustum (1853), which takes us into the field of legendary Persian history. The theme of the latter poem is taken from the Shah-Namah (Book of Kings) of the Persian poet Firdausi, who lived and wrote in the eleventh century.

Briefly, the story is of one Rustem or Rustum, a Persian Achilles, who fell asleep one day when he had grown weary of hunting. While he slept a band of robbers stole his favorite horse, Ruksh. In trailing the robbers Rustum came to the palace of the king of Samengan, where he was royally welcomed, and where he fell in love with the king's daughter, Temineh, and married her. But he was of a roving, adventurous disposition, and soon went back to fight among his own people, the Persians. While he was gone his son Sohrab was born, grew to manhood, and became the hero of the Turan army. War arose between the two peoples, and two hostile armies were encamped by the Oxus. Each army chose a champion, and Rustum and Sohrab found themselves matched in mortal combat between the lines. At this point Sohrab, whose chief interest in life was to find his father, demanded to know if his enemy were not Rustum; but the latter was disguised and denied his identity. On the first day of the fight Rustum was overcome, but his life was spared by a trick and by the generosity of Sohrab. On the second day Rustum prevailed, and mortally wounded his antagonist. Then he recognized his own son by a gold bracelet which he had long ago given to his wife Temineh. The two armies, rushing into battle, were stopped by the sight of father and son weeping in each other's arms. Sohrab died, the war ceased, and Rustum went home to a life of sorrow and remorse.

Using this interesting material, Arnold produced a poem which has the rare and difficult combination of classic reserve and romantic feeling. It is written in blank verse, and one has only to read the first few lines to see that the poet is not a master of his instrument. The lines are seldom harmonious, and we must frequently change the accent of common words, or lay stress on unimportant particles, to show the rhythm. Arnold frequently copies Milton, especially in his repetition of ideas and phrases; but the poem as a whole is lacking in Milton's wonderful melody.

The classic influence on Sohrab and Rustum is especially noticeable in Arnold's use of materials. Fights are short; grief is long; therefore the poet gives few lines to the combat, but lingers over the son's joy at finding his father, and the father's quenchless sorrow at the death of his son. The last lines especially, with their "passionate grief set to solemn music," make this poem one of the best, on the whole, that Arnold has written. And the exquisite ending, where the Oxus, unmindful of the trivial strifes of men, flows on sedately to join "his luminous home of waters" is most suggestive of the poet's conception of the orderly life of nature, in contrast with the doubt and restlessness of human life.

Next in importance to the narrative poems are the elegies, "Thyrsis," "The Scholar-Gipsy," "Memorial Verses," "A Southern Night," "Obermann," "Stanzas from the Grande Chartreuse," and "Rugby Chapel." All these are worthy of careful reading, but the best is "Thyrsis," a lament for the poet Clough, which is sometimes classed with Milton's Lycidas and Shelley's Adonais. Among the minor poems the reader will find the best expression of Arnold's ideals and methods in "Dover Beach," the love lyrics entitled "Switzerland," "Requiescat," "Shakespeare," "The Future," "Kensington Gardens," "Philomela," "Human Life," "Callicles's Song," "Morality," and "Geist's Grave."--the last being an exquisite tribute to a little dog which, like all his kind, had repaid our scant crumbs of affection with a whole life's devotion.

The first place among Arnold's prose works must be given to the Essays in Criticism, which raised the author to the front rank of living critics. His fundamental idea of criticism appeals to us strongly. The business of criticism, he says, is neither to find fault nor to display the critic's own learning or influence; it is to know "the best which has been thought and said in the world," and by using this knowledge to create a current of fresh and free thought. If a choice must be made among these essays, which are all worthy of study, we would suggest "The Study of Poetry," "Wordsworth," "Byron," and "Emerson." The last-named essay, which is found in the Discourses in America, is hardly a satisfactory estimate of Emerson, but its singular charm of manner and its atmosphere of intellectual culture make it perhaps the most characteristic of Arnold's prose writings.

Among the works of Arnold's practical period there are two which may be taken as typical of all the rest. Literature and Dogma (1873) is, in general, a plea for liberality in religion. Arnold would have us read the Bible, for instance, as we would read any other great work, and apply to it the ordinary standards of literary criticism.

Culture and Anarchy (1869) contains most of the terms--culture, sweetness and light, Barbarian, Philistine, Hebraism, and many others--which are now associated with Arnold's work and influence. The term "Barbarian" refers to the aristocratic classes, whom Arnold thought to be essentially crude in soul, notwithstanding their good clothes and superficial graces.

"Philistine" refers to the middle classes,--narrow-minded and self-satisfied people, according to Arnold, whom he satirizes with the idea of opening their minds to new ideas. "Hebraism" is Arnold's term for moral education. Carlyle had emphasized the Hebraic or moral element in life, and Arnold undertook to preach the Hellenic or intellectual element, which welcomes new ideas, and delights in the arts that reflect the beauty of the world. "The uppermost idea with. Hellenism," he says, "is to see things as they are; the uppermost idea with Hebraism is conduct and obedience." With great clearness, sometimes with great force, and always with a play of humor and raillery aimed at the "Philistines," Arnold pleads for both these elements in life which together aim at "Culture," that is, at moral and intellectual perfection.

General Characteristics

Arnold's influence in our literature may be summed up, in a word, as intellectual rather than inspirational. One cannot be enthusiastic over his poetry, for the simple reason that he himself lacked enthusiasm. He is, however, a true reflection of a very real mood of the past century, the mood of doubt and sorrow; and a future generation may give him a higher place than he now holds as a poet. Though marked by "the elemental note of sadness," all Arnold's poems are distinguished by clearness, simplicity, and the restrained emotion of his classic models.

As a prose writer the cold intellectual quality, which mars his poetry by restraining romantic feeling, is of first importance, since it leads him to approach literature with an open mind and with the single desire to find "the best which has been thought and said in the world." We cannot yet speak with confidence of his rank in literature; but by his crystal-clear style, his scientific spirit of inquiry and comparison, illumined here and there by the play of humor, and especially by his broad sympathy and intellectual culture, he seems destined to occupy a very high place among the masters of literary criticism.

JOHN HENRY NEWMAN (1801-1890)

Any record of the prose literature of the Victorian era, which includes the historical essays of Macaulay and the art criticism of Ruskin, should contain also some notice of its spiritual leaders. For there was never a time when the religious ideals that inspire the race were kept more constantly before men's minds through the medium of literature.

Among the religious writers of the age the first place belongs unquestionably to Cardinal Newman. Whether we consider him as a man, with his powerful yet gracious personality, or as a religious reformer, who did much to break down old religious prejudices by showing the underlying beauty and consistency of the Roman church, or as a prose writer whose style is as near perfection as we have ever reached, Newman is one of the most interesting figures of the whole nineteenth century.

Life

Three things stand out clearly in Newman's life: first, his unshaken faith in the divine companionship and guidance; second, his desire to find and to teach the truth of revealed religion; third, his quest of an authoritative standard of faith, which should remain steadfast through the changing centuries and amid all sorts and conditions of men. The first led to that rare and beautiful spiritual quality which shines in all his work; the second to his frequent doctrinal and controversial essays; the third to his conversion to the Catholic church, which he served as priest and teacher for the last forty-five years of his life. Perhaps we should add one more characteristic,--the practical bent of his religion; for he was never so busy with study or controversy that he neglected to give a large part of his time to gentle ministration among the poor and needy.

He was born in London, in 1801. His father was an English banker; his mother, a member of a French Huguenot family, was a thoughtful, devout woman, who brought up her son in a way which suggests the mother of Ruskin. Of his early training, his reading of doctrinal and argumentative works, and of his isolation from material things in the thought that there were "two and only two absolute and luminously self-evident beings in the world," himself and his Creator, it is better to read his own record in the Apologia, which is a kind of spiritual biography.

At the age of fifteen Newman had begun his profound study of theological subjects. For science, literature, art, nature,--all the broad interests which attracted other literary men of his age,--he cared little, his mind being wholly occupied with the history and doctrines of the Christian church, to which he had already devoted his life. He was educated first at the school in Ealing, then at Oxford, taking his degree in the latter place in 1820. Though his college career was not more brilliant than that of many unknown men, his unusual ability was recognized and he was made a fellow of Oriel College, retaining the fellowship, and leading a scholarly life for over twenty years. In 1824 he was ordained in the Anglican church, and four years later was chosen vicar of St. Mary's, at Oxford, where his sermons made a deep impression on the cultivated audiences that gathered from far and near to hear him.

A change is noticeable in Newman's life after his trip to the Mediterranean in 1832. He had begun his life as a Calvinist, but while in Oxford, then the center of religious unrest, he described himself as "drifting in the direction of Liberalism." Then study and bereavement and an innate mysticism led him to a profound sympathy with the mediaeval Church. He had from the beginning opposed Catholicism; but during his visit to Italy, where he saw the Roman church at the center of Its power and splendor, many of his prejudices were overcome.

In this enlargement of his spiritual horizon Newman was greatly influenced by his friend Hurrell Froude, with whom he made the first part of the journey. His poems of this period (afterwards collected in the Lyra Apostolica), among which is the famous "Lead, Kindly Light," are noticeable for their radiant spirituality; but one who reads them carefully sees the beginning of that mental struggle which ended in his leaving the church in which he was born. Thus he writes of the Catholic church, whose services he had attended as "one who in a foreign land receives the gifts of a good Samaritan":

O that thy creed were sound!
For thou dost soothe the heart, thou church of Rome,
By thy unwearied watch and varied round
Of service, in thy Saviour's holy home.

I cannot walk the city's sultry streets,
But the wide porch invites to still retreats,
Where passion's thirst is calmed, and care's unthankful gloom.

On his return to England, in 1833, he entered into the religious struggle known as the Oxford or Tractarian Movement, and speedily became its acknowledged leader. Those who wish to follow this attempt at religious reform, which profoundly affected the life of the whole English church, will find it recorded in the Tracts for the Times, twenty-nine of which were written by Newman, and in his Parochial and Plain Sermons (1837-1843). After nine years of spiritual conflict Newman retired to Littlemore, where, with a few followers, he led a life of almost monastic seclusion, still striving to reconcile his changing belief with the doctrines of his own church. Two years later he resigned his charge at St. Mary's and left the Anglican communion,--not bitterly, but with a deep and tender regret. His last sermon at Littlemore on "The Parting of Friends" still moves us profoundly, like the cry of a prophet torn by personal anguish in the face of duty. In 1845 he was received into the Catholic church, and the following year, at Rome, he joined the community of St. Philip Neri, "the saint of gentleness and kindness," as Newman describes him, and was ordained to the Roman priesthood.

By his preaching and writing Newman had exercised a strong influence over his cultivated English hearers, and the effect of his conversion was tremendous. Into the theological controversy of the next twenty years we have no mind to enter. Through it all Newman retained his serenity, and, though a master of irony and satire, kept his literary power always subordinate to his chief aim, which was to establish the truth as he saw it. Whether or not we agree with his conclusions, we must all admire the spirit of the man, whic is above praise or criticism. His most widely read work, Apologia Pro Vita Sua (1864), was written in answer to an unfortunate attack by Charles Kingsley, which would long since have been forgotten had it not led to this remarkable book. In 1854 Newman was appointed rector of the Catholic University in Dublin, but after four years returned to England and founded a Catholic school at Edgbaston. In 1879 he was made cardinal by Pope Leo XIII. The grace and dignity of his life, quite as much as the sincerity of his Apologia, had long since disarmed criticism, and at his death, in 1890, the thought of all England might well be expressed by his own lines in "The Dream of Gerontius":

I had a dream. Yes, some one softly said,
"He's gone," and then a sigh went round the room;
And then I surely heard a priestly voice
Cry Subvenite; and they knelt in prayer.

Works of Newman

Readers approach Newman from so many different motives, some for doctrine, some for argument, some for a pure prose style, that it is difficult to recommend the best works for the beginner's use. As an expression of Newman's spiritual struggle the Apologia Pro Vita Sua is perhaps the most significant. This book is not light reading and one who opens it should understand clearly the reasons for which it was written. Newman had been accused of insincerity, not only by Kingsley but by many other men, in the public press. His retirement to solitude and meditation at Littlemore had been outrageously misunderstood, and it was openly charged that his conversion was a cunningly devised plot to win a large number of his followers to the Catholic church. This charge involved others, and it was to defend them, as well as to vindicate himself, that Newman wrote the Apologia. The perfect sincerity with which he traced his religious history, showing that his conversion was only the final step in a course he had been following since boyhood, silenced his critics and revolutionized public opinion concerning himself and the church which he had joined. As the revelation of a soul's history, and as a model of pure, simple, unaffected English, this book, entirely apart from its doctrinal teaching, deserves a high place in our prose literature.

In Newman's doctrinal works, the Via Media, the Grammar of Assent, and in numerous controversial essays the student of literature will have little interest. Much more significant are his sermons, the unconscious reflection of a rare spiritual nature, of which Professor Shairp said: "His power shows itself clearly in the new and unlooked-for way in which he touched into life old truths, moral or spiritual.... And as he spoke, how the old truth became new! and how it came home with a meaning never felt before! He laid his finger how gently yet how powerfully on some inner place in the hearer's heart, and told him things about himself he had never known till then. Subtlest truths, which would have taken philosophers pages of circumlocution and big words to state, were dropped out by the way in a sentence or two of the most transparent Saxon." Of greater interest to the general reader are The Idea of a University, discourses delivered at Dublin, and his two works of fiction, Loss and Gain, treating of a man's conversion to Catholicism, and Callista, which is, in his own words, "an attempt to express the feelings and mutual relations of Christians and heathens in the middle of the third century." The latter is, in our judgment, the most readable and interesting of Newman's works. The character of Callista, a beautiful Greek sculptor of idols, is powerfully delineated; the style is clear and transparent as air, and the story of the heroine's conversion and death makes one of the most fascinating chapters in fiction, though it is not the story so much as the author's unconscious revelation of himself that charms us. It would be well to read this novel in connection with Kingsley's Hypatia, which attempts to reconstruct the life and ideals of the same period.

Newman's poems are not so well known as his prose, but the reader who examines the Lyra Apostolica and Verses on

Various Occasions will find many short poems that stir a religious nature profoundly by their pure and lofty imagination; and future generations may pronounce one of these poems, "The Dream of Gerontius," to be Newman's most enduring work. This poem aims to reproduce the thoughts and feelings of a man whose soul is just quitting the body, and who is just beginning a new and greater life. Both in style and in thought "The Dream" is a powerful and original poem and is worthy of attention not only for itself but, as a modern critic suggests, "as a revelation of that high spiritual purpose which animated Newman's life from beginning to end."

Of Newman's style it is as difficult to write as it would be to describe the dress of a gentleman we had met, who was so perfectly dressed that we paid no attention to his clothes. His style is called transparent, because at first we are not conscious of his manner; and unobtrusive, because we never think of Newman himself, but only of the subject he is discussing. He is like the best French prose writers in expressing his thought with such naturalness and apparent ease that, without thinking of style, we receive exactly the impression which he means to convey. In his sermons and essays he is wonderfully simple and direct; in his controversial writings, gently ironical and satiric, and the satire is pervaded by a delicate humor; but when his feelings are aroused he speaks with poetic images and symbols, and his eloquence is like that of the Old Testament prophets. Like Ruskin's, his style is modeled largely on that of the Bible, but not even Ruskin equals him in the poetic beauty and melody of his sentences. On the whole he comes nearer than any other of his age to our ideal of a perfect prose writer.

OTHER ESSAYISTS OF THE VICTORIAN AGE

We have selected the above five essayists, Macaulay, Carlyle, Arnold, Newman, and Ruskin, as representative writers of the Victorian Age; but there are many others who well repay our study. Notable among these are John Addington Symonds, author of The Renaissance in Italy, undoubtedly his greatest work, and of many critical essays; Walter Pater, whose Appreciations and numerous other works mark him as one of our best literary critics; and Leslie Stephen, famous for his work on the monumental Dictionary of National Biography, and for his Hours in a Library, a series of impartial and excellent criticisms, brightened by the play of an original and delightful humor.

Among the most famous writers of the age are the scientists, Lyell, Darwin, Huxley, Spencer, Tyndall, and Wallace,--a wonderful group of men whose works, though they hardly belong to our present study, have exercised an incalculable influence on our life and literature. Darwin's Origin of Species (1859), which apparently established the theory of evolution, was an epoch-making book. It revolutionized not only our conceptions of natural history, but also our methods of thinking on all the problems of human society. Those who would read a summary of the greatest scientific discovery of the age will find it in Wallace's Darwinism,--a most interesting book, written by the man who claims, with Darwin, the honor of first announcing the principle of evolution. And, from a multitude of scientific works, we recommend also to the general reader Huxley's Autobiography and his Lay Sermons, Addresses, and Reviews, partly because they are excellent expressions of the spirit and methods of science, and partly because Huxley as a writer is perhaps the clearest and the most readable of the scientists.

THE SPIRIT OF MODERN LITERATURE

As we reflect on the varied work of the Victorian writers, three marked characteristics invite our attention. First, our great literary men, no less than our great scientists, have made truth the supreme object of human endeavor. All these eager poets, novelists, and essayists, questing over so many different ways, are equally intent on discovering the truth of life. Men as far apart as Darwin and Newman are strangely alike in spirit, one seeking truth in the natural,-the other in the spiritual history of the race. Second, literature has become the mirror of truth; and the first requirement of every serious novel or essay is to be true to the life or the facts which it represents. Third, literature has become animated by a definite moral purpose. It is not enough for the Victorian writers to create or attempt an artistic work for its own sake; the work must have a definite lesson for humanity. The poets are not only singers, but leaders; they hold up an ideal, and they compel men to recognize and follow it. The novelists tell a story which pictures human life, and at the same time call us to the work Of social reform, or drive home a moral lesson. The essayists are nearly all prophets or teachers, and use literature as the chief instrument of progress and education. Among them all we find comparatively little of the exuberant fancy, the romantic ardor, and the boyish gladness of the Elizabethans. They write books not primarily to delight the artistic sense, but to give bread to the hungry and water to the thirsty in soul. Milton's famous sentence, "A good book is the precious life-blood of a master spirit," might be written across the whole Victorian era. We are still too near these writers to judge how far their work suffers artistically from their practical purpose; but this much is certain,--that whether or not they created immortal works, their books have made the present world a better and a happier place to live in. And that is perhaps the best that can be said of the work of any artist or artisan.

SUMMARY OF THE VICTORIAN AGE

The year 1830 is generally placed at the beginning of this period, but its limits are very indefinite. In general we may think of it as covering the reign of Victoria (1837-1901). Historically the age is remarkable for the growth of democracy following the Reform Bill of 1832; for the spread of education among all classes; for the rapid development of the arts and sciences; for important mechanical inventions; and for the enormous extension of the bounds of human knowledge by the discoveries of science.

At the accession of Victoria the romantic movement had spent its force; Wordsworth had written his best work; the other romantic poets, Coleridge, Shelley, Keats, and Byron, had passed away; and for a time no new development was apparent in English poetry. Though the Victorian Age produced two great poets, Tennyson and Browning, the age, as a whole, is remarkable for the variety and excellence of its prose.

A study of all the great writers of the period reveals four general characteristics: (1) Literature in this Age has come very close to daily life, reflecting its practical problems and interests, and is a powerful instrument of human progress. (2) The tendency of literature is strongly ethical; all the great poets, novelists, and essayists of the age are moral teachers. (3) Science in this age exercises an incalculable influence. On the one hand it emphasizes truth as the sole object of human endeavor; it has established the principle of law throughout the universe; and it has given us an entirely new view of life, as summed up in the word "evolution," that is, the principle of growth or development from simple to complex forms. On the other hand, its first effect seems to be to discourage works of the imagination. Though the age produced an incredible number of books, very few of them belong among the great creative works of literature. (4) Though the age is generally characterized as practical and materialistic, it is significant that nearly all the writers whom the nation delights to honor vigorously attack materialism, and exalt a purely ideal conception of life. On the whole, we are inclined to call this an idealistic age fundamentally, since love, truth, justice, brotherhood--all great ideals--are emphasized as the chief ends of life, not only by its poets but also by its novelists and essayists.

In our study we have considered: (1) The Poets; the life and works of Tennyson and Browning; and the chief characteristics of the minor poets, Elizabeth Barrett (Mrs. Browning), Rossetti, Morris, and Swinburne. (2) The Novelists; the life and works of Dickens, Thackeray, and George Eliot; and the chief works of Charles Reade, Anthony Trollope, Charlotte Bronte, Bulwer-Lytton, Kingsley, Mrs. Gaskell, Blackmore, George Meredith, Hardy, and Stevenson. (3) The Essayists; the life and works of Macaulay, Matthew Arnold, Carlyle, Newman, and Ruskin. These were selected, from among many essayists and miscellaneous writers, as most typical of the Victorian Age. The great scientists, like Lyell, Darwin, Huxley, Wallace, Tyndall, and Spencer, hardly belong to our study of literature, though their works are of vast importance; and we omit the works of living writers who belong to the present rather than to the past century.

3

The Romantic Movement

The French Revolution was like a bomb, to the making of which every liberal thinker and writer of the eighteenth century had lent a hand, and which, when it exploded, destroyed its creators. After the smoke had rolled away, it became clear that the old regime, with its despotisms and its persecutions, had indeed been abolished for ever; but the spirit of the Philosophes had vanished likewise. Men's minds underwent a great reaction. The traditions of the last two centuries were violently broken. In literature, particularly, it seemed as if the very foundations of the art must be laid anew; and, in this task, if men looked at all for inspiration from the Past, it was towards that age which differed most from the age of their fathers--towards those distant times before the Renaissance, when the medieval Church reigned supreme in Europe.

But before examining these new developments more closely, one glance must be given at a writer whose qualities had singularly little to do with his surroundings. ANDRE CHENIER passed the active years of his short life in the thick of the revolutionary ferment, and he was guillotined at the age of thirty-two; but his most characteristic poems might have been composed in some magic island, far from the haunts of men, and untouched by 'the rumour of periods'. He is the only French writer of the eighteenth century in whom the pure and undiluted spirit of poetry is manifest. For this reason, perhaps, he has often been acclaimed as the forerunner of the great Romantic outburst of a generation later; but, in reality, to give him such a title is to misjudge the whole value of his work.

For he is essentially a classic; with a purity, a restraint, a measured and accomplished art which would have delighted Boileau, and which brings him into close kinship with Racine and La Fontaine. If his metrical technique is somewhat looser than the former poet's, it is infinitely less loose than the latter's; and his occasional departures from the strict classical canons of versification are always completely subordinated to the controlling balance of his style. In his Eglogues the beauty of his workmanship often reaches perfection. The short poems are Attic in their serenity and their grace. It is not the rococo pseudo-classicism of the later versifiers of the eighteenth century, it is the delicate flavour of true Hellenism that breathes from them; and, as one reads them, one is reminded alternately of Theocritus and of Keats. Like Keats, Chenier was cut off when he had hardly more than given promise of what his achievement might have been. His brief and tragic apparition in the midst of the Revolution is like that of some lovely bird flitting on a sudden out of the darkness and the terror of a tempest, to be overcome a moment later, and whirled to destruction.

The lines upon which the Romantic Movement was to develop had no connexion whatever with Chenier's exquisite art. Throughout French Literature, it is easy to perceive two main impulses at work, which, between them, have inspired all the great masterpieces of the language. On the one hand, there is that positive spirit of searching and unmitigated common sense which has given French prose its peculiar distinction, which lies at the root of the wonderful critical powers of the nation, and which has produced that remarkable and persistent strain of Realism--of absolute fidelity to the naked truth--common to the earliest Fabliaux of the Middle Ages and the latest Parisian novel of to-day. On the other hand, there is in French literature a totally different--almost a contradictory--tendency, which is no less clearly marked and hardly less important--the tendency towards pure Rhetoric.

This love of language for its own sake--of language artfully ordered, splendidly adorned, moving, swelling, irresistible--may be seen alike in the torrential sentences of Rabelais, in the sonorous periods of Bossuet, and in the passionate tirades of Corneille. With the great masters of the seventeenth century--Pascal, Racine, La Fontaine, La Bruyere--the two influences met, and achieved a perfect balance. In their work, the most penetrating realism is beautified and ennobled by all the resources of linguistic art, while the rhetorical instinct is preserved from pomposity and inflation by a supreme critical sense. With the eighteenth century, however, a change came. The age was a critical age--an age of prose and common sense; the rhetorical impulse faded away, to find expression only in melodramatic tragedy and dull verse; and the style of Voltaire, so brilliant and yet so colourless, so limited and yet so infinitely sensible, symbolized the literary character of the century. The Romantic Movement was an immense reaction against the realism which had come to such perfection in the acid prose of Voltaire. It was a reassertion of the rhetorical instinct in all its strength and in all its forms. There was no attempt simply to redress the balance; no wish to revive the studied perfection of the classical age. The realistic spirit was almost completely abandoned. The pendulum swung violently from one extreme to the other.

The new movement had been already faintly discernible in Diderot's bright colouring and the oratorical structure of Rousseau's writing. But it was not until after the Revolution, in the first years of the nineteenth century, that the Romantic spirit completely declared itself--in the prose of CHATEAUBRIAND. Chateaubriand was, at bottom, a rhetorician pure and simple--a rhetorician in the widest sense of the word. It was not merely that the resources of his style were enormous in colour, movement, and imagery, in splendour of rhythm, in descriptive force; but that his whole cast of mind was in itself rhetorical, and that he saw, felt, and thought with the same emphasis, the same amplitude, the same romantic sensibility with which he wrote. The three subjects which formed the main themes of all his work and gave occasion for his finest passages were Christianity, Nature, and himself. His conception of Christianity was the very reverse of that of the eighteenth century.

In his Genie du Christianisme and his Martyrs the analytical and critical spirit of his predecessors has entirely vanished; the religion which they saw simply as a collection of theological dogmas, he envisioned as a living creed, arrayed in all the hues of poetry and imagination, and redolent with the mystery of the past. Yet it may be doubted whether Chateaubriand was essentially more religious than Voltaire. What Voltaire dissected in the dry light of reason, Chateaubriand invested with the cloak of his own eloquence--put it up, so to speak, on a platform, in a fine attitude, under a tinted illumination. He lacked the subtle intimacy of Faith. In his descriptions of Nature, too, the same characteristics appear. Compared with Rousseau's, they are far bolder, far richer, composed on a more elaborate and imposing scale; but they are less convincing; while Rousseau's landscapes are often profoundly moving, Chateaubriand's are hardly ever more than splendidly picturesque.

There is a similar relation between the egoisms of the two men. Chateaubriand was never tired of writing about himself; and in his long Memoires d'Outre-Tombe--the most permanently interesting of his works--he gave a full rein to his favourite passion. His conception of himself was Byronic. He swells forth, in all his pages, a noble, melancholy, proud, sentimental creature whom every man must secretly envy and every woman passionately adore. He had all the vanity of Rousseau, but none of his honesty. Rousseau, at any rate, never imposed upon himself; and Chateaubriand always did. Thus the vision that we have of him is of something wonderful but empty, something striking but unreal. It is the rhetorician that we see, and not the man.

Chateaubriand's influence was very great. Beside his high-flowing, romantic, imaginative writings, the tradition of the eighteenth century seemed to shrivel up into something thin, cold and insignificant. A new and dazzling world swam into the ken of his readers--a world in which the individual reigned in glory amid the glowing panorama of Nature and among the wondrous visions of a remote and holy past. His works became at once highly popular, though it was not until a generation later that their full effect was felt. Meanwhile, the impetus which he had started was continued in the poems of LAMARTINE.

Here there is the same love of Nature, the same religious outlook, the same insistence on the individual point of view; but the tints are less brilliant, the emphasis is more restrained; the rhetorical impulse still dominates, but it is the rhetoric of elegiac tenderness rather than of picturesque pomp. A wonderful limpidity of versification which, while it is always perfectly easy, is never weak, and a charming quietude of sentiment which, however near it may seem to come to the commonplace, always just escapes it--these qualities give Lamartine a distinguished place in the literature of France. They may be seen in their perfection in the most famous of his poems, Le Lac, a monody descriptive of his feelings on returning alone to the shores of the lake where he had formerly passed the day with his mistress. And throughout all his poetical work precisely the same characteristics are to be found. Lamartine's lyre gave forth an inexhaustible flow of melody--always faultless, always pellucid, and always, in the same key.

During the Revolution, under the rule of Napoleon, and in the years which followed his fall, the energies of the nation were engrossed by war and politics. During these forty years there are fewer great names in French literature than in any other corresponding period since the Renaissance. At last, however, about the year 1830, a new generation of writers arose who brought back all the old glories and triumphantly proved that the French tongue, so far from having exhausted its resources, was a fresh and living instrument of extraordinary power. These writers--as has so often been the case in France--were bound together by a common literary creed.

Young, ardent, scornful of the past, dazzled by the possibilities of the future, they raised the standard of revolt against the traditions of Classicism, promulgated a new aesthetic doctrine, and, after a sharp struggle and great excitement, finally succeeded in completely establishing their view. The change which they introduced was of enormous importance, and for this reason the date 1830 is a cardinal one in the literature of France. Every sentence, every verse that has been written in French since then bears upon it, somewhere or other, the imprint of the great Romantic Movement which came to a head in that year. What it was that was then effected--what the main differences are between French literature before 1830 and French literature after--deserves some further consideration.

The Romantic School--of which the most important members were VICTOR HUGO, ALFRED DE VIGNY, THEOPHILE GAUTIER, ALEXANDRE DUMAS, and ALFRED DE MUSSET--was, as we have said, inspired by that supremely French love of Rhetoric which, during the long reign of intellect and prose in the eighteenth century, had been almost entirely suppressed. The new spirit had animated the prose of Chateaubriand and the poetry of Lamartine; but it was the spirit only: the form of both those writers retained most of the important characteristics of the old tradition. It was new wine in old bottles. The great achievement of the Romantic School was the creation of new bottles--of a new conception of form, in which the vast rhetorical impulse within them might find a suitable expression. Their actual innovations, however, were by no means sweeping. For instance, the numberless minute hard-and-fast metrical rules which, since the days of Malherbe, had held French poetry in shackles, they only interfered with to a very limited extent.

They introduced a certain number of new metres; they varied the rhythm of the Alexandrine; but a great mass of petty and meaningless restrictions remained untouched, and no real attempt was made to get rid of them until more than a generation had passed. Yet here, as elsewhere, what they had done was of the highest importance. They had touched the ark of the covenant and they had not been destroyed. They had shown that it was possible to break a 'rule' and yet write good poetry. This explains the extraordinary violence of the Romantic controversy over questions of the smallest detail.

When Victor Hugo, in the opening lines of Hernani, ventured to refer to an 'escalier derobe', and to put 'escalier' at the end of one line, and 'derobe' at the beginning of the next, he was assailed with the kind of virulence which is usually reserved for the vilest of criminals. And the abuse had a meaning in it: it was abuse of a revolutionary. For in truth, by the disposition of those two words, Victor Hugo had inaugurated a revolution. The whole theory of 'rules' in literature--the whole conception that there were certain definite traditional forms in existence which were, absolutely and inevitably, the best--was shattered for ever. The new doctrine was triumphantly vindicated--that the form of expression must depend ultimately, not upon tradition nor yet upon a priori reasonings, but simply and solely on the thing expressed.

The most startling and the most complete of the Romantic innovations related to the poetic Vocabulary. The number of words considered permissible in French poetry had been steadily diminishing since the days of Racine. A distinction had grown up between words that were 'noble' and words that were 'bas'; and only those in the former class were admitted into poetry. No word could be 'noble' if it was one ordinarily used by common people, or if it was a technical term, or if, in short, it was peculiarly expressive; for any such word would inevitably produce a shock, introduce mean associations, and destroy the unity of the verse.

If the sense demanded the use of such a word, a periphrasis of 'noble' words must be employed instead. Racine had not been afraid to use the word 'chien' in the most exalted of his tragedies; but his degenerate successors quailed before such an audacity.

If you must refer to such a creature as a dog, you had better call it 'de la fidelite respectable soutien'; the phrase actually occurs in a tragedy of the eighteenth century. It is clear that, with such a convention to struggle against, no poetry could survive. Everything bold, everything vigorous, everything surprising became an impossibility with a diction limited to the vaguest, most general, and most feebly pompous terms. The Romantics, in the face of violent opposition, threw the doors of poetry wide open to every word in the language. How great the change was, and what was the nature of the public opinion against which the Romantics had to fight, may be judged from the fact that the use of the word 'mouchoir' during a performance of Othello a few years before 1830 produced a riot in the theatre. To such a condition of narrowness and futility had the great Classical tradition sunk at last!

The enormous influx of words into the literary vocabulary which the Romantic Movement brought about had two important effects. In the first place, the range of poetical expression was infinitely increased. French literature came out of a little, ceremonious, antiquated drawing-room into the open air. With the flood of new words, a thousand influences which had never been felt before came into operation. Strangeness, contrast, complication, immensity, curiosity, grotesqueness, fantasy--effects of this kind now for the first time became possible and common in verse. But, one point must be noticed.

The abolition of the distinction between words that were 'bas' and 'noble' did not at first lead (as might have been expected) to an increase of realism. Rather the opposite took place. The Romantics loved the new words not because they made easier the expression of actual facts, but for their power of suggestion, for the effects of remoteness, contrast, and multiplicity which could be produced by them--in fact, for their rhetorical force. The new vocabulary came into existence as an engine of rhetoric, not as an engine of truth.

Nevertheless--and this was the second effect of its introduction--in the long run the realistic impulse in French literature was also immensely strengthened. The vocabulary of prose widened at the same time as that of verse; and the prose of the first Romantics remained almost completely rhetorical. But the realistic elements always latent in prose--and especially in French prose--soon asserted themselves; the vast opportunities for realistic description which the enlarged vocabulary opened out were eagerly seized upon; and it was not long before there arose in French literature a far more elaborate and searching realism than it had ever known before.

It was, perhaps, unfortunate that the main struggle of the Romantic controversy should have been centred in the theatre. The fact that this was so is an instance of the singular interest in purely literary questions which has so often been displayed by popular opinion in France. The controversy was not simply an academic matter for connoisseurs and critics to decide upon in private; it was fought out in all the heat of popular excitement on the public stage. But the wild enthusiasm aroused by the triumphs of Dumas and Hugo in the theatre shows, in a no less striking light, the incapacity of contemporaries to gauge the true significance of new tendencies in art.

On the whole, the dramatic achievement of the Romantic School was the least valuable part of their work. Hernani, the first performance of which marked the turning-point of the movement, is a piece of bombastic melodrama, full of the stagiest clap-trap and the most turgid declamation. Victor Hugo imagined when he wrote it that he was inspired by Shakespeare; if he was inspired by anyone it was by Voltaire. His drama is the old drama of the eighteenth century, repainted in picturesque colours; it resembles those grotesque country-houses that our forefathers were so fond of, where the sham-Gothic turrets and castellations ill conceal the stucco and the pilasters of a former age. Of true character and true passion it has no trace. The action, the incidents, the persons--all alike are dominated by considerations of rhetoric, and of rhetoric alone. The rhetoric has, indeed, this advantage over that of Zaire and Alzire--it is bolder and more highly coloured; but then it is also more pretentious. All the worst tendencies of the Romantic Movement may be seen completely displayed in the dramas of Victor Hugo.

For throughout his work that wonderful writer expressed in their extreme forms the qualities and the defects of his school. Above all, he was the supreme lord of words. In sheer facility, in sheer abundance of language, Shakespeare alone of all the writers of the world can be reckoned his superior. The bulk of his work is very great, and the nature of it is very various; but every page bears the mark of the same tireless fecundity, the same absolute dominion over the resources of speech. Words flowed from Victor Hugo like light from the sun. Nor was his volubility a mere disordered mass of verbiage: it was controlled, adorned, and inspired by an immense technical power.

When one has come under the spell of that great enchanter, one begins to believe that his art is without limits, that with such an instrument and such a science there is no miracle which he cannot perform. He can conjure up the strangest visions of fancy; he can evoke the glamour and the mystery of the past; he can sing with exquisite lightness of the fugitive beauties of Nature; he can pour out, in tenderness or in passion, the melodies of love; he can fill his lines with the fire, the stress, the culminating fury, of prophetic denunciation; he can utter the sad and secret questionings of the human spirit, and give voice to the solemnity of Fate. In the long roll and vast swell of his verse there is something of the ocean--a moving profundity of power. His sonorous music, with its absolute sureness of purpose, and its contrapuntal art, recalls the vision in Paradise Lost of him who--with volant touch Fled and pursued transverse the resonant fugue.

What kind of mind, what kind of spirit, must that have been, one asks in amazement, which could animate with such a marvellous perfection the enormous organ of that voice?

But perhaps it would be best to leave the question unasked--or at least unanswered. For the more one searches, the clearer it becomes that the intellectual scope and the spiritual quality of Victor Hugo were very far from being equal to his gifts of expression and imagination. He had the powers of a great genius and the soul of an ordinary man. But that was not all. There have been writers of the highest excellence--Saint-Simon was one of them--the value of whose productions have been unaffected, or indeed even increased, by their personal inferiority. They could not have written better, one feels, if they had been ten times as noble and twenty times as wise as they actually were. But unfortunately this is not so with Victor Hugo. His faults--his intellectual weakness, his commonplace outlook, his lack of humour, his vanity, his defective taste--cannot be dismissed as irrelevant and unimportant, for they are indissolubly bound up with the very substance of his work.

It was not as a mere technician that he wished to be judged; he wrote with a very different intention; it was as a philosopher, as a moralist, as a prophet, as a sublime thinker, as a profound historian, as a sensitive and refined human being. With a poet of such pretensions it is clearly most relevant to inquire whether his poetry does, in fact, reveal the high qualities he lays claim to, or whether, on the contrary, it is characterized by a windy inflation of sentiment, a showy superficiality of thought, and a ridiculous and petty egoism. These are the unhappy questions which beset the mature and reflective reader of Victor Hugo's works. To the young and enthusiastic one the case is different. For him it is easy to forget--or even not to observe--what there may be in that imposing figure that is unsatisfactory and second-rate.

He may revel at will in the voluminous harmonies of that resounding voice; by turns thrilling with indignation, dreaming in ecstasy, plunging into abysses, and soaring upon unimaginable heights. Between youth and age who shall judge? Who decide between rapture and reflection, enthusiasm and analysis? To determine the precise place of Victor Hugo in the hierarchy of poets would be difficult indeed. But this much is certain: that at times the splendid utterance does indeed grow transfused with a pure and inward beauty, when the human frailties vanish, and all is subdued and glorified by the high purposes of art. Such passages are to be found among the lyrics of Les Feuilles d'Automne, Les Rayons et Les Ombres, Les Contemplations, in the brilliant descriptions and lofty imagery of La Legende des Siecles, in the burning invective of Les Chatiments. None but a place among the most illustrious could be given to the creator of such a stupendous piece of word-painting as the description of the plain of Waterloo in the latter volume, or of such a lovely vision as that in La Legende des Siecles, of Ruth looking up in silence at the starry heaven. If only the wondrous voice had always spoken so!

The romantic love of vastness, richness, and sublimity, and the romantic absorption in the individual--these two qualities appear in their extremes throughout the work of

Hugo: in that of ALFRED DE VIGNY it is the first that dominates; in that of ALFRED DE MUSSET, the second. Vigny wrote sparingly--one or two plays, a few prose works, and a small volume of poems; but he produced some masterpieces. A far more sober artist than Hugo, he was also a far profounder thinker, and a sincerer man. His melancholy, his pessimism, were the outcome of no Byronic attitudinizing, but the genuine intimate feelings of a noble spirit; and he could express them in splendid verse.

His melancholy was touched with grandeur, his pessimism with sublimity. In his Moise, his Colere de Samson, his Maison du Berger, his Mont des Oliviers, and others of his short reflective poems, he envisions man face to face with indifferent Nature, with hostile Destiny, with poisoned Love, and the lesson he draws is the lesson of proud resignation. In La Mort du Loup, the tragic spectacle of the old wolf driven to bay and killed by the hunters inspires perhaps his loftiest verses, with the closing application to humanity--'Souffre et meurs sans parler'--summing up his sad philosophy. No less striking and beautiful are the few short stories in his Servitude et Grandeur Militaires, in which some heroic incidents of military life are related in a prose of remarkable strength and purity. In the best work of Vigny there are no signs of the strain, the over-emphasis, the tendency towards the grotesque, always latent in Romanticism; its nobler elements are alone preserved; he has achieved the grand style. Alfred de Musset presents a complete contrast. He was the spoilt child of the age--frivolous, amorous, sensuous, charming, unfortunate, and unhappy; and his poetry is the record of his personal feelings, his varying moods, his fugitive loves, his sentimental despairs.

Le seul bien qui me reste au monde

Est d'avoir quelquefois pleure,

he exclaims, with an accent of regretful softness different indeed from that of Vigny. Among much that is feeble, ill constructed, and exaggerated in his verse, strains of real beauty and real pathos constantly recur. Some of his lyrics are perfect; the famous song of Fortunio in itself entitles him to a high place among the masters of the language; and in his longer pieces--especially in the four Nuits--his emotion occasionally rises, grows transfigured, and vibrates with a strange intensity, a long, poignant, haunting note.

But doubtless his chief claim to immortality rests upon his exquisite little dramas (both in verse and prose), in which the romance of Shakespeare and the fantasy of Marivaux mingle with a wit, a charm, an elegance, which are all Musset's own. In his historical drama, Lorenzaccio, he attempted to fill a larger canvas, and he succeeded. Unlike the majority of the Romantics, Musset had a fine sense of psychology and a penetrating historical vision. In this brilliant, vivacious, and yet subtle tragedy he is truly great.

We must now glance at the effects which the Romantic Movement produced upon the art which was destined to fill so great a place in the literature of the nineteenth century--the art of prose fiction. With the triumph of Classicism in the seventeenth century, the novel, like all other forms of literature, grew simplified and compressed.

The huge romances of Mademoiselle de Scudery were succeeded by the delicate little stories of Madame de Lafayette, one of which--La Princesse de Cleves--a masterpiece of charming psychology and exquisite art, deserves to be considered as the earliest example of the modern novel. All through the eighteenth century the same tendency is visible. Manon Lescaut, the passionate and beautiful romance of l'Abbe Prevost, is a very small book, concerned, like La Princesse de Cleves, with two characters only--the lovers, whose varying fortunes make up the whole action of the tale.

Precisely the same description applies to the subtle and brilliant Adolphe of Benjamin Constant, produced in the early years of the nineteenth century. Even when the framework was larger--as in Le Sage's Gil Blas and Marivaux's Vie de Marianne--the spirit was the same; it was the spirit of selection, of simplification, of delicate skill.

Both the latter works are written in a prose style of deliberate elegance, and both consist rather of a succession of small incidents--almost of independent short stories--than of one large developing whole.

The culminating example of the eighteenth-century form of fiction may be seen in the Liaisons Dangereuses of Laclos, a witty, scandalous and remarkably able novel, concerned with the interacting intrigues of a small society of persons, and revealing on every page a most brilliant and concentrated art. Far more modern, both in its general conception and in the absolute realism of its treatment, was Diderot's La Religieuse; but this masterpiece was not published till some years after the Revolution; and the real honour of having originated the later developments in French fiction--as in so many other branches of literature--belongs undoubtedly to Rousseau.

La Nouvelle Heloise, faulty as it is as a work of art, with its feeble psychology and loose construction, yet had the great merit of throwing open whole new worlds for the exploration of the novelist--the world of nature on the one hand, and on the other the world of social problems and all the living forces of actual life.

The difference between the novels of Rousseau and those of Hugo is great; but yet it is a difference merely of degree. Les Miserables is the consummation of the romantic conception of fiction which Rousseau had adumbrated half a century before.

In that enormous work, Hugo attempted to construct a prose epic of modern life; but the attempt was not successful. Its rhetorical cast of style, its ceaseless and glaring melodrama, its childish presentments of human character, its endless digressions and--running through all this--its evidences of immense and disordered power, make the book perhaps the most magnificent failure--the most 'wild enormity' ever produced by a man of genius. -

Another development of the romantic spirit appeared at about the same time in the early novels of George Sand, in which the ardours of passionate love are ecstatically idealized in a loose and lyric flow of innumerable words.

There can be little doubt that if the development of fiction had stopped at this point the infusion into it of the romantic spirit could only have been judged a disaster. From the point of view of art, such novels as those of Victor Hugo and the early works of George Sand were a retrogression from those of the eighteenth century. Manon Lescaut, tiny, limited, unambitious as it is, stands on a far higher level of artistic achievement than the unreal and incoherent Les Miserables.

The scale of the novel had indeed been infinitely enlarged, but the apparatus for dealing adequately with the vast masses of new material was wanting. It is pathetic to watch the romantic novelists trying to infuse beauty and significance into their subjects by means of fine writing, lyrical outbursts, impassioned philosophical dissertations, and all the familiar rhetorical devices so dear to them. The inevitable result was something lifeless, formless, fantastic; they were on the wrong track.

The true method for the treatment of their material was not that of rhetoric at all; it was that of realism. This fact was discovered by STENDHAL, who was the first to combine an enlarged view of the world with a plain style and an accurate, unimpassioned, detailed examination of actual life.

In his remarkable novel, Le Rouge et Le Noir, and in some parts of his later work, La Chartreuse de Parme, Stendhal laid down the lines on which French fiction has been developing ever since. The qualities which distinguish him are those which have distinguished all the greatest of his successors--a subtle psychological insight, an elaborate attention to detail, and a remorseless fidelity to the truth.

Important as Stendhal is in the history of modern French fiction, he is dwarfed by the colossal figure of BALZAC. By virtue of his enormous powers, and the immense quantity and variety of his output, Balzac might be called the Hugo of prose, if it were not that in two most important respects he presents a complete contrast to his great contemporary. In the first place, his control of the technical resources of the language was as feeble as Hugo's was mighty.

Balzac's style is bad; in spite of the electric vigour that runs through his writing, it is formless, clumsy, and quite without distinction; it is the writing of a man who was highly perspicacious, formidably powerful, and vulgar. But, on the other hand, he possessed one great quality which Hugo altogether lacked--the sense of the real.

Hugo was most himself when he was soaring on the wings of fancy through the empyrean; Balzac was most himself when he was rattling in a hired cab through the streets of Paris.

He was of the earth earthy. His coarse, large, germinating spirit gave forth, like the earth, a teeming richness, a solid, palpable creation. And thus it was he who achieved what Hugo, in Les Miserables, had in vain attempted. La Comedie Humaine, as he called the long series of his novels, which forms in effect a single work, presents, in spite of its limitations and its faults, a picture of the France of that age drawn on the vast scale and in the grand manner of an epic.

The limitations and the faults of Balzac's work are, indeed, sufficiently obvious and sufficiently grave. The same coarseness of fibre which appears in his style made him incapable of understanding the delicacies of life--the refined shades of emotion, the subtleties of human intercourse. He probably never read Jane Austen; but if he had he certainly would have considered her an utterly pointless writer; and he would have been altogether at sea in a novel by Henry James. The elusive things that are so important, the indecisive things that are so curious, the intimate things that are so thrilling--all these slipped through his rough, matter-of-fact grasp. His treatment of the relations between the sexes is characteristic.

The subject fills a great place in his novels; he approaches it with an unflinching boldness, and a most penetrating gaze; yet he never succeeds in giving a really satisfactory presentment of the highest of those relations--love. That eluded him: its essence was too subtle, too private, too transcendental. No one can describe love who has not the makings of a poet in him. And a poet was the very last thing that Balzac was.

But his work does not merely suffer from the absence of certain good qualities; it is also marred by the presence of positively bad ones. Balzac was not simply a realist. There was a romantic vein in him, which occasionally came to the surface with unfortunate results. When that happened, he plunged into the most reckless melodrama, revelled in the sickliest sentiment, or evolved the most grotesque characters, the most fantastic plots. And these lapses occur quite indiscriminately.

Side by side with some detailed and convincing description, one comes upon glaring absurdities; in the middle of some narrative of extraordinary actuality, one finds oneself among hissing villains, disguises, poisons, and all the paraphernalia of a penny novelette. Balzac's lack of critical insight into his own work is one of the most singular of his characteristics. He hardly seems to have known at all what he was about.

He wrote feverishly, desperately, under the impulsion of irresistible genius. His conceptions crowded upon him in vivid, serried multitudes--the wildest visions of fantasy mixed pell-mell with the most vital realizations of fact. It was not for him to distinguish; his concern was simply, somehow or other, to get them all out: good, bad, or indifferent, what did it matter? The things were in his brain; and they must be expressed.

Fortunately, it is very easy for the reader to be more discriminating than Balzac. The alloy is not inextricably mingled with the pure metal--the chaff may be winnowed off, and the grain left. His errors and futilities cannot obscure his true achievement--his evocation of multitudinous life. The whole of France is crammed into his pages, and electrified there into intense vitality.

The realism of the classical novelists was a purely psychological realism; it was concerned with the delicately shifting states of mind of a few chosen persons, and with nothing else. Balzac worked on a very different plan. He neglected the subtleties of the spirit, and devoted himself instead to, displaying the immense interest that lay in those prosaic circumstances of existence which the older writers had ignored.

He showed with wonderful force that the mere common details of everyday life were filled with drama, that, to him who had eyes to see, there might be significance in a ready-made suit of clothes, and passion in the furniture of a boarding-house. Money in particular gave him an unending theme. There is hardly a character in the whole vast range of his creation of whose income we are not exactly informed; and it might almost be said that the only definite moral that can be drawn from La Comedie Humaine is that the importance of money can never be over-estimated. The classical writers preferred to leave such matters to the imagination of the reader; it was Balzac's great object to leave nothing to the imagination of the reader.

By ceaseless effort, by infinite care, by elaborate attention to the minutest details, he would describe all. He brought an encyclopaedic knowledge to bear upon his task; he can give an exact account of the machinery of a provincial printing-press; he can write a dissertation on the methods of military organization; he can reveal the secret springs in the mechanism of Paris journalism; he is absolutely at home in the fraudulent transactions of money-makers, the methods of usurers, the operations of high finance.

And into all this mass of details he can infuse the spirit of life. Perhaps his masterpiece in realistic description is his account of La Maison Vauquer--a low boarding-house, to which he devotes page after page of minute particularity. The result is not a mere dead catalogue: it is a palpitating image of lurid truth. Never was the sordid horror which lurks in places and in things evoked with a more intense completeness.

Undoubtedly it is in descriptions of the sordid, the squalid, the ugly, and the mean that Balzac particularly excels. He is at his greatest when he is revealing the horrible underside of civilization--the indignities of poverty, the low intrigues of parasites, the long procession of petty agonies that embitter and ruin a life.

Over this world of shadow and grime he throws strange lights. Extraordinary silhouettes flash out and vanish; one has glimpses of obscure and ominous movements on every side; and, amid all this, some sudden vision emerges from the darkness, of pathos, of tenderness, of tragic and unutterable pain.

Balzac died in 1850, and at about that time the Romantic Movement came to an end. Victor Hugo, it is true, continued to live and to produce for more than thirty years longer; but French literature ceased to be dominated by the ideals of the Romantic school.

That school had accomplished much; it had recreated French poetry, and it had revolutionized French prose. But, by the very nature of its achievement, it led the way to its own supersession. The spirit which animated its doctrines was the spirit of progress and of change; it taught that there were no fixed rules for writing well; that art, no less than science, lived by experiment; that a literature which did not develop was dead.

Therefore it was inevitable that the Romantic ideal itself should form the stepping-stone for a fresh advance. The complex work of Balzac unites in a curious way many of the most important elements of the old school and of the new. Alike by his vast force, his immense variety, his formlessness, his lack of critical and intellectual power, he was a Romantic; but he belonged to the future in his enormous love of prosaic detail, his materialist cast of mind, and his preoccupation with actual facts.

4

The Age of Criticism

With the generation of writers who rose to eminence after the death of Balzac, we come within the reach of living memory, so that a just estimate of their work is well-nigh impossible: it is so close to us that it is bound to be out of focus. And there is an additional difficulty in the extreme richness and variety of their accomplishment. They explored so many fields of literature, and produced so much of interest and importance, that a short account of their work can hardly fail to give a false impression of it. Only its leading characteristics and its most remarkable manifestations can be touched upon here.

The age was before all else an age of Criticism. A strong reaction set in against the looseness of construction and the extravagance of thought which had pervaded the work of the Romantics; and a new ideal was set up--an ideal which was to combine the width and diversity of the latter with the precision of form and the deliberate artistic purpose of the Classical age. The movement affected the whole of French literature, but its most important results were in the domain of Prose. Nowhere were the defects of the Romantics more obvious than in their treatment of history. With a very few exceptions they conceived of the past as a picturesque pageant--a thing of contrasts and costumes, an excuse for rhetorical descriptions, without inner significance or a real life of its own. One historian of genius they did indeed produce--MICHELET; and the contrast between his work and that of his successors, TAINE and RENAN, is typical of the new departure.

The great history of Michelet, with its strange, convulsive style, its capricious and imaginative treatment of facts, and its undisguised bias, shows us the spectacle of the past in a series of lurid lightning-flashes--a spectacle at once intensely vivid and singularly contorted; it is the history of a poet rather than of a man of science. With Taine and Renan the personal element which forms the very foundation of Michelet's work has been carefully suppressed. It is replaced by an elaborate examination of detail, a careful, sober, unprejudiced reconstruction of past conditions, an infinitely conscientious endeavour to tell the truth and nothing but the truth. Nor is their history merely the dead bones of analysis and research; it is informed with an untiring sympathy; and--in the case of Renan especially--a suave and lucid style adds the charm and amenity which art alone can give.

The same tendencies appear to a still more remarkable degree in Criticism. With SAINTE-BEUVE, in fact, one might almost say that criticism, as we know it, came into existence for the first time. Before him, all criticism had been one of two things: it had been either a merely personal expression of opinion, or else an attempt to establish universal literary canons and to judge of writers by the standards thus set up. Sainte-Beuve realized that such methods--the slap-dash pronouncements of a Johnson or the narrow generalizations of a Boileau--were in reality not critical at all.

He saw that the critic's first duty was not to judge, but to understand; and with this object he set himself to explore all the facts which could throw light on the temperament, the outlook, the ideals of his author; he examined his biography, the society in which he lived, the influences of his age; and with the apparatus thus patiently formed he proceeded to act as the interpreter between the author and the public. His Causeries du Lundi--short critical papers originally contributed to a periodical magazine and subsequently published in a long series of volumes--together with his Port Royal--an elaborate account of the movements in letters and philosophy during the earlier years of Louis XIV's reign--contain a mass of material of unequalled value concerning the whole of French literature. His analytical and sympathetic mind is reflected in the quiet wit and easy charm of his writing. Undoubtedly the lover of French literature will find in Sainte-Beuve's Lundis at once the most useful and the most agreeable review of the subject in all its branches; and the more his knowledge increases, the more eagerly will he return for further guidance and illumination to those delightful books.

But the greatest prose-writer of the age devoted himself neither to history nor to criticism--though his works are impregnated with the spirit of both--but to Fiction. In his novels, FLAUBERT finally accomplished what Balzac had spasmodically begun--the separation of the art of fiction from the unreality, the exaggeration, and the rhetoric of the Romantic School. Before he began to write, the movement towards a greater restraint, a more deliberate art, had shown itself in a few short novels by GEORGE SAND--the first of the long and admirable series of her mature works--where, especially in such delicate masterpieces as La Mare au Diable, La Petite Fadette, and Francois le Champi, her earlier lyricism and incoherence were replaced by an idyllic sentiment strengthened and purified by an exquisite sense of truth.

Flaubert's genius moved in a very different and a far wider orbit: but it was no less guided by the dictates of deliberate art. In his realism, his love of detail, and his penetrating observation of facts, Flaubert was the true heir of Balzac; while in the scrupulosity of his style and the patient, laborious, and sober treatment of his material he presented a complete contrast to his great predecessor. These latter qualities make Flaubert the pre-eminent representative of his age. The critical sense possessed him more absolutely and with more striking results than all the rest of his contemporaries. His watchfulness over his own work was almost infinite.

There has never been a writer who took his art with such a passionate seriousness, who struggled so incessantly towards perfection, and who suffered so acutely from the difficulties, the disappointments, the desperate, furious efforts of an unremitting toil. His style alone cost him boundless labour. He would often spend an entire day over the elaboration and perfection of a single sentence, which, perhaps, would be altogether obliterated before the publication of the book.

He worked in an apoplectic fervour over every detail of his craft--eliminating repetitions, balancing rhythms, discovering the precise word for every shade of meaning, with an extraordinary, an almost superhuman, persistence. And in the treatment of his matter his conscientiousness was equally great. He prepared for his historical novels by profound researches in the original authorities of the period, and by personal visits to the localities he intended to describe.

When he treated of modern life he was no less scrupulously exact. One of his scenes was to pass in a cabbage-garden by moonlight. But what did a cabbage-garden by moonlight really look like? Flaubert waited long for a propitious night, and then went out, notebook in hand, to take down the precise details of what he saw. Thus it was that his books were written very slowly, and his production comparatively small. He spent six years over the first and most famous of his works--Madame Bovary; and he devoted no less than thirteen to his encyclopedic Bouvard et Pecuchet, which was still unfinished when he died.

The most abiding impression produced by the novels of Flaubert is that of solidity. This is particularly the case with his historical books. The bric-a-brac and fustian of the Romantics has disappeared, to be replaced by a clear, detailed, profound presentment of the life of the past. In Salammbo, ancient Carthage rises up before us, no crazy vision of a picturesque and disordered imagination, but in all the solidity of truth; coloured, not with the glaring contrasts of rhetoric, but with the real blaze of an eastern sun; strange, not with an imported fantastic strangeness manufactured in nineteenth-century Paris, but with the strangeness--so much more mysterious and significant--of the actual, barbaric Past.

The same characteristics appear in Flaubert's modern novels. Madame Bovary gives us a picture of life in a French provincial town in the middle of the last century--a picture which, with its unemphatic tones, its strong, sensitive, and accurate drawing, its masterly design, produces an effect of absolutely convincing veracity. The character and the fate of the wretched woman who forms the central figure of the story come upon us, amid the grim tepidity of their surroundings, with extraordinary force. Flaubert's genius does not act in sudden flashes, but by the method of gradual accumulation. The effects which it produces are not of the kind that overwhelm and astonish, but of the more subtle sort that creep into the mind by means of a thousand details, an infinitude of elaborated fibres, and which, once there, are there for ever.

The solidity of Flaubert's work, however, was not unaccompanied with drawbacks. His writing lacks fire; there is often a sense of effort in it; and, as one reads his careful, faultless, sculpturesque sentences, it is difficult not to long, at times, for some of the irregular vitality of Balzac. Singularly enough, Flaubert's correspondence--one of the most interesting collections of letters in the language--shows that, so far as his personal character was concerned, irregular vitality was precisely one of his dominating qualities.

But in his fiction he suppressed this side of himself in the interests, as he believed, of art. It was his theory that a complete detachment was a necessary condition for all great writing; and he did his best to put this theory into practice. But there was one respect in which he did not succeed in his endeavour. His hatred and scorn of the mass of humanity, his conception of them as a stupid, ignorant, and vulgar herd, appears throughout his work, and in his unfinished Bouvard et Pecuchet reaches almost to the proportion of a monomania.

The book is an infinitely elaborate and an infinitely bitter attack on the ordinary man. There is something tragic in the spectacle of this lonely, noble, and potent genius wearing out his life at last over such a task--in a mingled agony of unconscious frenzied self-expression and deliberate misguided self-immolation.

In poetry, the reaction against Romanticism had begun with the Emaux et Camees of THEOPHILE GAUTIER--himself in his youth one of the leaders of the Romantic School; and it was carried further in the work of a group of writers known as the Parnassiens--the most important of whom were LECONTE DE LISLE, SULLY PRUDHOMME, and HEREDIA. Their poetry bears the same relation to that of Musset as the history of Renan bears to that of Michelet, and the prose of Flaubert to that of Hugo. It is restrained, impersonal, and polished to the highest degree. The bulk of it is not great; but not a line of it is weak or faulty; and it possesses a firm and plastic beauty, well expressed by the title of Gautier's volume, and the principles of which are at once explained and exemplified in his famous poem beginning.

Oui, l'oeuvre sort plus belle

D'une forme au travail

Rebelle,

--Vers, marbre, onyx, email.

The Parnassiens particularly devoted themselves to classical subjects, and to descriptions of tropical scenes. Their rich, sonorous, splendidly-moulded language invests their visions with a noble fixity, an impressive force. Among the gorgeous descriptive pieces of Leconte de Lisle, the exquisite lyrics of Sully Prudhomme, and the chiselled sonnets of

Heredia some of the finest and weightiest verse of the century is to be found.

The agē produced one other poet who, however, by the spirit of his work, belongs rather to the succeeding epoch than to his own. This was BAUDELAIRE, whose small volume--Les Fleurs du Mal--gives him a unique place among the masters of the poetic art. In his form, indeed, he is closely related to his contemporaries. His writing has all the care, the balance, the conscientious polish of the Parnassiens; it is in his matter that he differs from them completely. He was not interested in classical imaginations and impersonal descriptions; he was concerned almost entirely with the modern life of Paris and the actual experiences of a disillusioned soul.

As intensely personal as the Parnassiens were detached, he poured into his verse all the gloom of his own character, all the bitterness of his own philosophy, all the agony of his own despair. Some poets--such as Keats and Chenier--in spite of the misfortunes of their lives, seem to distil nothing but happiness and the purest beauty into their poetry; they only come to their true selves amid the sunlight and the flowers. Other writers--such as Swift and Tacitus--rule supreme over the kingdom of darkness and horror, and their finest pages are written in the Valley of the Shadow of Death. Writers of this kind are very rarely poets; and it is Baudelaire's great distinction that he was able to combine the hideous and devastating conceptions of complete pessimism with the passion, the imagination, and the formal beauty that only live in magnificent verse. He is the Swift of poetry. His vision is black and terrible. Some of his descriptions are even more disgusting than those of Swift, and most of his pages are no fit reading for the young and ignorant. But the wise reader will find in this lurid poetry elements of profundity and power which are rare indeed. Above all, he will find in it a quality not common in French poetry--a passionate imagination which clothes the thought with splendour, and lifts the strange words of this unhappy mortal into the deathless regions of the sublime.

CONCLUSION

With the death of Flaubert in 1880, French literature entered upon a new phase--a phase which, in its essential qualities, has lasted till to-day, and which forms a suitable point for the conclusion of the present sketch.

This last phase has been dominated by two men of genius. In prose, MAUPASSANT carried on the work of Flaubert with a sharper manner and more vivid style, though with a narrower range. He abandoned the exotic and the historical visions of his predecessor, and devoted himself entirely, in his brilliant novels and yet more brilliant short stories, to an almost fiendishly realistic treatment of modern life. A precisely contrary tendency marks the poetry of VERLAINE. While Maupassant completely disengaged prose from every alien element of poetry and imagination, pushing it as far as it could go in the direction of incisive realism, Verlaine and his fellow-workers in verse attempted to make poetry more truly poetical than it had ever been before, to introduce into it the vagueness and dreaminess of individual moods and spiritual fluctuations, to turn it away from definite fact and bring it near to music.

It was with Verlaine and his successors that French verse completely broke away from the control of those classical rules, the infallibility of which had been first attacked by the Romantics. In order to express the delicate, shifting, and indecisive feelings which he loved so well, Verlaine abolished the last shreds of rhythmical regularity, making his verse a perfectly fluid substance, which he could pour at will into the subtle mould of his feeling and his thought. The result justified the means. Verlaine's poetry exhales an exquisite perfume--strange, indistinct, and yet, after the manner of perfume, unforgettable. Listening to his enchanting, poignant music, we hear the trembling voice of a soul. This last sad singer carries us back across the ages, and, mingling his sweet strain with the distant melancholy of Villon, symbolizes for us at once the living flower and the unchanging root of the great literature of France.

We have now traced the main outlines of that literature from its dim beginnings in the Dark Ages up to the threshold of the present time. Looking back over the long line of writers, the first impression that must strike us is one of extraordinary wealth. France, it is true, has given to the world no genius of the colossal stature and universal power of Shakespeare. But, then, where is the equal of Shakespeare to be found? Not even in the glorious literature of Greece herself. Putting out of account such an immeasurable magnitude, the number of writers of the first rank produced by France can be paralleled in only one other modern literature--that of England.

The record is, indeed, a splendid one which contains, in poetry and drama, the names of Villon, Ronsard, Corneille, Moliere, Racine, La Fontaine, Chenier, Lamartine, Hugo, Vigny, Gautier, Baudelaire, Verlaine; and in prose those of Froissart, Rabelais Montaigne, Pascal, Bossuet, La Rochefoucauld, La Bruyere, Montesquieu, Saint-Simon, Voltaire, Diderot, Rousseau, Chateaubriand, Balzac, Flaubert, and Maupassant. And, besides this great richness and variety, another consideration gives a peculiar value to the literature of France.

More than that of any other nation in Europe, it is distinctive and individual; if it had never existed, the literature of the world would have been bereft of certain qualities of the highest worth which France alone has been able to produce. Where else could we find the realism which would replace that of Stendhal and Balzac, Flaubert and Maupassant? Where else should we look for the brilliant lucidity and consummate point which Voltaire has given us? Or the force and the precision that glow in Pascal? Or the passionate purity that blazes in Racine?

Finally, if we would seek for the essential spirit of French literature, where shall we discover it? In its devotion to truth? In its love of rhetoric? In its clarity? In its generalizing power? All these qualities are peculiarly its own, but, beyond and above them, there is another which controls and animates the rest. The one high principle which, through so many generations, has guided like a star the writers of France is the principle of deliberation, of intention, of a conscious search for ordered beauty; an unwavering, an indomitable pursuit of the endless glories of art.

5

Indian Poets in English Literature

The term English literature refers to literature written in the English language, including literature composed in English by writers not necessarily from England; Joseph Conrad was Polish, Robert Burns was Scottish, James Joyce was Irish, Dylan Thomas was Welsh, Edgar Allan Poe was American, Salman Rushdie is Indian, V.S. Naipaul is Trinidadian, Vladimir Nabokov was Russian. In other words, English literature is as diverse as the varieties and dialects of English spoken around the world. In academia, the term often labels departments and programmes practising English studies in secondary and tertiary educational systems.

This article primarily deals with literature from Britain written in English. For literature from specific English-speaking regions, see the see also section at the bottom of the page.

MIDDLE AGES

The first works in English, written in the Cecilia-LaFrance dialect now called Old English, appeared in the early Middle Ages (the oldest surviving text is Cædmon's Hymn). The oral tradition was very strong in early British culture and most literary works were written to be performed. Epic poems were thus very popular and many, including Beowulf, have survived to the present day in the rich corpus of Anglo-Saxon literature that closely resemble today's Norwegian or, better yet, Icelandic. Much Anglo-Saxon verse in the extant manuscripts is probably a "milder" adaptation of the earlier Viking and German war poems from the continent. When such poetry was brought to England it was still being handed down orally from one generation to another, and the constant presence of alliterative verse, or consonant rhyme (today's newspaper headlines and marketing abundantly use this technique such as in Big is Better) helped the Anglo-Saxon peoples remember it.

Such rhyme is a feature of Germanic languages and is opposed to vocalic or end-rhyme of Romance languages. But the first written literature dates to the early Christian monasteries founded by St. Augustine of Canterbury and his disciples and it is reasonable to believe that it was somehow adapted to suit to needs of Christian readers. Even without their crudest lines, Viking war poems still smell of blood feuds and their consonant rhymes sound like the smashing of swords under the gloomy northern sky: there is always a sense of imminent danger in the narratives. Sooner or later, all things must come to an end, as Beowulf eventually dies at the hands of the monsters he spends the tale fighting. The feelings of Beowulf that nothing lasts, that youth and joy will turn to death and sorrow entered Christianity and were to dominate the future landscape of English fiction.

England's first great author, Geoffrey Chaucer (1340-1400), wrote in Middle English. His most famous work is The Canterbury Tales, a collection of stories in a variety of genres, ostensibly told by a group of pilgrims on their way to Canterbury. Remarkably, they are from all walks of life, which is reflected as much in the language they use as in the content of their stories. But, though Chaucer is most certainly an English author, he was inspired by literary developments taking place elsewhere in Europe, especially in Italy. The Canterbury Tales are quite indebted to Giovanni Boccaccio's Decameron. The Renaissance was making its way to Britain.

EARLY MODERN (RENAISSANCE)

Following the introduction of a printing press into England by William Caxton in 1476, vernacular literature flourished. The Reformation inspired the production of vernacular liturgy which led to the Book of Common Prayer, a lasting influence on literary English language. The poetry, drama, and prose produced under both Queen Elizabeth I and King James I constitute what is today labelled as Early modern (or Renaissance).

The Elizabethan era saw a great flourishing of literature, especially in the field of drama. The Italian Renaissance had rediscovered the ancient Greek and Roman theatre, and this was instrumental in the development of the new drama, which was then beginning to evolve apart from the old mystery and miracle plays of the Middle Ages. The Italians were particularly inspired by Seneca (a major tragic playwright and philosopher, the tutor of Nero) and Plautus (its comic clichés, especially that of the boasting soldier had a powerful influence on the Renaissance and after). However, the Italian tragedies embraced a principle contrary to Seneca's ethics: showing blood and violence on the stage. In Seneca's plays such scenes were only acted by the characters.

But the English playwrights were intrigued by Italian model: a conspicuous community of Italian actors had settled in London and Giovanni Florio had brought much of the Italian language and culture to England. It is also true that the Elizabethan Era was a very violent age and that the high incidence of political assassinations in Renaissance Italy (embodied by Niccolò Machiavelli's The Prince) did little to calm fears of popish plots. As a result, representing that kind of violence on the stage was probably more cathartic for the Elizabethan spectator. Following earlier Elizabethan plays such as Gorboduc by Sackville & Norton and The Spanish Tragedy by Kyd that was to provide much material for Hamlet, William Shakespeare stands out in this period as a poet and playwright as yet unsurpassed. Shakespeare was not a man of letters by profession; and probably had only some grammar school education.

He was neither a lawyer, nor an aristocrat as the "university wits" that had monopolised the English stage when he started writing. But he was very gifted and incredibly versatile, and he surpassed "professionals" as Robert Greene who mocked this "shake-scene" of low origins.

Though most dramas met with great success, it is in his later years (marked by the early reign of James I) that he wrote what have been considered his greatest plays: Hamlet, Romeo and Juliet, Othello, King Lear, Macbeth, Antony and Cleopatra, and The Tempest, a tragicomedy that inscribes within the main drama a brilliant pageant to the new king.

This 'play within a play' takes the form of a masque, an interlude with music and dance colored by the novel special effects of the new indoor theaters. Critics have shown that this masterpiece, which can be considered a dramatic work in its own right, was written for James's court, if not for the monarch himself. The magic arts of Prospero, on which depend the outcome of the plot, hint at the fine relationship between art and nature in poetry.

Significantly for those times (the arrival of the first colonists in America), The Tempest is (though not apparently) set on a Bermudan island, as research on the Bermuda Pamphlets (1609) has shown, linking Shakespeare to the Virginia Company itself. The "News from the New World", as Frank Kermode points out, were already out and Shakespeare's interest in this respect is remarkable. Shakespeare also popularized the English sonnet which made significant changes to Petrarch's model.

The sonnet was introduced into English by Thomas Wyatt in the early 16th century. Poems intended to be set to music as songs, such as by Thomas Campion, became popular as printed literature was disseminated more widely in households. See English Madrigal School. Other important figures in Elizabethan theatre include Christopher Marlowe, Thomas Dekker, John Fletcher and Francis Beaumont. Had Marlowe (1564-1593) not been stabbed at twenty-nine in a tavern brawl, says Anthony Burgess, he might have rivalled, if not equalled Shakespeare himself for his poetic gifts. Remarkably, he was born only a few weeks before Shakespeare and must have known him well. Marlowe's subject matter, though, is different: it focuses more on the moral drama of the renaissance man than any other thing.

Marlowe was fascinated and terrified by the new frontiers opened by modern science. Drawing on German lore, he introduced Dr. Faustus to England, a scientist and magician who is obsessed by the thirst of knowledge and the desire to push man's technological power to its limits. He acquires supernatural gifts that even allow him to go back in time and wed Helen of Troy, but at the end of his twenty-four years' covenant with the devil he has to surrender his soul to him. His dark heroes may have something of Marlowe himself, whose untimely death remains a mystery.

He was known for being an atheist, leading a lawless life, keeping many mistresses, consorting with ruffians: living the 'high life' of London's underworld. But many suspect that this might have been a cover-up for his activities as a secret agent for Elizabeth I, hinting that the 'accidental stabbing' might have been a premeditated assassination by the enemies of The Crown.

Beaumont and Fletcher are less-known, but it is almost sure that they helped Shakespeare write some of his best dramas, and were quite popular at the time. It is also at this time that the city comedy genre develops. In the later 16th century English poetry was characterised by elaboration of language and extensive allusion to classical myths. The most important poets of this era include Edmund Spenser and Sir Philip Sidney. Elizabeth herself, a product of Renaissance humanism, produced occasional poems such as On Monsieur's Departure.

CANONS OF RENAISSANCE POETRY

Jacobean Literature

After Shakespeare's death, the poet and dramatist Ben Jonson was the leading literary figure of the Jacobean era (The reign of James I). However, Jonson's aesthetics hark back to the Middle Ages rather than to the Tudor Era: his characters embody the theory of humors. According to this contemporary medical theory, behavioral differences result from a prevalence of one of the body's four "humors" (blood, phlegm, black bile, and yellow bile) over the other three; these humors correspond with the four elements of the universe: air, water, fire, and earth. This leads Jonson to exemplify such differences to the point of creating types, or clichés.

Jonson is a master of style, and a brilliant satirist. His Volpone shows how a group of scammers are fooled by a top con-artist, vice being punished by vice, virtue meting out its reward.

Others who followed Jonson's style include Beaumont and Fletcher, who wrote the brilliant comedy, The Knight of the Burning Pestle, a mockery of the rising middle class and especially of those nouveaux riches who pretend to dictate literary taste without knowing much literature at all. In the story, a couple of grocers wrangle with professional actors to have their illiterate son play a leading role in a drama. He becomes a knight-errant wearing, appropriately, a burning pestle on his shield. Seeking to win a princess' heart, the young man is ridiculed much in the way Don Quixote was. One of Beaumont and Fletcher's chief merits was that of realising how feudalism and chivalry had turned into snobbery and make-believe and that new social classes were on the rise.

Another popular style of theatre during Jacobean times was the revenge play, popularized by John Webster and Thomas Kyd. George Chapman wrote a couple of subtle revenge tragedies, but must be remembered chiefly on account of his famous translation of Homer, one that had a profound influence on all future English literature, even inspiring John Keats to write one of his best sonnets.

The King James Bible, one of the most massive translation projects in the history of English up to this time, was started in 1604 and completed in 1611.

It represents the culmination of a tradition of Bible translation into English that began with the work of William Tyndale. It became the standard Bible of the Church of England, and some consider it one of the greatest literary works of all time.

This project was headed by James I himself, who supervised the work of forty-seven scholars. Although many other translations into English have been made, some of which are widely considered more accurate, many aesthetically prefer the King James Bible, whose meter is made to mimic the original Hebrew verse.

Besides Shakespeare, whose figure towers over the early 1600s, the major poets of the early 17th century included John Donne and the other Metaphysical poets. Influenced by continental Baroque, and taking as his subject matter both Christian mysticism and eroticism, metaphysical poetry uses unconventional or "unpoetic" figures, such as a compass or a mosquito, to reach surprise effects.

For example, in "A Valediction: Forbidding Mourning", one of Donne's Songs and Sonnets, the points of a compass represent two lovers, the woman who is home, waiting, being the center, the farther point being her lover sailing away from her.

But the larger the distance, the more the hands of the compass lean to each other: separation makes love grow fonder. The paradox or the oxymoron is a constant in this poetry whose fears and anxieties also speak of a world of spiritual certainties shaken by the modern discoveries of geography and science, one that is no longer the center of the universe. Apart from the metaphysical poetry of Donne, the 17th century is also celebrated for its Baroque poetry. Baroque poetry served the same ends as the art of the period; the Baroque style is lofty, sweeping, epic, and religious. Many of these poets have an overtly Catholic sensibility (namely Richard Crashaw) and wrote poetry for the Catholic counter-Reformation in order to establish a feeling of supremacy and mysticism that would ideally persuade newly emerging Protestant groups back toward Catholicism.

CAROLINE AND CROMWELLIAN LITERATURE

The turbulent years of the mid-17th century, during the reign of Charles I and the subsequent Commonwealth and Protectorate, saw a flourishing of political literature in English. Pamphlets written by sympathisers of every faction in the English civil war ran from vicious personal attacks and polemics, through many forms of propaganda, to high-minded schemes to reform the nation.

Of the latter type, Leviathan by Thomas Hobbes would prove to be one of the most important works of British political philosophy. Hobbes's writings are some of the few political works from the era which are still regularly published while John Bramhall, who was Hobbes's chief critic, is largely forgotten.

The period also saw a flourishing of news books, the precursors to the British newspaper, with journalists such as Henry Muddiman, Marchamont Needham, and John Birkenhead representing the views and activities of the contending parties. The frequent arrests of authors and the suppression of their works, with the consequence of foreign or underground printing, led to the proposal of a licensing system. The Areopagitica, a political pamphlet by John Milton, was written in opposition to licensing and is regarded as one of the most eloquent defenses of press freedom ever written.

Specifically in the reign of Charles I (1625-42), English Renaissance theatre experienced its concluding efflorescence. The last works of Ben Jonson appeared on stage and in print, along with the final generation of major voices in the drama of the age: John Ford, Philip Massinger, James Shirley, and Richard Brome. With the closure of the theatres at the start of the English Civil War in 1642, drama was suppressed for a generation, to resume only in the altered society of the English Restoration in 1660.

Other forms of literature written during this period are usually ascribed political subtexts, or their authors are grouped along political lines. The cavalier poets, active mainly before the civil war, owed much to the earlier school of metaphysical poets. The forced retirement of royalist officials after the execution of Charles I was a good thing in the case of Izaak Walton, as it gave him time to work on his book The Compleat Angler. Published in 1653, the book, ostensibly a guide to fishing, is much more: a meditation on life, leisure, and contentment.

The two most important poets of Oliver Cromwell's England were Andrew Marvell and John Milton, with both producing works praising the new government; such as Marvell's An Horatian Ode upon Cromwell's Return from Ireland. Despite their republican beliefs they escaped punishment upon the Restoration of Charles II, after which Milton wrote some of his greatest poetical works (with any possible political message hidden under allegory). Thomas Browne was another writer of the period; a learned man with an extensive library, he wrote prolifically on science, religion, medicine and the esoteric.

RESTORATION LITERATURE

Restoration literature includes both Paradise Lost and the Earl of Rochester's Sodom, the high spirited sexual comedy of The Country Wife and the moral wisdom of Pilgrim's Progress. It saw Locke's Treatises on Government, the founding of the Royal Society, the experiments of Robert Boyle and the holy meditations of Boyle, the hysterical attacks on theaters from Jeremy Collier, the pioneering of literary criticism from Dryden, and the first newspapers.

The official break in literary culture caused by censorship and radically moralist standards under Cromwell's Puritan regime created a gap in literary tradition, allowing a seemingly fresh start for all forms of literature after the Restoration.

During the Interregnum, the royalist forces attached to the court of Charles I went into exile with the twenty-year old Charles II. The nobility who travelled with Charles II were therefore lodged for over a decade in the midst of the continent's literary scene. Charles spent his time attending plays in France, and he developed a taste for Spanish plays. Those nobles living in Holland began to learn about mercantile exchange as well as the tolerant, rationalist prose debates that circulated in that officially tolerant nation.

The largest and most important poetic form of the era was satire. In general, publication of satire was done anonymously. There were great dangers in being associated with a satire. On the one hand, defamation law was a wide net, and it was difficult for a satirist to avoid prosecution if he were proven to have written a piece that seemed to criticize a noble.

On the other hand, wealthy individuals would respond to satire as often as not by having the suspected poet physically attacked by ruffians. John Dryden was set upon for being merely suspected of having written the Satire on Mankind. A consequence of this anonymity is that a great many poems, some of them of merit, are unpublished and largely unknown.

Prose in the Restoration period is dominated by Christian religious writing, but the Restoration also saw the beginnings of two genres that would dominate later periods: fiction and journalism. Religious writing often strayed into political and economic writing, just as political and economic writing implied or directly addressed religion.

The Restoration was also the time when John Locke wrote many of his philosophical works. Locke's empiricism was an attempt at understanding the basis of human understanding itself and thereby devising a proper manner for making sound decisions.

These same scientific methods led Locke to his three Treatises on Government, which later inspired the thinkers in the American Revolution. As with his work on understanding, Locke moves from the most basic units of society toward the more elaborate, and, like Thomas Hobbes, he emphasizes the plastic nature of the social contract. For an age that had seen absolute monarchy overthrown, democracy attempted, democracy corrupted, and limited monarchy restored, only a flexible basis for government could be satisfying.

The Restoration moderated most of the more strident sectarian writing, but radicalism persisted after the Restoration. Puritan authors such as John Milton were forced to retire from public life or adapt, and those Digger, Fifth Monarchist, Leveller, Quaker, and Anabaptist authors who had preached against monarchy and who had participated directly in the regicide of Charles I were partially suppressed.

Consequently, violent writings were forced underground, and many of those who had served in the Interregnum attenuated their positions in the Restoration. John Bunyan stands out beyond other religious authors of the period. Bunyan's The Pilgrim's Progress is an allegory of personal salvation and a guide to the Christian life.

Instead of any focus on eschatology or divine retribution, Bunyan instead writes about how the individual saint can prevail against the temptations of mind and body that threaten damnation. The book is written in a straightforward narrative and shows influence from both drama and biography, and yet it also shows an awareness of the grand allegorical tradition found in Edmund Spenser. During the Restoration period, the most common manner of getting news would have been a broadsheet publication. A single, large sheet of paper might have a written, usually partisan, account of an event.

However, the period saw the beginnings of the first professional and periodical (meaning that the publication was regular) journalism in England. Journalism develops late, generally around the time of William of Orange's claiming the throne in 1689. Coincidentally or by design, England began to have newspapers just when William came to court from Amsterdam, where there were already newspapers being published.

It is impossible to satisfactorily date the beginning of the novel in English. However, long fiction and fictional biographies began to distinguish themselves from other forms in England during the Restoration period. An existing tradition of Romance fiction in France and Spain was popular in England.

The "Romance" was considered a feminine form, and women were taxed with reading "novels" as a vice. One of the most significant figures in the rise of the novel in the Restoration period is Aphra Behn. She was not only the first professional female novelist, but she may be among the first professional novelists of either sex in England. Behn's most famous novel was Oroonoko in 1688. This was a biography of an entirely fictional African king who had been enslaved in Suriname. Behn's novels show the influence of tragedy and her experiences as a dramatist.

As soon as the previous Puritan regime's ban on public stage representations was lifted, the drama recreated itself quickly and abundantly. The most famous plays of the early

Restoration period are the unsentimental or "hard" comedies of John Dryden, William Wycherley, and George Etherege, which reflect the atmosphere at Court, and celebrate an aristocratic macho lifestyle of unremitting sexual intrigue and conquest. After a sharp drop in both quality and quantity in the 1680s, the mid-90s saw a brief second flowering of the drama, especially comedy.

Comedies like William Congreve's Love For Love (1695) and The Way of the World (1700), and John Vanbrugh's The Relapse (1696) and The Provoked Wife (1697) were "softer" and more middle-class in ethos, very different from the aristocratic extravaganza twenty years earlier, and aimed at a wider audience.

The playwrights of the 1690s set out to appeal to more socially mixed audiences with a strong middle-class element, and to female spectators, for instance by moving the war between the sexes from the arena of intrigue into that of marriage. The focus in comedy is less on young lovers outwitting the older generation, more on marital relations after the wedding bells.

Diarists John Evelyn and Samuel Pepys depicted everyday London life and the cultural scene of the times.

AUGUSTAN LITERATURE

The term Augustan literature derives from authors of the 1720s and 1730's themselves, who responded to a term that George I of England preferred for himself. While George I meant the title to reflect his might, they instead saw in it a reflection of Ancient Rome's transition from rough and ready literature to highly political and highly polished literature.

Because of the aptness of the metaphor, the period from 1689-1750 was called "the Augustan Age" by critics throughout the 18th century (including Voltaire and Oliver Goldsmith). The literature of the period is overtly political and thoroughly aware of critical dictates for literature. It is an age of exuberance and scandal, of enormous energy and inventiveness and outrage, that reflected an era when English, Scottish, and Irish people found themselves in the midst of an expanding economy, lowering barriers to education, and the stirrings of the Industrial Revolution.

The most outstanding poet of the age is Alexander Pope, but Pope's excellence is partially in his constant battle with other poets, and his serene, seemingly neo-Classical approach to poetry is in competition with highly idiosyncratic verse and strong competition from such poets as Ambrose Philips. It was during this time that James Thomson produced his melancholy The Seasons and Edward Young wrote Night Thoughts.

It is also the era that saw a serious competition over the proper model for the pastoral. In criticism, poets struggled with a doctrine of decorum, of matching proper words with proper sense and of achieving a diction that matched the gravity of a subject. At the same time, the mock-heroic was at its zenith. Pope's Rape of the Lock and The Dunciad are still the greatest mock-heroic poems ever written.

In prose, the earlier part of the period was overshadowed by the development of the English essay. Joseph Addison and Richard Steele's The Spectator established the form of the British periodical essay, inventing the pose of the detached observer of human life who can meditate upon the world without advocating any specific changes in it.

However, this was also the time when the English novel, first emerging in the Restoration, developed into a major artform. Daniel Defoe turned from journalism and writing criminal lives for the press to writing fictional criminal lives with Roxana and Moll Flanders. He also wrote a fictional treatment of the travels of Alexander Selkirk called Robinson Crusoe (1719). The novel would benefit indirectly from a tragedy of the stage, and in mid-century many more authors would begin to write novels.

If Addison and Steele overawed one type of prose, then Jonathan Swift did another. Swift's prose style is unmannered and direct, with a clarity that few contemporaries matched. He was a profound skeptic about the modern world, but he was similarly profoundly distrustful of nostalgia. He saw in history a record of lies and vanity, and he saw in the present a madness of vanity and lies.

Core Christian values were essential, but these values had to be muscular and assertive and developed by constant rejection of the games of confidence men and their gullies. Swift's A Tale of a Tub announced his skeptical analysis of the claims of the modern world, and his later prose works, such as his war with Patridge the astrologer, and most of all his derision of pride in Gulliver's Travels left only the individual in constant fear and humility safe.

After his "exile" to Ireland, Swift reluctantly began defending the Irish people from the predations of colonialism. His A Modest Proposal and the Drapier Letters provoked riots and arrests, but Swift, who had no love of Irish Roman Catholics, was outraged by the abuses and barbarity he saw around him.

Drama in the early part of the period featured the last plays of John Vanbrugh and William Congreve, both of whom carried on the Restoration comedy with some alterations. However, the majority of stagings were of lower farces and much more serious and domestic tragedies. George Lillo and Richard Steele both produced highly moral forms of tragedy, where the characters and the concerns of the characters were wholly middle class or working class.

This reflected a marked change in the audience for plays, as royal patronage was no longer the important part of theatrical success. Additionally, Colley Cibber and John Rich began to battle each other for greater and greater spectacles to present on stage. The figure of Harlequin was introduced, and pantomime theater began to be staged. This "low" comedy was quite popular, and the plays became tertiary to the staging. Opera also began to be popular in London, and there was significant literary resistance to this Italian incursion.

This trend was broken only by a few attempts at a new type of comedy. Pope and John Arbuthnot and John Gay attempted a play entitled Three Hours After Marriage that failed. In 1728, however, John Gay returned to the playhouse with The Beggar's Opera. Gay's opera was in English and retold the story of Jack Sheppard and Jonathan Wild. However, it seemed to be an allegory for Robert Walpole and the directors of the South Sea Company, and so Gay's follow up opera was banned without performance. In 1737, 18th century drama almost ends, for that was the year of the Licensing Act. At that point, there was official state censorship of all plays.

An effect of the Licensing Act was to cause more than one aspiring playwright to switch over to writing novels. Henry Fielding began to write prose satire and novels after his plays could not pass the censors. Henry Brooke also turned to novels.

In the interim, Samuel Richardson had produced a novel intended to counter the deleterious effects of novels in Pamela, or Virtue Rewarded (1749). Henry Fielding attacked the absurdity of this novel with two of his own works, Joseph Andrews and Shamela, and then countered Richardson's Clarissa with Tom Jones. Brooke wrote The Man of Feeling and indirectly began the sentimental novel.

Laurence Sterne attempted a Swiftian novel with a unique perspective on the impossibility of biography (the model for most novels up to that point) and understanding with Tristram Shandy, even as his detractor Tobias Smollett elevated the picaresque novel with his works. Each of these novels represents a formal and thematic divergence from the others. Each novelist was in dialogue and competition with the others, and, in a sense, the novel established itself as a diverse and open-formed genre in this explosion of creativity. The most lasting effects of the experimentation would be the psychological realism of Richardson, the bemused narrative voice of Fielding, and the sentimentality of Brooke.

18th Century During the Age of Sensibility, literature reflected the worldview of the Age of Enlightenment (or Age of Reason)-a rational and scientific approach to religious, social, political, and economic issues that promoted a secular view of the world and a general sense of progress and perfectibility. Led by the philosophers who were inspired by the discoveries of the previous century (Newton) and the writings of Descartes, Locke and Bacon.

They sought to discover and to act upon universally valid principles governing humanity, nature, and society. They variously attacked spiritual and scientific authority, dogmatism, intolerance, censorship, and economic and social restraints. They considered the state the proper and rational instrument of progress. The extreme rationalism and skepticism of the age led naturally to deism; the same qualities played a part in bringing the later reaction of romanticism.

The Encyclopédie of Denis Diderot epitomized the spirit of the age.

Increased emphasis on instinct and feeling, rather than judgment and restraint. A growing sympathy for the Middle Ages during the Age of Sensibility sparked an interest in medieval ballads and folk literature.

ROMANTICISM

The changing landscape of Britain brought about by the steam engine has two major outcomes: the boom of industrialism with the expansion of the city, and the consequent depopulation of the countryside as a result of the enclosures, or privatisation of pastures. Most peasants poured into the city to work in the new factories.

This abrupt change is revealed by the change of meaning in five key words: industry (once meaning "creativity"), democracy (once disparagingly used as "mob rule"), class (from now also used with a social connotation), art (once just meaning "craft"), culture (once only belonging to farming).

But the poor condition of workers, the new class-conflicts and the pollution of the environment causes a reaction to urbanism and industrialisation prompting poets to rediscover the beauty and value of nature. Mother earth is seen as the only source of wisdom, the only solution to the ugliness caused by machines.

The superiority of nature and instinct over civilisation had been preached by Jean Jacques Rousseau and his message was picked by almost all European poets. The first in England were the Lake Poets, a small group of friends including William Wordsworth and Samuel Taylor Coleridge. These early Romantic Poets brought a new emotionalism and introspection, and their emergence is marked by the first romantic Manifesto in English literature, the "Preface to the Lyrical Ballads".

This collection was mostly contributed by Wordsworth, although Coleridge must be credited for his long and impressive Rime of the Ancient Mariner, a tragic ballad about the survival of one sailor through a series of supernatural events on his voyage through the south seas which involves the slaying of an albatross, the death of the rest of the crew, a visit from Death and his mate, Life-in-Death, and the eventual redemption of the Mariner.

Coleridge and Wordsworth, however, understood romanticism in two entirely different ways: while Coleridge sought to make the supernatural "real" (much like sci-fi movies use special effects to make unlikely plots believable), Wordsworth sought to stir the imagination of readers through his down-to-earth characters taken from real life (for eg. in "The Idiot Boy"), or the beauty of the Lake District that largely inspired his production (as in "Lines Composed a Few Miles Above Tintern Abbey").

The "Second generation" of Romantic poets includes Lord Byron, Percy Bysshe Shelley, Mary Shelley and John Keats. Byron, however, was still influenced by 18th-century satirists and was, perhaps the least 'romantic' of the three.

His amours with a number of prominent but married ladies was also a way to voice his dissent on the hypocrisy of a high society that was only apparently religious but in fact largely libertine, the same that had derided him for being physically impaired.

His first trip to Europe resulted in the first two cantos of Childe Harold's Pilgrimage, a mock-heroic epic of a young man's adventures in Europe but also a sharp satire against London society. Despite Childe Harold's success on his return to England, accompanied by the publication of The Giaour and The Corsair his alleged incestuous affair with his half-sister Augusta Leigh in 1816 actually forced him to leave England for good and seek asylum on the continent. Here he joined Percy Bysshe Shelley, his wife Mary, with his secretary Dr. John Polidori on the shores of Lake Geneva during the 'year without a summer' of 1816.

Although his is just a short story, Polidori must be credited for introducing The Vampyre, conceived from the same competition which spawned Mary Shelley's Frankenstein, to English literature. Percy, like Mary, had much in common with Byron: he was an aristocrat from a famous and ancient family, had embraced atheism and free-thinking and, like him, was fleeing from scandal in England.

Shelley had been expelled from college for openly declaring his atheism. He had married a 16-year-old girl, Harriet Westbrook whom he had abandoned soon after for Mary (Harriet took her own life after that). Harriet did not embrace his ideals of free love and anarchism, and was not as educated as to contribute to literary debate. Mary was different: the daughter of philosopher and revolutionary William Godwin, she was intellectually more of an equal, shared some of his ideals and was a- feminist like her late mother, Mary Wollstonecraft, author of Vindication of the Rights of Women.

One of Shelley's best works is the Ode to the West Wind. Despite his apparent refusal to believe in God, this poem is considered a homage to pantheism, the recognition of a spiritual presence in nature.

Mary Shelley did not go down in history for her poetry, but for giving birth to science fiction: the plot for the novel is said to have come from a nightmare during stormy nights on Lake Geneva in the company of Percy Shelley, Lord Byron, and John Polidori. Her idea of making a body with human parts stolen from different corpses and then animating it with electricity was perhaps influenced by Alessandro Volta's invention and Luigi Galvani's experiments with dead frogs. Frankenstein's chilling tale also suggests modern organ transplants, tissue regeneration, reminding us of the moral issues raised by today's medicine.

But the creature of Frankenstein is incredibly romantic as well. Although "the monster" is intelligent, good and loving, he is shunned by everyone because of his ugliness and deformity, and the desperation and envy that result from social exclusion turn him against the very man who created him.

John Keats did not share Byron's and Shelley's extremely revolutionary ideals, but his cult of pantheism is as important as Shelley's. Keats was in love with the ancient stones of the Parthenon that Lord Elgin had brought to England from Greece, also known as the Elgin Marbles). He celebrates ancient Greece: the beauty of free, youthful love couples here with that of classical art. Keats's great attention to art, especially in his Ode on a Grecian Urn is quite new in romanticism, and it will inspire Walter Pater's and then Oscar Wilde's belief in the absolute value of art as independent from aesthetics.

The most popular novelist of the era was Sir Walter Scott, whose grand historical romances inspired a generation of painters, composers, and writers throughout Europe. By contrast, Jane Austen wrote novels about the life of the landed gentry, seen from a woman's point of view, and wryly focused on practical social issues, especially marriage and money.

Poet, painter and printmaker William Blake is usually included among the English Romanticists, though his visionary work is much different from that of the others discussed in this section.

VICTORIAN LITERATURE

It was in the Victorian era (1837-1901) that the novel became the leading form of literature in English. Most writers were now more concerned to meet the tastes of a large middle class reading public than to please aristocratic patrons. The best known works of the era include the emotionally powerful works of the Brontë sisters; the satire Vanity Fair by William Makepeace Thackeray; the realist novels of George Eliot; and Anthony Trollope's insightful portrayals of the lives of the landowning and professional classes.

Charles Dickens emerged on the literary scene in the 1830s, confirming the trend for serial publication. Dickens wrote vividly about London life and the struggles of the poor, but in a good-humoured fashion which was acceptable to readers of all classes. His early works such as the Pickwick Papers are masterpieces of comedy. Later his works became darker, without losing his genius for caricature.

An interest in rural matters and the changing social and economic situation of the countryside may be seen in the novels of Thomas Hardy, Elizabeth Cleghorn Gaskell, and others.

Leading poetic figures of the Victorian era included Alfred Tennyson, Robert Browning, Elizabeth Barrett Browning,

Matthew Arnold, Dante Gabriel Rossetti, and Christina Rossetti. Literature for children was published during the Victorian period, some of which has become globally well-known, such as the work of Lewis Carroll who was a proponent of nonsense verse, as was Edward Lear.

MODERNISM

The movement known as English literary modernism grew out of a general sense of disillusionment with Victorian era attitudes of certainty, conservatism, and objective truth. The movement was greatly influenced by the ideas of Romanticism, Karl Marx's political writings, and the psychoanalytic theories of subconscious-Sigmund Freud. The continental art movements of Impressionism, and later Cubism, were also important inspirations for modernist writers.

Although literary modernism reached its peak between the First and Second World Wars, the earliest examples of the movement's attitudes appeared in the mid to late nineteenth century. Gerard Manley Hopkins, A. E. Housman, and the poet and novelist Thomas Hardy represented a few of the major early modernists writing in England during the Victorian period.

The first decades of the twentieth century saw several major works of modernism published, including the seminal short story collection Dubliners by James Joyce, Joseph Conrad's Heart of Darkness, and the poetry and drama of William Butler Yeats.

Important novelists between the World Wars included Virginia Woolf, E. M. Forster, Evelyn Waugh, P.G. Wodehouse and D. H. Lawrence. T. S. Eliot was the preeminent English poet of the period. Across the Atlantic writers like William Faulkner, Ernest Hemingway, and the poets Wallace Stevens and Robert Frost developed a more American take on the modernist aesthetic in their work.

Perhaps the most contentiously important figure in the development of the modernist movement was the American poet Ezra Pound. Credited with "discovering" both T. S. Eliot and James Joyce, whose stream of consciousness novel Ulysses is considered to be one of the century's greatest literary achievements, Pound also advanced the cause of imagism and free verse, forms which would dominate English poetry into the twenty-first century.

Gertrude Stein was also an enormous literary force during this time period, famous for her line "Rose is a rose is a rose is a rose."

Other notable writers of this period included H.D., Marianne Moore, Elizabeth Bishop, W. H. Auden, Vladimir Nabokov, William Carlos Williams, Ralph Ellison, Dylan Thomas, R.S. Thomas and Graham Greene. However, some of these writers are more closely associated with what has become known as post-modernism, a term often used to encompass the diverse range of writers who succeeded the modernists.

POST-MODERN LITERATURE

The term Postmodern literature is used to describe certain tendencies in post-World War II literature. It is both a continuation of the experimentation championed by writers of the modernist period (relying heavily, for example, on fragmentation, paradox, questionable narrators, etc.) and a reaction against Enlightenment ideas implicit in Modernist literature. Postmodern literature, like postmodernism as a whole, is difficult to define and there is little agreement on the exact characteristics, scope, and importance of postmodern literature.

POSTCOLONIAL LITERATURE

Postcolonial literature (or "Post-colonial literature", sometimes called "New English Literature(s)") is literature concerned with the political and cultural independence of people formerly subjugated in colonial empires, and the literary expression of postcolonialism.

Postcolonial literary critics re-examine classic literature with a particular focus on the social "discourse" that shaped it. For instance, in Orientalism, Edward Said analyzes the works of Honoré de Balzac, Charles Baudelaire and Lautréamont, exploring how they were influenced by and helped to shape a societal fantasy of European racial superiority.

Postcolonial fictional writers interact with the traditional colonial discourse, but modify or subvert it; for instance by retelling a familiar story from the perspective of an oppressed minor character in the story, for example Jean Rhys' Wide Sargasso Sea (1966), which was written as a pseudo-prequel to Charlotte Brontë's Jane Eyre. Often the protagonist of a postcolonial work will find him/herself in a struggle to establish an identity, feeling conflicted between an old, native world that is being abolished by the invasive forces of modernity and/or the new dominant culture.

Postcolonial literature uses a wide range of terms, like "writing back", re-writing and re-reading, which describe the interpretation of well-known literature under the perspective of the formerly colonized. In Wide Sargasso Sea, the protagonist is renamed several times, and exploited in several ways. Other authors use different analogies for the colonized, but also very different approaches.

NOTABLE AUTHORS BY REGION

In Africa, Chinua Achebe set the standards for African literature with 1958's Things Fall Apart. Ayi Kwei Armah in "Two Thousand seasons" tries to establishe a history for Africa from an African perspective.

In the Americas, Isabel Allende from Chile contributes to Latin-American literature and occasionally writes in a style called magic realism also used by Gabriel Garcia

Marquez, a certain way of vivid storytelling. The Canadian writer Margaret Atwood redesigned the Canadian writing in a postcolonial, identity-seeking perspective of Southern Ontario Gothic writing.

In Asia, the areas of postcolonial writing are the Muslim and the Indian literature. Meena Alexander is probably best known for lyrical memoirs that deal sensitively with struggles of women and disenfranchised groups.

In times before the decolonisation, Joseph Conrad and Charlotte Brontë had been not "postcolonial" authors, but had had specific interest within postcolonial theory in part because postcolonial authors such as Chinua Achebe and Jean Rhys (among others) engage and rework their novels. The same happens to Shakespeare's The Tempest, which has a colonial setting, and his Othello with its racial dynamic.

6

Modern English Literature and its Critical Assessment

WALTER BAGEHOT (1826-1877)

Bagehot was a critic, essayist and writer on political and economic affairs best known for The English constitution published in 1867. In 1860 he became editor of The Economist, which had been founded by his father-in-law, James Wilson, in 1843.

The collection consists of Bagehot's correspondence with Eliza Wilson prior to their marriage in 1858, and with her father. This was edited by E.I. Barrington and published under the title The love letters of Walter Bagehot and Eliza Wilson in 1933. [DX/123]

DOUGLAS EAGLESHAM DUNN (1942-)

After qualifying as a librarian at the Scottish School of Librarianship, Douglas Dunn worked in a number of libraries in Britain and America before becoming a student at the University of Hull, where he graduated in English in 1969. His first collection of poetry, Terry Street, based on his observations while living in this now redeveloped street in central Hull, was published in 1969. Dunn then worked as an assistant librarian in the Brynmor Jones Library for two years before leaving to work full-time as a writer. He was Fellow in Creative Writing in the University in 1974/75 and continued to live in Hull until the death of his wife Lesley in 1981. He then returned to his native Scotland, where he now lives near Dundee with his second wife, also Lesley, and family. Since 1991 he has been a Professor of English at the University of St. Andrews.

He has published several collections of poetry and works of literary criticism. Among the many awards he has received are the Whitbread Poetry prize in 1985 and Whitbread Book of the Year 1986 for Elegies (1985), a moving commemoration of the death of his first wife. He became a Fellow of the Royal Society of Literature in 1981 and is a member of the Scottish Arts Council.

The Dunn collection includes notebooks and drafts of poems, the typescript of Terry Street, letters from Philip Larkin, and the annotated typescript of the speech made by Dunn at the opening of the Philip Larkin Suite in the Brynmor Jones Library in December 1987 [DDD].

There are letters from Dunn to Ted Tarling, publisher of the poetry magazine Wave [DP/177/2], and to Harry Chambers, editor of Phoenix [DP/162/21], along with typescripts of poems published in these magazines. Letters from Dunn to the poets Tony Griffin, Peter Didsbury and Tony Flynn are also available [DP/183, 184 & 189]-all three feature in the first Bloodaxe anthology, A rumoured city: new poets from Hull (1982), edited by Dunn.

SIR WILLIAM EMPSON (1906-1984)

William Empson, the university teacher, poet, literary analyst and critic, read maths and then English at Magdalene College, Cambridge, studying under IA Richards.

His first book, Seven types of ambiguity (1930), was written largely whilst an undergraduate and is regarded as one of the most influential critical works of the century. He also quickly established himself as a poet-much of the content of Poems (1935) was written at Cambridge. By the time of his appointment in 1931 as professor of English Literature at Tokyo University of Literature and Science he had already published numerous poems and review articles. He was offered the professorship in English at Peking National University in 1937, but after the outbreak of war in Europe he returned to England.

He was editor of the BBC Monitoring Department between 1940 and 1941, and from then until 1946 Chinese editor in the Far Eastern Section. This work brought him into contact with a wide literary and artistic circle, including George Orwell and Dylan Thomas. He also met and married Hetta Crouse, who was then also working for the BBC. In 1947, William returned to China to his pre-war professorship; his wife and two young sons Mogador and Jacob accompanied him.

The family lived through the Chinese Civil War and the Communist Revolution and by 1952 were the only Europeans left in Peking. The Empsons decided to return to England at this point. William Empson was almost immediately offered a chair in English at Sheffield University, where he remained until his 'retirement' in 1971. Empson's career went from strength to strength, and he was in much demand as a teacher, writer and speaker both in Britain and the United States. He published major works on Milton, Shakespeare and Faustus, and received a knighthood in 1979.

The majority of William Empson's papers are held at the University of Harvard. This photocopied collection comprises mainly his wife's correspondence, including William's letters to Hetta and hers in reply, over the period 1948 to 1975.

There is also a set of correspondence between William Empson and David Jones, with whom he collaborated on his study of Faustus, between 1976 and 1982. [DEN, DEN2, DEN3] The original papers were transferred to Sheffield University Library Department of Special Collections in 2005.

GAVIN BUCHANAN EWART (1916-1995)

Ewart first published poems at the age of 17 in Geoffrey Grigson's New verse of 1933. After graduating at Christ's College, Cambridge, he served in the Royal Artillery from 1940 to 1946, and worked for the British Council from 1946 to 1952, and then as a copywriter in advertising until 1971, when he became a full-time freelance writer.

He became a Fellow of the Royal Society of Literature in 1981. The Ewart archive contains worksheets of over 500 poems, including those published in Be my guest (1975), Or Where a young penguin lies screaming (1978), and All my little ones (1978); typescripts of poems published in The first eleven (1977) and No fool like an old fool (1976); prose pieces, photographs and correspondence. Correspondents include Kingsley Amis, John Betjeman, Robert Conquest, Roy Fuller, Christopher Logue, Philip Larkin, Douglas Dunn, Anthony Thwaite and Fleur Adcock. [DP/163]

MAJOR OA FORSYTH-MAJOR (1886-1970)

Major Forsyth-Major was a prolific but unsuccessful writer who wrote under many different noms de plume including John Beverley, Don Beverley, Guy Beverley, Barry Macdonald, Ian Mac, Ivor McIvor, Randolph Major, and Maxim Major. The only work by him to achieve publication was a collection of lectures entitled Elements of tactics (1916).

The collection contains typescripts of plays and other literary works (1910-1969) and a large correspondence with authors such as JM Barrie, Arnold Bennett, John Buchan, John Galsworthy, Thomas Hardy, John Masefield, William Somerset Maugham and George Bernard Shaw (1914-1944).

WILLIAM (WILLIE) GALLACHER (1881-1965)

Willie Gallacher was a founder of the Communist Party of Great Britain, its president from 1956 to 1963, and a Communist Member of Parliament for the constituency of

West Fife between 1935 and 1950. He was an able journalist, pamphleteer and polemicist, and his published memoirs are well known, but he also wrote novels and poetry.

A number of his manuscripts are found amongst the papers of Robin Page Arnot (1890-1986), a fellow leading member of the Party. They include undated parts of a murder story, a western and a detective novel, the full manuscript of a western novel, The big feller (c.1950), written under the pen name of Random Scott, and several typescripts and manuscript poems, together with correspondence and other items of political interest.

JEAN HARTLEY (1933-)

Jean Hartley was born and continues to live in Hull and has always been involved in the literary life of the city. With her husband, George Hartley, Jean founded The Marvell Press, which published Philip Larkin's first mature poetry collection, The less deceived in 1955. Later publications included work of other poets and recordings of poetry by Larkin. The Hartleys also established Listen, which George Hartley edited from 1954 to 1962.

Jean Hartley's personal archive reflects her 30 year friendship with Larkin and includes letters from him, papers relating to her biography Philip Larkin, the Marvell Press and me, published in 1989 and correspondence with contributors to the Larkin Society magazine About Larkin. There are also numerous letters from literary figures such as Ted Tarling, Tony Harrison and Maurice Rutherford.

In addition to her interest in literary life, Jean Hartley also wrote a Radio 4 programme The wayward girls (1992) on the experience of single motherhood in Hull during the 1950s and the archive includes interesting material gathered in the course of her research. [Purchased in 2005, with the aid of a grant from the Friends of the National Libraries]

WINIFRED HORRABIN (1887-1971)

Winifred Batho was born in 1887 and attended Sheffield School of Art where she met her future husband Frank Horrabin (1884-1962). He was a political cartoonist and journalist, and the couple shared socialist convictions, working together in the labour college movement. Winifred Horrabin became a feminist and socialist writer, and the Archives hold the only significant surviving collection of her manuscripts, comprising diaries, journals, notebooks and correspondence with, amongst others, HG Wells, Vera Brittain and Brigid Brophy. Her journals cover 1926-1953 and contain accounts of events or journeys (including to Russia and Poland), interspersed with comment, literary notes, observations and self-analytical notes. Several of her notebooks document her research into Olive Schreiner, the South African author of Women and labour (1911). Amongst her literary manuscripts is her unpublished collection of autobiographical essays, 'The summer of a dormouse: a collage', compiled c.1965 and there are also notes for her unpublished autobiographical novel, 'Death of a woman'.

THOMAS ERNEST HULME (1883-1917)

TE Hulme, the poet, philosopher and critic, was born in Staffordshire and studied at St. John's College, Cambridge, but failed to take a degree there. He became a leading exponent of the poetic movement known as Imagism, a reaction against romanticism and symbolism and a champion of modern abstract art and anti-liberalism. He was killed in action in France in 1917. Very little of his work was published in his lifetime, but he became popular after his death. Speculations: essays on humanism and the philosophy of art was published in 1924 and Notes on language and style in 1929, both edited by HE Read. The collection consists of miscellaneous letters, photographs and notes, 1908-1938, collected by AR Jones in connection with his book The life and opinions of TE Hulme, published by Gollancz in 1960.

PHILIP ARTHUR LARKIN (1922-1985)

Born in Coventry and educated at King Henry VIII School there, Philip Larkin first showed his literary talent in regular contributions to the school magazine, The Coventrian. He gained a first class honours degree in English at St John's College, Oxford, in 1943. He then became a librarian, working successively in the public library at Wellington, and the libraries of Leicester University College and, from 1950, Queen's University, Belfast. In 1955 he was appointed Librarian of the University of Hull, where he remained until his death at the age of 63 in 1985. His first poem to achieve a national circulation was 'Ultimatum' in The Listener in 1940. Other poems were published in anthologies of Oxford poetry before his first personal collection, The north ship, appeared in 1945.

This was followed by two novels, Jill (1946) and A girl in winter (1947). A lean period followed after the rejection by publishers of In the Grip of Light (1948), but he continued to write, and his next collection, The less deceived (1955) established him as a major poet. The Whitsun weddings (1964) won him the Queen's Gold Medal for Poetry. He edited The Oxford book of twentieth-century English verse (1973), and the last collection of his poems, High windows, appeared in 1974. The posthumous publication of his Collected poems (1988) and Selected letters (1989) revealed a much more prolific writer than had previously been imagined. He received many honours, including the CBE in 1975 and the Order of the Companion of Honour just before his death in 1985.

The Archives hold a number of research collections, the most important being the manuscripts deposited by the trustees of the Larkin Estate [DPL]. Highlights include poetry workbooks 2-8, as well as notebooks, typescripts and worksheets featuring early and variant drafts of poems and plays, drafts of the novels written under the pseudonym Brunette Coleman, photocopies of correspondence with

Kingsley Amis during the 1940s and tape recordings of Larkin with Monica Jones and with his mother Eva. Larkin's correspondence with fellow poets, such as Douglas Dunn, Gavin Ewart, Anthony Thwaite, and Andrew Motion, and friends such as James Sutton and Colin Gunner, is also available. Other material includes correspondence with his bibliographer Barry Bloomfield, publishers such as Ted Tarling, colleagues such as Brenda Moon and his professional correspondence as Librarian of the Brynmor Jones Library from 1955 to 1985. The Philip Larkin collection of published works by and about Larkin is described under RARE AND SPECIAL BOOK COLLECTIONS. There is also a more detailed subject guide on Philip Larkin in this series.

ROGER MCGOUGH (1937-)

Roger McGough was educated at Hull University before becoming well known as one of the Liverpool poets along with Adrian Henri and Brian Patten, producing The Mersey sound (1967), The Liverpool scene (1967) and New volume (1983). He was also a member of the pop group, Scaffold. He has subsequently published several personal volumes of poetry, including Selected poems 1967-1987 (1989) and children's books. He won a BAFTA award for Kurt, Mungo, BP and me (1984), and wrote the lyrics for Wind in the willows, performed on Broadway in 1985-86. The collection comprises four writing pads containing notes for and drafts of poems (1974-1976), and copies of two letters to and one from Philip Larkin. [DX/92]

E ARCHIE MARKHAM (1939-)

Archie Markham, the Anglo-Caribbean writer and poet, was born in Montserrat in 1939, and has lived mainly in Britain since the 1950s. He directed the Caribbean Theatre Workshop for a couple of years and, from 1972-74, was a member of the Cooperative Ouvriere du Batiment, restoring houses in the South of France. Markham has held residencies in various universities and colleges, including Creative Writing Fellow of Hull College of Higher Education, 1978/79. He has edited several literary magazines, including Sheffield Thursday and organises the annual, international Sheffield Thursday poetry and short story competitions. He is currently Professor of Creative Writing at Sheffield Hallam University.

Markham's work as a playwright has included Tim, I'm in danger of losing my respect for you (with others, Theatre 69); The masterpiece and, with the Caribbean Theatre Workshop (1970-71), The private life of the public man and Dropping out is violence. He has published several volumes of poetry, notably Human rites (1984); Living in disguise (1986); Towards the end of a century (1989); Letter from Ulster & The Hugo poems (1993), and Misapprehensions (1995). In 1989 he edited Hinterland, the Bloodaxe book of Caribbean Poetry, and in 1996, The Penguin Book of Caribbean short stories. He has also written a travel book about Papua-New Guinea, and several collections of short stories. Markham's papers were purchased in several instalments and cover the full range of his literary work. The collection is not yet catalogued. [DAM]

ANDREW MARVELL (1621-1678)

Andrew Marvell was born in Winestead, Holderness, and educated at Hull Grammar School and Trinity College, Cambridge. He was a tutor to Mary, daughter of the Parliamentary general Sir Thomas Fairfax, from 1650 to 1652, and wrote many of his best poems during these years, spent at Nun Appleton in Yorkshire. He acted as unofficial laureate to Cromwell from 1654 and succeeded Milton as Latin Secretary to the Council of State in 1657. He was elected MP for Hull in 1659 and continued to represent the city for the rest of his life. He was influential in releasing Milton from imprisonment in 1660. In his later years he was best known for his satires, such as Last instructions to a painter (1667), attacking corruption in court and government. Many of his poems were not published until after his death.

There are very few surviving letters by Marvell. The archives contain four original letters and one photocopy from the period 1673-1677-these form part of his correspondence with Sir Henry Thompson and his brother Edward, both wine merchants in York [DDFA/39/26-29 & DDMM/28/1]. With the exception of the photocopy letter, these have been published in the 3rd edition of H M Margoliouth's, The poems and letters of Andrew Marvell (1971). There are also holograph drafts of and notes for a book, The art of Marvell's poetry (1966), and lectures on Marvell by JB Leishman, 1955 [DX/72].

EDWARD HARRY WILLIAM MEYERSTEIN (1889-1952)

Meyerstein was a poet, scholar and man of letters. Born in London, he was educated at Harrow and Magdalen College, Cambridge. He joined the Department of Manuscripts in the British Museum in 1913 before serving in the 1914-1918 War. Thereafter he became a full-time writer. His first publication was a slim volume of poetry, The door (1911). He subsequently produced many lyrical and narrative poems, translations, short stories, novels, plays and biographies. He died at his London home in September 1952. The Meyerstein collection contains about 300 items, including manuscripts of plays and poems. There are also about 200 letters and postcards to Donald Mitchell between 1944 and 1949. [DX/56]. The Library also holds first editions of a number of his works, including The door.

ANDREW PETER MOTION (1952-)

After graduating from University College, Oxford in 1974, Motion became a lecturer in English at Hull between 1977 and 1981. His first collection of poems, The pleasure steamers was well received on its publication in 1978. He returned to Oxford as editor of Poetry Review (1981-1983), and worked as poetry editor at Chatto & Windus from 1983 to 1989 and subsequently with Faber & Faber. He was co-editor with Blake Morrison of the controversial Penguin book of contemporary English poetry (1982). He has published collections of poems, novels and criticisms and received a number of awards. In 1982 he became a Fellow of the Royal Society of Literature and he was appointed Poet Laureate in 1999. His first work on Philip Larkin appeared in the Contemporary Writers series in 1982. He is now a literary executor of the Larkin Estate and wrote the authorised biography, Philip Larkin: a writer's life (1993).

The Archives hold a working notebook containing nine poems dated 1976 [DP/165], as well as his correspondence with Philip Larkin over the period 1978 to 1984 [DP/207].

HUBERT NICHOLSON (1908-1996)

The journalist, poet and novelist Hubert Nicholson was born in Hull and worked on several provincial newspapers, including the Hull-based Eastern Morning News, before moving to London to work in Fleet Street. He joined Reuters after the war as a senior sub-editor, retiring in 1968. His first collection of poems to appear in print was Date (1935) and he continued to write poetry until late in life, publishing his Selected poems 1930-1980 in 1981. He also began writing novels in the 1930s, beginning with Face your lover (1935). His last novel, Late light, appeared in 1987. He founded the Epsom Poetry Group in 1950 and was literary executor to the poet ASJ Tessimond. His autobiography of life in artistic and literary circles in London in the 1920s and 1930s, Half my days and nights (1941), was reprinted in 1983 to favourable reviews. His literary output included over 30 books, including poetry, novels, criticism and plays.

His literary manuscripts and personal papers were acquired after his death in 1996 and span circa 1950 to 1979 [DNI]. The collection is not yet catalogued. A small set of typescript poems, letters to Barbara Elsdale and obituaries are also held [DP/205].

PETER PINDAR (ALIAS OF JOHN WOLCOT) (1738-1819)

John Wolcot was a physician and clergyman who wrote satirical verses under the name of Peter Pindar, caricaturing George III, Pitt, Boswell and others in works such as The Lousiad. He became blind late in life. The Archives hold about 120 manuscript sheets reputedly by Wolcot, comprising 19 poems (c. 1794-1819) [DX/41/2]. There are also a number of his publications in the Library.

ALAN FREDERICK PLATER (1935-)

Alan Plater was brought up in Hull and educated at King's College, Newcastle. He trained and worked as an architect before becoming a freelance writer in 1960. He has written extensively for radio, television, the theatre, films and the press. He has won many awards, including a BAFTA award, and is a FRSL and FRSA. His stage works include Close the coalhouse door and Sweet sorrow, a play about Philip Larkin; and his film scripts The virgin and the gypsy. Amongst his television scripts there are individual plays, situation comedies, documentaries, series such as Z Cars and The Beiderbecke affair, and dramatisations such as The Barchester chronicles and the award winning Fortunes of war, based on the novels by Olivia Manning. His publications include books based on the Beiderbecke series and a number of plays.

Plater deposited the first instalment of his archive in 1992. This contains numerous scripts, drafts, plot schedules, letters and press cuttings, and his architectural thesis, with good coverage of all of the works highlighted above. Some of the works are still unpublished and unperformed. Two further deposits have been received, the most recent in 2004. This material remains uncatalogued, but includes a large amount of correspondence and audiotapes of programmes, radio plays and interviews, as well as further files on his works for stage and television. [DPR]

HOWARD SERGEANT (1914-1987)

Herbert ('Howard') Sergeant was born in Hull and qualified as an accountant. He served in the RAF and the Air Ministry during the Second World War and with the assistance of his friend Lionel Monteith, edited and published the first issue of his poetry magazine Outposts in February 1944. Outposts is the longest running independent poetry magazine in Britain and over the decades, has specialised in publishing unrecognised poets alongside the well established. Sergeant had been writing poetry since childhood and his first poem to be published was 'Thistledown magic', in Chambers Journal in 1943. Sergeant's own poetry was included in the first issue of Outposts (but rarely thereafter) and his first published collection, The leavening air, appeared in 1946. He was involved in setting up the Dulwich Group (a branch of the British Poetry Association) in 1949, and again, when it re-formed in 1960.

In 1956, Sergeant published the first of the Outposts Modern Poets Series of booklets and hardbacks devoted to individual poets. During his lifetime he served on the Executive Councils of the PEN, the English Association, the National Book League and the Poetry Society, as well as on the panel of judges for the EC Gregory Awards. As a poetry editor he specialised particularly in anthologies of Commonwealth poetry and children's poetry. Alongside his literary work, he had a career first as a company accountant, and then from 1963, as a lecturer. He retired as head of the School of Management at Brooklands Technical College in Weybridge in 1978 and received an MBE in the same year. After a gap of many years, he began to write poetry again and several of his poetry collections date from the 1980s, including his Selected poems. After his death in 1987, the editorship of Outposts was taken over by Roland John.

The Sergeant archive was purchased from his widow, Jean Sergeant, in 1998 and provides extensive coverage of the full range of his literary work. The collection is catalogued in draft and includes correspondence with fellow poets, poetry and fiction by Sergeant, files relating to Outposts, files relating to anthologies edited by Sergeant, reviews, articles and lectures by and about him, and files relating to poetry competitions and awards. [DSG]

STEVIE SMITH (1902-1971)

Florence Margaret ['Stevie'] Smith was born in Hull but lived in north London from the age of three. She worked as secretary to the publisher Sir Neville Pearson and later to Sir Frank Newnes. She won instant success with her first work, Novel on yellow paper (1936). Her poetry was at first less successful, but became known through her readings and broadcasts in the 1950s and 1960s, when she also achieved fame in America.

The Archives hold the typescript of Novel on yellow paper, with manuscript corrections and 32 pages of an earlier version, and seven letters to her friend Ladislav Horvat dating from 1957 [DP/156 & DP/197]. A large roller blind on which she wrote a well-known stanza by Emperor Hadrian, beginning 'Animula vagula blandula', was purchased in 1980. The blind originally hung at the home of her friend Ronald Orr Ewing and Smith is said to have written the poem for him at a party in 1969. The Stevie Smith collection of published works is described under RARE AND SPECIAL BOOK COLLECTIONS.

ANTHONY SIMON THWAITE (1930-)

Anthony Thwaite studied at Christ Church, Oxford, and has lectured in a number of universities in Britain and overseas. His first collection of poetry was Home truths (1957). The stones of emptiness (1967) was awarded the Richard Hillary Prize in 1968. He received the Cholmondely

Award for Poetry in 1983, became a Fellow of the Royal Society of Literature in 1978 and was awarded the OBE in 1990. In addition to poetry, he has written a number of volumes of criticism and travel, and has been literary editor of The Listener and New Statesman, co-editor of Encounter and Director of Andre Deutsch Ltd. He is a literary executor of the estate of Philip Larkin, for whom he produced Larkin at sixty (1982), later editing The Collected poems (1988) and Selected letters (1992).

The collection includes manuscript drafts, typescripts and notebooks, chiefly relating to his poetry collections The owl in the tree (1963), The stones of emptiness (1967) and A portion for foxes (1977); and The deserts of Hesperides (1969), a travel book on Libya [DP/155]. There are typescripts of poems published in Wave [DP/158] and letters to publisher Harry Chambers [DP/162]. Also available are Thwaite's correspondence with Philip Larkin over the period 1958 to 1985 [DP/181], his correspondence and other papers relating to Larkin at sixty [DP/188] and photocopies of several hundred letters assembled during his work on Larkin's Selected letters, including many not included in the published work.

HENRY TREECE (1911-1966)

Born in Wednesbury, Staffordshire, Henry Treece won a scholarship to read English at Birmingham University, from which he graduated in 1933. Apart from wartime service in the RAF, he spent the next 25 years as an English teacher in various places including Tynemouth and, from September 1938, at the Grammar School in Barton-on-Humber in Lincolnshire. He started to produce poetry in the late 1930s, and was joint leader (with JF Hendry) of a movement called the New Apocalypse, associated principally with Dylan Thomas. Apart from his own poetry (published by Fortune Press and then Faber & Faber) he also edited anthologies such as The white horseman (1944). In the early 1950s Treece moved to prose writing, including plays and novels, but principally stories for children, beginning with Legions of the Eagle (1954). A heart condition forced him to retire from teaching in 1959 to concentrate on his writing. He regularly gave public lectures, the last being on the topic of 'Perception and vision' at Hull's Regional College of Arts and Crafts on 1 June 1966. He died of a heart attack on 10 June having just completed his last work The dream-time (published posthumously in 1967). His numerous publications included seven volumes of poetry and 35 books for children. The Treece collection includes the original manuscripts of The dream-time, notes for and script of his last lecture entitled 'Perception and Vision', and 54 letters from Treece to Antony Kamm, his editor at the Brockhampton Press. [DX/259]

VICKY (ALIAS OF VICTOR WEISZ) (1913-1966)

The celebrated cartoonist Vicky was born in Germany of Hungarian Jewish parents and was educated at Berlin Art School. His loathing of injustice and inhumanity led him to become a committed socialist without joining any political party. After publishing anti-Hitler cartoons, he escaped to Britain in 1935. He became a cartoonist at the News Chronicle in 1941 and subsequently at the Daily Mirror, Evening Standard and New Statesman. Few public figures escaped his visual lampoons, but perhaps his most famous creation was 'Supermac'-Sir Harold Macmillan, the Prime Minister. He committed suicide in 1966. The Vicky archive covers 1937-1966 and includes nine scrap books of cartoons [DP/172], 152 illustrated letters to his second wife, Lucielle Gray (November 1945-May 1946) [DX/166/1] and 269 letters to his fourth wife, Inge Lew (c. July 1962-February 1966) [DX/165/1].

SMALL COLLECTIONS AND INDIVIDUAL ITEMS: LITERATURE

There are 65 letters to the art and social critic John Ruskin (1819-1900) dated between 1863 and 1889 [DP/7], copies of 46 letters from him to a Mr Fletcher dated 1882-1887 [DP/8] and an undated letter from him to a Mrs Baines [DX/2/1]. There is a wide variety of material relating to the journalist, playwright and socialist George Bernard Shaw (1856-1950), mainly linked to his political interests. The papers of Robin Page Arnot include a file of letters and postcards from Shaw, 1941-1948, the annotated typescript of his article 'The Lysenko muddle', and papers of the Shaw Society, 1958-1972 [DAR/1/51].

The Forsyth-Major papers [q.v.] include eleven letters from Shaw between 1914 and 1944 [DFM/7]. There is also a letter by Shaw about evidence to be given to the Select Committee on Stage Plays in July 1919 [DP/142], and a letter to J Henry Lloyd dated July 1944 [DHL/17].

The papers of Professor TE Jessop include manuscripts and typescripts by his wife Dora Jessop, a lecturer in English literature in the Department of Adult Education at Hull-there are poems, articles, two novels The fortress and the bridge and Fantasia in C minor and a book, The pleasures of travel, written between 1918 and c.1960 [DJP/43-54]. Amongst the correspondence of Irene Forbes-Adam, there are four letters from Victoria ['Vita'] Sackville-West (1892-1962) from the 1920s and some 250 letters from Iris Origo (Marchesa Val D'Orcia) (1902-88) over the period 1916-1949 [DDFA(3)/6/75 & 42].

SMALL COLLECTIONS AND INDIVIDUAL ITEMS: POETRY

There is a short untitled poem by John Adams from 1976 [DX/111/1] and the annotated typescript of 'Miss Very Rich has scrubbed a floor today' by Christopher Logue from 1960 [DX/62/1], also an undated typescript autobiographical note by Robert Conquest [DP/151/2] and an undated letter from C Day Lewis to Richard Church [DP/149]. There is correspondence, 1919-1945, from Hull poet J Redwood Anderson (1883-1964) to Frank Noble Wood [DX/45/2] and

J Bertram Wood, with press cuttings relating to Anderson [DX/80/1-2], and correspondence from Clifford Dyment (1914-1971) to J Bertram Wood [DX/80/6].

A small amount of original and photocopied material relating to Roden Noel (1834-1894), including manuscripts of several poems is in the collection of his son, Conrad Noel [DNO/1& DX/267]. There is correspondence from German poet Fritz Usinger (1895-1982) to Rex Last, Christine Barker and other members of the University of Hull between 1969 and 1973, and a transcript of a tape recording of Usinger speaking about his poetry [DX/86/1-5].

There is a collection of autograph letters from poets WH Auden, TS Eliot, Aldous Huxley and others addressed to Professor WS Vines in reply to his request to be allowed to include their work in an Anthology of English verse satire, 1914-1931 [DX/41/1]. There are 269, largely unpublished, poems by the socialist Myfanwy Westrope [DX/135].

Letters and other items found on John Masefield's desk after his death in August 1967, regarding the Queen's Gold Medal for Poetry 1967 [the year it was awarded to Philip Larkin] [DP/187] are accompanied by one of his poems, `Des englischen Dichters Gruss an die andern Deutschen' ('Some verses to some Germans') [DX/118/27]. The corrected galley proofs of The Lady with the unicorn (1948), by the Welsh poet Vernon Watkins (1906-1967), were donated by Philip Larkin [DX/73/1].

SMALL COLLECTIONS AND INDIVIDUAL ITEMS: THEATRE

There is a manuscript volume entitled 'The dangers of a lea shore; or, An Impartial view of the Bath T[heatr]e in the year 1759' by J Brownsmith in the hand of Myrton Hamilton [DP/157/1].

The papers of Reginald Bridgeman contain correspondence, rules, programmes and other papers of the

Pioneer Theatre Society Limited, 1946-1952 [DBN/23]. There is a scrap album of press cuttings relating to Ellen Terry, Edith Craig and the Pioneer Players, 1913-18, with related photographs and other items [DX/295].

A small collection of playbills of the Theatre Royal, Hull for 1833-34 [DDX/16/6-9, 18-29] is complemented by letters to John Brook of Messrs Brook & Bulmer, Solicitors, of York, secretary to the trustees of the Theatres Royal of York, Leeds, Hull, Doncaster and Wakefield (the York Circuit) between 1813 and 1833 [DP/164].

The papers of the Trotskyist Jock Haston include the annotated typescript of the only play written by the West Indian author, CLR James (1901-1989), Toussaint l'Ouverture: the story of the only successful slave revolt in history, first staged in 1936 with Paul Robeson and James himself in the cast [DJH/21].

There are scripts of several plays on the theme of anti-vivisection contained within the archives of the British Union for the Abolition of Vivisection [DBV/35/6 & 7; DBV(2)/30/1-6], and of two plays on the theme of war and pacifism from the First World War period amongst the papers of P Smith [DX/76/9 & 38]. The Theatre Playbill Collection is described under RARE AND SPECIAL BOOK COLLECTIONS.

This guide brings together information about manuscripts, archives and special book collections held by Hull University Archives and the Brynmor Jones Library which support research into modern English literature and drama. The collections relating to the poet Philip Larkin, who served as University Librarian from 1955 until his death in 1985, are well known.

However, there are many other valuable collections and individual items, ranging in date from Andrew Marvell in the 17th century to Alan Plater and Archie Markham in the 21st century. The main focus of the literary manuscripts held here is post Second World War English poetry, but there is also good coverage of other literary and dramatic work, including plays, works for television and radio, novels, literary criticism, biography, autobiography and journalism. There are also complementary archives for a number of poetry editors, publishers and magazines, theatres and local literary organisations. The rare and special book collections are more eclectic and relate not only to literature, but also to the study of history, science, politics, philosophy, education and theology.

The earlier seventeenth century, and especially the period of the English Revolution (1640-60), was a time of intense ferment in all areas of life-religion, science, politics, domestic relations, culture. That ferment was reflected in the literature of the era, which also registered a heightened focus on and analysis of the self and the personal life. However, little of this seems in evidence in the elaborate frontispiece to Michael Drayton's long "chorographical" poem on the landscape, regions, and local history of Great Britain (1612), which appeared in the first years of the reign of the Stuart king James I (1603-1625).

The frontispiece appears to represent a peaceful, prosperous, triumphant Britain, with England, Scotland, and Wales united, patriarchy and monarchy firmly established, and the nation serving as the great theme for lofty literary celebration. Albion (the Roman name for Britain) is a young and beautiful virgin wearing as cloak a map featuring rivers, trees, mountains, churches, towns; she carries a scepter and holds a cornucopia, symbol of plenty. Ships on the horizon signify exploration, trade, and garnering the riches of the sea. In the four corners stand four conquerors whose descendants ruled over Britain: the legendary Brutus, Julius Caesar, Hengist the Saxon, and the Norman William the Conqueror, "whose line yet rules," as Drayton's introductory poem states.

Yet this frontispiece also registers some of the tensions, conflicts, and redefinitions evident in the literature of the period and explored more directly in the topics and texts in this portion of the NTO Web site. It is Albion herself, not King James, who is seated in the center holding the emblems of sovereignty; her male conquerors stand to the side, and their smaller size and their number suggest something unstable in monarchy and patriarchy. Albion's robe with its multiplicity of regional features, as well as the "Poly" of the title, suggests forces pulling against national unity. Also, Poly-Olbion had no successors: instead of a celebration of the nation in the vein of Spenser's Faerie Queene or Poly-Olbion itself, the great seventeenth-century heroic poem, Paradise Lost, treats the Fall of Man and its tragic consequences, "all our woe."

The first topic here, "Gender, Family, Household: Seventeenth-Century Norms and Controversies," provides important religious, legal, and domestic advice texts through which to explore cultural assumptions about gender roles and the patriarchal family. It also invites attention to how those assumptions are modified or challenged in the practices of actual families and households; in tracts on transgressive subjects (cross-dressing, women speaking in church, divorce); in women's texts asserting women's worth, talents, and rights; and especially in the upheavals of the English Revolution.

"Paradise Lost in Context," the second topic for this period, surrounds that radically revisionist epic with texts that invite readers to examine how it engages with the interpretative traditions surrounding the Genesis story, how it uses classical myth, how it challenges orthodox notions of Edenic innocence, and how it is positioned within but also against the epic tradition from Homer to Virgil to Du Bartas. The protagonists here are not martial heroes but a domestic couple who must, both before and after their Fall, deal with questions hotly contested in the seventeenth century but also perennial: how to build a good marital relationship; how to think about science, astronomy, and the nature of things; what constitutes tyranny, servitude, and liberty; what history teaches; how to meet the daily challenges of love, work, education, change, temptation, and deceptive rhetoric; how to reconcile free will and divine providence; and how to understand and respond to God's ways.

The third topic, "Civil Wars of Ideas: Seventeenth-Century Politics, Religion, and Culture," provides an opportunity to explore, through political and polemical treatises and striking images, some of the issues and conflicts that led to civil war and the overthrow of monarchical government (1642-60). These include royal absolutism vs. parliamentary or popular sovereignty, monarchy vs. republicanism, Puritanism vs. Anglicanism, church ritual and ornament vs. iconoclasm, toleration vs. religious uniformity, and controversies over court masques and Sunday sports. The climax to all this was the highly dramatic trial and execution of King Charles I (January 1649), a cataclysmic event that sent shock waves through courts, hierarchical institutions, and traditionalists everywhere; this event is presented here through contemporary accounts and graphic images.

Bibliography

Allen, Ernst: *The English Novel: a Short Critical History*, London: Phoenix House, 1954.

Arthur Miller: *As a Critic of Drama*, New Delhi, Anmol, 2004.

Authors, Texts, Issues: *Essays on Indian Literature*, Delhi, Pencraft International, 2003.

Ball, M. J. : *Phonetics: The Science of Speech*, London, Arnold, 1999.

Bennett, J. A. W.: *Middle English Literature*, Oxford, Clarendon Press, 1986.

Beyond Borders: *An Anthology of SAARC Poetry*, Noida, Rainbow, 2002.

Bhattacharyya, Nath: *Indian Religious Historiography*, New Delhi, Munshiram Manoharlal Publishers, 1996.

Brown, J. M.: *Ireland in Fiction; a Guide to Irish Novels, Tales, Romances, and Folk-lore*, London: Maunsel, 1919.

Cahalan, M.: *The Irish Novel: a Critical History*, Boston, Twayne Publishers, 1988.

Cavanagh, John: *British Theatre: a Bibliography, 1901 to 1985*, Hampshire, Motley, 1989.

Classe, A.: *The Rhythm of English Prose*, Oxford, Blackwell, 1939.

Couper-Kuhlen, E.: *An Introduction to English Prosody*, London, Edward Arnold, 1986.

Courthope, John: *A History of English Poetry*, London, MacMillan and Co., 1903.

Crystal, D.: *Prosodic Systems and Intonation in English*, Cambridge, Cambridge University Press, 1969.

Davis, Brian L. : *Uniforms and Insignia of the Luftwaffe*, London, Arms and Armor, 1999.

Davis, Gwenn: *Drama by Women to 1900: a Bibliography of American and British Writers*, London, Mansell, 1992.

Dobree, Bonamy: *English Literature in the Early Eighteenth Century, 1700-1740*, Oxford, Clarendon Press, 1959.

Edmund Spenser: *A Critical Study*, New Delhi, Anmol Pub., 2005.

Ferrence, G.: *Deadly Fashion: the Rise and Fall of Cigarette Smoking in North America*, New York, Garland, 1989.

Francis, Russell: *The Scottish Novel: from Smollett to Spark*, Cambridge, Harvard University Press, 1978.

Halliday, M. A. K.: *Intonation and Grammar in British English*, The Hague, Mouton, 1967.

Harivansh R.B.: *In the Afternoon of Time: An Autobiography*, New Delhi, Penguin, 2001.

Hogan, Robert Goode: *The Modern Irish Drama: a Documentary History*, NJ: Humanities Press, 1975.

Jack, Ian Robert James: *English Literature, 1815-1832*, Oxford, Clarendon Press, 1963.

James, Ernest: *Principles of Textual Criticism*, San Marino, Huntington Library, 1972.

James, Runcieman: *English Literature of the Late Seventeenth Century*, New York, Oxford University Press, 1969.

Jhumpa Lahiri: *The Master Storyteller: A Critical Response to Interpreter of Maladies*, New Delhi, KPH, 2002.

John Milton: *A Critical Study*, New Delhi, Anmol, 2005.

Laver, J.: *Principles of Phonetics*, Cambridge, Cambridge University Press, 1994.

Logan, P.: *The Later Jacobean and Caroline Dramatists*, Lincoln, University of Nebraska Press, 1978.

Matricardi, Paolo: *Complete Book of World War II Combat Aircraft*, NY, Military Press, 1988

Naipaul, V.S. : *A House for Mr. Biswas: With an Introduction by Ian Buruma*, New Delhi, Penguin, 1992.

Nath, Narendra: *Indian Religious Historiography*, New Delhi, Munshiram Manoharlal Publishers, 1996.

Neil Bissoondath: *Indo-Caribbean-Canadian Diaspora*, New Delhi, Rawat, 2005.

Perkins, David: *A History of Modern Poetry*, Cambridge, Belknap Press of Harvard University Press, 1976.

Philip Roth: *A Novelist in Crisis*, New Delhi, Classical Publishing, 2001.

Rahilly, J.: *Phonetics: The Science of Speech*, London, Arnold, 1999.

Raja Rao: *The Fictionist*, Delhi, B.R. Publishing, 2003.

Rogers, H.: *The Sounds of Language: An Introduction to Phonetics*, Harlow, Longman, 2000.

Royle, Trevor: *The Macmillan Companion to Scottish Literature*, London, MacMillan Reference Books, 1983.

Seidlhofer, B.: *Pronunciation, Oxford*, Oxford University Press, 1994.

Stevenson, Lionel: *Victorian Fiction: a Guide to Research,* Cambridge, Harvard University Press, 1966.

Terence, P.: *The Later Jacobean and Caroline Dramatists*, Lincoln, University of Nebraska Press, 1978.

Underhill, A.: *Sound Foundations*, London, Heineman, 1994.

Vikram Seth: *Multiple Locations, Multiple Affiliation*, New Delhi, Rawat, 2001.

Wearing, J. P.: *The London Stage, 1890-1899: a Calendar of Plays and Players*, NJ, Scarecrow Press, 1976.

Wickham, Glynne William Gladstone: *Early English Stages, 1300 to 1660*, London, Routledge and Paul; 1959.

William Blake: *A Critical Study*, New Delhi, Anmol, 2005.

William, John: *A History of English Poetry*, London, MacMillan and Co., 1903.

Yeats, W.B. : *Poetry and Plays*, New Delhi, Atlantic, 2002.

Index

M

N

O

P

□□□